-h from
- to

The Science of Enlightenment

Enlightenment, Liberation and God

Contemporary Researches in
Hindu Philosophy & Religion

(ISSN 0971-9628)

1. Idealistic Thought in Indian Philosophy: Rise and grow[illegible] the Vedic Times to the Kevlādvaita Vedānta u[illegible] Prakāśānanda of 16th century, including as propounded in the Mahāyāna Buddhism; by Shuchita C. Divatia (ISBN 81-246-0021-X)
2. Karma and Reincarnation: The Vedāntic Perspective; by Muni Narayana Prasad (ISBN 81-246-0022-8)
3. Stonemill and Bhakti: From the Devotion of Peasant Women to the Philosophy of Swamies; by Guy Poitevin and Hema Rairkar (ISBN 81-246-0059-7)
4. Śaivism: Some Glimpses; by G.V. Tagare (ISBN 81-246-0076-7)
5. Advaita: A Conceptual Analysis; by A. Ramamurty (ISBN 81-246-0067-8)
6. Mind-Body Dualism: A Philosophic Investigation; by Alpana Chakraborty (ISBN 81-246-0071-6)
7. Hinduism and Scientific Quest; by T.R.R. Iyengar (ISBN 81-246-0077-5)
8. Indra and Other Vedic Deities — A Euhemeristic Study; by Uma Chakravarty (ISBN 81-246-0080-5)
9. Brahma-Vāda: Doctrine of Śri Vallabhācārya; by G.V. Tagare (ISBN 81-246-0112-7)
10. The Science of Enlightenment: Enlightenment, Liberation and God — A Scientific Explanation; by Nitin Trasi (ISBN 81-246-0130-5)
11. Retrieval of Sāṁkhya History: an Ascent from Dawn to Meridian; by Lallanji Gopal (ISBN 81-246-0143-7)
12. The Philosophical Foundations of Hinduism; by A. Ramamurty (ISBN 81-246-0163-1)
13. The Eternal Hinduism; by B. Saraswati (ISBN 81-246-0249-2)

Contemporary Researches in Hindu Philosophy & Religion, no. 10

The Science of Enlightenment

Enlightenment, Liberation and God

— A Scientific Explanation —

Nitin Trasi

D.K.Printworld(P)Ltd.
NEW DELHI - 110 015

Cataloging in Publication Data — DK
[Courtesy: D.K. Agencies (P) Ltd. <docinfo@dkagencies.com>]

Trasi, Nitin, 1953 -
The Science of Enlightenment.
(Contemporary researches in Hindu philosophy & religion; no. 10).
Includes bibliographical references (p.)

1. Enlightenment — Religious aspects.
2. Liberation — Religious aspects. 3. Spirituality.
I. Title. II. Series: Contemporary researches in Hindu philiosophy & religion; no. 10.

ISBN 13: 978-81-246-0130-3 (Hardbound)
ISBN 13: 978-81-246-0276-8 (Paperback)
ISBN 10: 81-246-0130-5 (Hardbound)
ISBN 10: 81-246-0276-X (Paperback)

First Published in India in 1999
Second impression in 2004
Third impression in 2009

Published and printed by:
D.K. Printworld (P) Ltd.
Regd. office : *'Sri Kunj'*, F-52, Bali Nagar
New Delhi - 110 015
Phones : (011) 2545-3975; 2546-6019; *Fax* : (011) 2546-5926
E-mail: dkprintworld@vsnl.net
Web: www.dkprintworld.com

Dedicated
to
Sri Ramesh Balsekar

What they Say . . .

". . . the book is most exceptional . . . (Dr. Trasi) clearly writes about a subject he knows about from experience, knowledge, and much thought. He writes well and clearly . . . a reviewer is expected to find and tell the weaknesses in a book review, and it is hard to fault this book."

Henry Swift
for Science Within Consciousness, USA

"This book is not only for the intellectually curious; it is, in my opinion, a necessary companion for all those who are seriously pursuing the path of enlightenment. If approached correctly, this book can literally take decades off the search, given all the wrong turns that one is prone to take before waking up to the simplicity of what is."

Kriben Pillay
for The Noumenon Journal, Wandsbek, South Africa

"Trasi's clarity of thought and lucidity of expression makes his work highly readable and thought-provoking." "For the average man, with his familiar comforting concepts of a benevolent God, of Rebirth, After-life, Heaven and Hell and so on, this book comes as a jolt. He may resist instant conversion. But he can't remain unaffected by the force of Trasi's logic and conviction. . . . This book is a must for the true seeker's shelf."

Savitri Babulkar
for The Kanara Saraswat, Mumbai, India

". . . a unique contribution. . . . the author has successfully decoded the mystic language of the saints . . . providing new and deepened insight into theories of Enlightenment and Liberation. . . . makes a complete and in-depth psychological study of the Enlightened and Liberated person, a task perhaps never attempted before."

Dr. S.G. Desai
Bhavan's Journal

Foreword

THIS work, *The Science of Enlightenment* by Dr. Nitin Trasi is an attempt to find a scientific basis for consciousness and spirituality. There are at least two questions for which answers have been eluding us for thousands of years: Why is there anything instead of Nothing? And why are there living and non-living things? The above two questions can be further expanded to include: Why is there again a difference between various forms of living beings, particularly regarding Consciousness? Do animals have consciousness, or is it that Man alone is gifted with consciousness? And when did Man become conscious that he is conscious? Is consciousness entirely due to material assemblage of things or is there something beyond materialism in consciousness?

One can go on with more and more questions of similar nature. To quote Immanuel Kant, "Two things fill the mind with awe and wonder. The starry heavens above me and the moral laws within me."

Dr. Trasi has analysed some of the concepts connected with consciousness in great detail, collecting and expanding on the thoughts of great philosophers and saints. The writing is lucid and cogent. The author provokes thinking and one can elaborate further on the ideas suggested by Dr.Trasi. I find the book to be highly educative and it will certainly lead one to find spiritual solace. The extensive bibliography will also aid interested students to proceed further in the study. I wish the author all happiness in all his endeavours.

December 8, 1998 **Dr. V. S. Venkatavaradan**
Jt. Director, Ananthacharya Indological
Research Institute, Mumbai; and
former Director, Nehru Planetarium, Mumbai

Preface

FROM time immemorial, ever since he learned to speak and think, man has speculated and wondered about God, and about things spiritual. Ancient and prehistoric art and paintings testify to this fact. But never has a scientifically convincing answer been found so far for the vexed question — does God exist, and if he does, what is his nature? Now this crucial gap in our knowledge is sought to be filled by this book.

This book, then, is offered especially to those readers who may be plagued by the common existential questions about Life, God, and so on — in short, those who sometimes wish to know WHAT IS IT ALL ABOUT?

The subject of spirituality is generally considered highly esoteric, and has always been shrouded in myth, mystery, superstition and tradition. The aim and purpose of this book then is to demystify the entire subject of spirituality and the phenomena of Enlightenment and Liberation. It is to demonstrate that Enlightenment and Liberation do have a scientific basis, and can be precisely defined in scientific, psychological terms.

Although volumes of literature have already been written on the subject of spirituality, and there have also been books correlating spirituality with physics (notably *The Tao of Physics* by Fritjof Capra) and with psychology (*The Spectrum of Consciousness* and others by Ken Wilber), this book attempts to do something different in that it offers for the first time a completely cohesive theory explaining spirituality from all angles — spiritual, scientific, anatomic, physiological, psychological, mystic, and practical — a sort of a **Grand Unified Theory** of spirituality. It is also shown how the traditional or conventional teachings can be reconciled with this theory.

This book defines precisely and explains in detail the phenomena of Enlightenment and Liberation in psychological terms, and makes a complete and in-depth psychological study of the Enlightened and Liberated person, a task perhaps never attempted before. It goes into the subject of death, and also describes the true nature of God and explores the possibility of proving (or disproving) his existence. It finally discusses in scientific detail the practical aspect of what a person is to do to reach his spiritual goal, and the relevance of the teacher — the *guru* — and of the various spiritual techniques, and also their scientific basis.

In short, this book attempts to provide a complete and comprehensive theoretical explanation as well as practical guide to all things spiritual. All that is asked of the reader is that he keep aside for a few moments his own existing notions and ideas on the subject and read the book with a completely open mind. At the same time, the reader is not being asked to accept the conclusions in this book as final and authoritative. All that he is asked to do is to at least *consider* this theory with an open mind, and perhaps use it as a sort of a working hypothesis during his own research on the subject, for ultimately, each has to find out and see for himself.

This, then, is a scientific study of spirituality — spirituality examined from the perspective of science, medicine, psychology. And it is shown that a convincing, consistent, cohesive scientific explanation *can* be given for spiritual phenomena. The spiritual message is restated here in the scientific idiom — in the language of science.

Perhaps, one hopes, the day is not far off when the phenomena of Enlightenment and Liberation may be found included in standard medical texts of psychology — and a Liberated or Enlightened person is seen not as a freak of Nature, but as the most normal, sane, uncomplicated human being that there can be. And if this text serves to contribute even a little to that end, I would consider my labour well rewarded.

Feb. 1, 1999 **Nitin M. Trasi**

Abbreviations used:

Bhagavad Gītā: BG

Literal: Lit.

Synonymous: Syn.

Acknowledgements

I MUST especially acknowledge my deep indebtedness to Ken Wilber, transpersonal psychologist, in whose ideas I have found extensive support and corroboration of my own. This I have demonstrated by appropriate references from time to time. (Publishers: The Theosophical Publishing House, Wheaton, Illinois, USA).

I also gratefully acknowledge the following sources :

Krishnamurti Foundation of India and Krishnamurti Foundation Trust Ltd., London for quotations of J. Krishnamurti.

Gujarat Sahitya Prakash Publications and Carlos G. Valles for some quotes of Fr. Anthony de Mello S.J.

Penguin Books for some quotations by Allan Watts.

Ramanasramam publications for quotations of Śrī Ramaṇa Maharṣi.

I also wish to express my gratitude to Yogesh Sharma of Zen Publications (Bombay), Wayne Liquorman of Advaita Press (California), and Dr. Kavi Arya of Chetana Pvt. Ltd. (Bombay) for use of quotations of Sri Ramesh S. Balsekar, and also for going through the draft and offering some extremely helpful comments and suggestions in preparing the final version of this book.

Last but not least, I must acknowledge all those well-wishers who helped to make this book possible, by their inspiration, encouragement, suggestions, guidance and assistance.

Transliteration Chart

a	ā	i	ī	u	ū	e	ai	o	au
अ	आ	इ	ई	उ	ऊ	ए	ऐ	ओ	औ

ṁ	ḥ	ṛ	ḷ
अं	अः	ऋ	ळ

k	kh	g	gh	ṅ
क्	ख्	ग्	घ्	ङ्
c	ch	j	jh	ñ
च्	छ्	ज्	झ्	ञ्
ṭ	ṭh	ḍ	ḍh	ṇ
ट्	ठ्	ड्	ढ्	ण्
t	th	d	dh	n
त्	थ्	द्	ध्	न्
p	ph	b	bh	m
प्	फ्	ब्	भ्	म्

y	r	l	v
य्	र्	ल्	व्
ś	ṣ	s	h
श्	ष्	स्	ह्

kṣ	tr	jñ
क्ष्	त्र्	ज्ञ्

Contents

Introduction

Science versus Spirituality[1]

SCIENCE and spirituality are commonly perceived to be divorced from each other; they are thought to be mutually exclusive. So much so that one normally does not look for scientific explanations for spiritual phenomena. Even those men of science who believe in the spiritual seem to have compartmentalised their minds, so that science and spirituality co-exist, but in an uneasy truce. It is presumed that one cannot demand scientific explanations in spiritual matters.

But in ancient times, both in India and the West, the two had

1. The word 'spirituality' has been used here in the sense of a genuine and earnest quest for the truth about spiritual matters, God, etc.

   Religion, on the other hand, is a set of traditional beliefs handed over from generation to generation, along with the attendant rites and rituals. Spirituality and religion are thus far removed from one another, and in fact, may have nothing at all to do with each other. A person may be truly spiritual without being religious, and religious persons are rarely, if ever, truly spiritual in the sense in which the word is used here. Religion implies belief, usually blind, whereas true spirituality requires that nothing be taken on trust. In fact, unquestioning faith is demanded by most religions, whereas a true spiritual quest primarily requires just the opposite — a questioning, enquiring mind. Although some religions state this as a principle (notably Hinduism and Buddhism), in actual practice, it is found that a religious person rarely questions his beliefs.

a common origin. In fact, science was called 'natural philosophy' in the West, and in the East too, spirituality was approached in a spirit of scientific enquiry. The *Brahma Sūtra* begins with the words, *athāto brahma jijñāsā* (now, therefore, an enquiry into *Brahman*). It was in later ages that the split occurred, science on the one side, spirituality on the other. Now, to reconcile the two is, as Dr. S. Radhakrishnan has said, the task set to our generation.[2]

Secondly, though some of the spiritual texts may have been written in a scientific manner, science itself has since advanced to an extent which could not have been possibly imagined in those early times. So it is now perhaps time to re-evaluate the spiritual contentions in the light of current scientific knowledge.

Finally, the distinctions between 'spirituality' and 'science', these very classifications, are themselves man-made and artificial. Nature is one, and knows no such distinctions. It follows therefore that if a phenomenon exists in Nature, it must submit to a 'scientific' explanation, however far we may be from discovering one. As men of science, it behoves us to look at such matters with a scientific perspective, in an objective manner.

Is it then possible to look into the matter of spirituality with a scientific eye? Is it possible to form a hypothesis which will broadly cover and explain these phenomena which, we will decide to agree, do undeniably exist — a theory which will satisfy both scientist and spiritualist?

This, then, is the problem which will be addressed in the succeeding pages.

A Note on the use of the word 'Consciousness': The word 'consciousness' (with a small c) is used in this book in its ordinary meaning, as a function or property of the living human brain.

---

2. *Religion and Culture*, pp. 154-6.

Etymologically the word 'consciousness' is derived from the Latin *scire* (to know) and *cum* (with). Thus 'consciousness' is "to know with". A lower life-form may be alive, but not really conscious in the sense of being aware. What is required for such conscious awareness is a nervous system sufficiently advanced with a collection of specialised nerve cells which we call the brain. The word 'awareness' is specifically used in this book to denote the active aspect of consciousness, or consciousness 'in action', so to speak. It denotes attention. Thus, there may be consciousness without awareness as with respect to subliminal stimuli, for example.

Thus, the word with the small c ('consciousness') has been used for the individual consciousness. On the other hand, we have used the word with a capital C ('Consciousness') to denote the collective or Universal Consciousness. When it is stated that "Consciousness is one" (chapter 1), it refers to the postulate that although we feel that we are each of us separate centres of awareness, each with our own individual, discrete, autonomous consciousness (with a small c), the actual reality is that there is only one Universal Consciousness or simply Consciousness (capital C).

Even so, at this point, we are still talking of Consciousness as if inanimate objects and the rest of the inanimate universe is something different. However, as we progress through the book, the word expands till it includes everything that exists and ultimately the word Consciousness comes to take an all-encompassing meaning synonymous with *Brahman*, **That**, Tao, All-That-Is, Mind, etc. Thus, later on in the book we will see that the 'external' world too can be said to be **within** Consciousness just as in a dream the entire world of objects is within the dream-consciousness.

This is the point where present-day science radically differs. In the presently accepted scientific world-view, matter is seen as the primary reality, and consciousness is considered secondary. That is, consciousness is seen as a property of matter, or an 'epiphenomenon'. On the other hand, in the philosophical world-view, Consciousness is primary, and matter is seen to exist only because Consciousness exists. That is, Consciousness is the primary reality, or the base or ground of all that exists ('the ground of all being'). Thus in the spiritual or philosophical reality, everything, including matter, exists **in** Consciousness. It only appears as if consciousness is a function of matter (of the brain) just as in a dream, the dream consciousness appears to be a function of the brain of the body seen in the dream. In short, the world exists in Consciousness and not the other way around.

Interestingly, exactly this same theory has now been propounded in detail by physicist Amit Goswami[3] who claims that it solves most or all the paradoxes of quantum physics.

However, the main purpose of this book is not really to speculate about such matters, but rather to establish that the phenomena of Enlightenment and Liberation do in fact exist, and that they can be explained very well in medical and psychological terms. In this book we are interested less in the theories of Consciousness and matter, and more in the condition of Enlightenment, the state of Liberation and the psychology of the sage, the Enlightened One.

Condensation: This is a chapter-wise condensation or summary of the main thesis as outlined in detail in the book. A brief reading of this may prepare the reader for what follows later.

Chapter 1 : This book is a scientific study of spirituality, and as a starting point we have taken the core of the teaching of all the sages over the centuries, which is that Consciousness is one, in other words, *we are not separate psychological entities*.

It is only man that suffers from this unique delusion of being a separate entity, of 'having' a 'soul'. How did this come to be? We find that it is the combined result of his symbolic way of

3. Goswami, Amit, *The Self-Aware Universe*.

thinking, language, ability to think of past and future, and fear of death. Symbolic thinking gives him the ability to symbolise and conceptualise 'himself' as a separate entity over and above the body-mind, and the fear of future death and annihilation gives him the incentive and reason to thus conceptualise. And so in his rejection of death, is born the idea of the separate soul or ego, which is considered to have existed as a separate entity even before the birth of that body-mind, and which will survive after its disintegration.

Occasionally, a rare human being sees through this illusion, and such a person is then said to be Illumined or Enlightened.

Chapter 2: Psychological suffering is shown to be related to this idea of being a separate entity. This idea leads to unnecessary conditioning, which in turn leads to unnecessary thinking, and avoidable (psychological) suffering. The Enlightened person, on the other hand, undergoes a process of de-conditioning leading eventually to his Liberation (from unnecessary suffering).

Chapter 3 : The idea of Liberation is dangled before the eyes of the common man by most religions as a sort of a panacea for all the ills of this world, and he is encouraged to pursue it as a goal. Thus, begins the seeking of Enlightenment by the person *for 'himself' as an entity*. As Enlightenment is, in fact, the realisation that he is not a separate entity, these very efforts thus become self-defeating, for such me-based efforts inevitably reinforce and perpetuate the illusion of the 'me'. This is the paradox of spiritual effort.

Common spiritual terminology is discussed from a scientific perspective.

Chapter 4 : Enlightenment is defined as the intuitive understanding that one is not a separate entity. The characteristics of Enlightenment are discussed, and its psychological, physiological and anatomic aspects.

Chapter 5 : 'Liberation' is the end-result of the process of deconditioning initiated by Enlightenment.

What are the characteristics of a Liberated person? How does he act and react? What does he do in life after Liberation? What does he think? How is his sleep? What does he dream? How does he see the world? What is his relationship with God? These and other questions are discussed, including the scientific aspects, brain waves, and awareness.

Mysticism and modern science (especially quantum physics) are shown to converge and so merge imperceptibly that it is often difficult to distinguish one from the other. Space and time are both seen as illusions, and consciousness is no more merely a function of the brain. It is seen as all-encompassing, all-inclusive.

Chapter 6 : Is a *guru* required? How exactly can he help? How does one select the proper *guru*? What must be the attitude of the seeker towards the *guru*?

Chapter 7 : What happens after death? If there is no soul in reality, then what survives after death? And why do the religions insist on life after death? What is rebirth and who is reborn? Revolutionary as the idea (that there is no separate individual 'soul') may seem, it is shown that this is exactly what the sages and even traditional scriptures have been trying to say.

Chapter 8: The practical aspect — what is one to do actually?

The second part dealing with the spontaneous processes is only of academic interest. It is included specially to point out that these are **not** directions to be actively followed, (which is how they are often misunderstood).

Chapter 9 : The previous chapter is here correlated with the traditional *mārga*s of *karma*, *bhakti* and *jñāna*. The dispute over their relative merits is discussed.

Chapter 10 : This chapter is on God. The common man's idea of God is first discussed, and then the reality of God as described by the mystic. The question of proving the existence of God is scientifically explored, and also the question of the reason for the existence of the universe. Finally, as a sample, the descriptions given by two well-known mystics of India are presented in some detail.

Appendix: The doctrine of *Advaita* is compared with the thesis outlined in this book. The matter of paranormal phenomena, miracles, telepathy, faith healing, instances of 'reincarnation', etc., are discussed in the light of our thesis, and it is shown that all these can be convincingly and satisfactorily explained in a scientific way. *Nirvikalpa samādhi* and *sahaja sthiti* are discussed, as also meditative techniques.

Finally some commonly asked questions are answered.

1

'Me' and the 'Other'

The Starting Point

As with any other investigation, we need to have a starting point. No one can deny that there are many things that are, even today, inadequately explained by science. Some of these, like black holes and other such phenomena, are nevertheless not considered to be outside the realm of science. But there are others to which the label 'spiritual', 'paranormal' or 'supernatural' is attached. One such is the existence of saints.

The fact that there have existed (and no doubt still do exist) some remarkable persons whom we call saints[1] or mystics, cannot perhaps be denied by science. Therefore, this could serve as the starting point of our investigation.

If we admit to the existence of saints, then we must also admit to the existence of such phenomena as 'Enlightenment' and 'Liberation' which these sages have always talked about.

1. The words 'saint', 'sage', 'mystic', have all been used synonymously in this book, to mean seers of the Truth — Enlightened or Liberated persons. Western writers often use the word 'saint' in a different sense. In the Christian world, sainthood is a sort of title conferred by the organised Church. Arthur Osborne differentiates between sainthood and self-realisation. (*The Teachings of Bhagavan Sri Ramana Maharshi in His Own Words*, ed. Arthur Osborne, 5th edn., pp. 213-14). Here no such distinction has been made, and the two terms have been used to mean the same thing.

Before proceeding, it must be made clear that we are here concerned with the basic core of the so-called spiritual phenomena, and not the peripheral events, many of which are apocryphal. We must delve deep into the lives and teachings of the saints, guided by our own insight, to sift the essential from the non-essential, and obtain the common thread running through their various lives and teachings, shorn of frills and trimmings. We have to take care not to pay undue importance to the inconsequential trivia of a saint's life, which are often highlighted by fond devotees — a form of well-meaning and respectful exaggeration which Max-Müller has called the 'Dialogic Process' and which inevitably occurs in the narration of every saint's life story.[2] These peripheral events, which include the so-called 'miraculous' manifestations, invariably tend to distract from and obfuscate the saint's central message.

It is not the intention here to deny or trivialise these happenings, but rather to place them in perspective, and to sift the essential and enduring from the decorative non-events which generally take away all the attention.

What then is this common thread which forms the core of the teaching of every saint from Kṛṣṇa to Kabīr, from Meister Eckhart to Jalāl-ud-dīn Rūmī, from Jñāneśvar to Ramaṇa Maharṣi?

The essence or central message or core of the teaching of all the sages (when speaking at the highest level of Reality), has been that *Consciousness is one*, in other words, that we are not separate psychological entities.

To quote J. Krishnamurti, perhaps the most articulate of the modern day sages,

> . . . you are not an individual; you are not a separate soul, a separate *ātman*. Your consciousness, which is what

2. Müller, Max, Prof. F., *Ramakrishna — His Life and Sayings*, pp. 25-30.

> you are — not physically, but psychologically, inwardly — is the consciousness of mankind.[3]

And again,

> The content of consciousness is the common ground of all humanity and therefore we are not individuals. We are not separate entities with separate psychological content; we are, each one of us, actually, the rest of humanity.[4]

The *Bhāgavat* says,

> There is but one Consciousness, though it appears as multiple in form.
>
> — *Śrīmad Bhāgavatam*, XI.28.6-7

The *Yoga Vāsiṣṭha* says

> . . . the distinction between 'I' and 'you' is imaginary. The distinction between the one and the many is verbal. All these do not exist at all even as darkness does not exist in the sun. . . . On enquiry, all these disappear and only the unmodified pure consciousness remains.
>
> — *Nirvāṇa Prakaraṇam*

The sage does not see anyone as 'other'. The state of *gyāna* is described by Ramaṇa Maharṣi as "the state in which no other is seen, no other heard, no other known". (*Guru Vachaka Kovai*, V.1005)

The *Bhagavad Gītā* says:

> The (one) Self abiding within all beings, and all beings within the Self; so does the man see, who is steadied in *Yoga*. . . .
>
> — VI.29, also see VI.30-31 and XIII.30

---

3. Krishnamurti, J., *The Last Talks*, p. 92.
4. Krishnamurti, J., *Sunday Times* article, quoted by Asit Chandmal.

In fact, the essence of the *Advaita* philosophy, which is the most generally accepted philosophy in Hinduism today, is that *Brahman* is One, and is all there is. There are no separate entities apart from *Brahman* (see Appendix: *Advaita*).

Also, the essence of *bhakti* or devotion, whether in Christianity (the teaching 'Thy will be done') or in Hinduism (self-surrender) implies ultimately, not that there is a separate entity who is perpetually to accept the Lord's will over his own, but rather that there is no separate, autonomous, independent entity apart from God to *have* any will of his own. Surrender does not mean constantly subjugating or subordinating our will to His, but rather understanding once for all that there is no separate 'we' to have any such separate will. This has been the teaching of all the mystics from St. Augustine and Meister Eckhart of the West, to Ramaṇa Maharṣi, Jñāneśvar, Tukārām or Jalāl-ud-dīn Rūmī of the East. Meister Eckhart said "God and I are one". Sūfi mystic Mansūr al-Hallaj declared "*Anal Haq* (I am the Truth)". Jesus said "My father and I are one". And Jalāl-ud-dīn Rūmī sang:

> I have put duality away,
> I have seen that the two worlds are one;
> One I seek, One I know,
> One I see, One I call.

Whether it is Vedānta, Sūfism or Christian mysticism, Taoism or Zen Buddhism, all are unanimous on this one point. And we will take this as the starting point of our exploration into the great mystery of Life.

So although we (the average people) see ourselves psychologically as distinct entities, each with our own distinct consciousness, the sages have always insisted that this feeling of separateness is an illusion. This illusory feeling of separateness clouds our vision and colours our entire lives, and forms the basis of the average person's motivations and ambitions which drive his normal activities in life. But in actual fact we are all one unified Consciousness, and if we can only perceive this truth, our perspective on life will change dramatically.

To summarise, though Consciousness is one, for some reason there has occurred in us an **illusion of separateness**. The significant point is that if we can actually realise this fact for ourselves (not just believe in it or understand it intellectually), our lives will be totally transformed (*parāvṛtti, metanoia*). Such realisation of this truth has been traditionally termed 'Enlightenment', and the resulting metamorphosis 'Liberation', because such a person is liberated from the psychological suffering which so bothers the rest of mankind.

> We are the world, psychologically, and the world is us. That is not a conviction, that is not a conclusion, that is not an intellectual theory, but an actuality, to be felt, to be realised and to be lived.[5]

Even Freud, the father of modern psychoanalysis, recognised this fact. He said:

> the ego-feeling we are aware of now is thus only a shrunken vestige of a far more extensive feeling — a feeling which embraced the universe and expressed an inseparable connection of the ego with the external world.[6]

If indeed Consciousness is one, then why has it (apparently) split into the many? Can we try to understand this from a scientific point of view?

The Genesis of Separateness

According to the most accepted scientific theory today, the

---

5. Krishnamurti, J., *The Wholeness of Life*, p. 183.
6. Quoted by Wilber, Ken, *The Spectrum of Consciousness*, p. 115.

universe has evolved from the Big-Bang, before which there was 'nothing', not even Space and Time. (In fact, since Time itself did not exist, there cannot really be a 'before' to the Big-Bang.)

In its early stages, the universe was unaware of itself. Over billions of years, the universe evolved. Life originated on earth (and possibly elsewhere), and developed into conscious and aware life-forms — conscious organisms able to perceive and be aware of their surroundings.

But, as far as we know, man is the only life-form **aware of itself, aware of its own consciousness**. The human brain is the only brain which can speculate about itself. How did this unique consciousness develop? As mankind evolved from lower animals, there was a progressive evolution of his nervous system over millions of years.

As the higher functions of the Central Nervous System (CNS) developed, there came a stage when the organism, constituted by a body with its CNS, became dimly aware of its surroundings, then consciously aware of them, and finally consciously aware of itself *as apart from its surroundings*.

At this stage of its evolution, the organism, though conscious of itself in a physical sense (as a physical body), was nevertheless unable or incapable of seeing itself as separate from (and in opposition to) its surroundings. In other words, it could see itself (its physical body) as **different**, but not **separate** from the rest of the world.

This is not to say that it saw itself as continuous or unified with the rest of the world. At this stage, it simply did not possess the faculty to consider the two as separate. That is to say, it was, in evolution, upstream of the point at which the two are seen as separate and in opposition to each other (which only comes with symbolic thought and conceptualisation — see later). The word 'inseparate' is suggested as a better description of the state.

At this stage then, man was still not psychologically separated from the rest of humanity, or for that matter, from the rest of the universe. Man was still living in actuality, devoid of conceptualisation. Human consciousness was still unitary, and not yet conceptually fragmented into separate psychological entities.

As development proceeded, there appeared the capacity for language because of the need to communicate its experiences. With language came verbalised thought. Where formerly there was only a conscious awareness of its surroundings and itself, now this awareness could be expressed in symbolical form. Where the person was aware of a tree, he now labelled it as a 'tree'.

The next step was to label the perceiving organism as a 'me', and automatically the rest of the world as the 'other'. *This is where the split started.* When there is the separation of a 'me' from the 'other', there is simultaneously a separation of interests — the interests of the 'me' as against the interests of the 'other'. In other words, the 'me' is not only seen as distinct from the rest of the world, but also generally in opposition to it and thus the conflict begins. "Thought has created me," said J. Krishnamurti.[7]

The separation of the 'me' from the rest of the world is a very significant development, and it has been termed here '**Entitification**'. J. Krishnamurti has called it 'fragmentation'.[8]

Interestingly, a rapid replay of the same process can be seen as a child grows into an adult human being. (This has been called an 'ontogenetic[9] recapitulation of phylogenetic history'). Ken Wilber has described this in detail.[10] To begin with, the newborn baby (and the foetus before that) has no concept of 'inside' and

7. Krishnamurti, J., *The Wholeness of Life*, p. 72.

8. *Ibid.*, p. 9.

9. Ontogeny or ontogenesis = development of an individual organism. Phylogeny or phylogenesis = evolutionary history of the organism.

10. Wilber, Ken, *The Atman Project*.

'outside', subject and object, self and other, and it therefore cannot distinguish or differentiate between these opposites. Nor does it have any concept of time. Its awareness is therefore said to be spaceless, timeless and objectless. This is the stage of 'absolute adualism'. Needless to say, the newborn is not aware of itself as a separate entity at this stage.

As the baby develops, because of the sensations perceived from the body, it learns the difference between its body and the environment. This stage lasting from approximately the seventh month to the end of the second year is characterised by the awareness of itself as a physical body. There is as yet no concept of time, but the child is aware of a simple 'passing present', and later (as it develops the capacity to form mental images), of an 'extended present'.

As the child learns language, a major transformation occurs. The child begins to **think** in **verbal** terms. It now has a mind proper and sees the world through it. It gains the concept of linear, sequential time. The child now begins to feel that it **has** (not **is**) a body. This stage lasts from approximately ages two to four.

Finally, from the age of four till full adulthood, the child slowly begins to be aware of its mind as well as its body. It then begins to think of itself as something **apart** from them both. This is the birth of the ego-entity, which we called 'entitification'. The child now thinks of itself as **having** a body **and** a mind. The idea of the separate self or ego is usually fully crystallised by the age of twenty-one.

How exactly this separation occurs is now described below.

Symbolic Thinking and 'Entitification'

We think by the use of symbols. This is what makes human thinking so sophisticated. The symbols used are often words or language (verbalised thought), but they may also be images.[11] However, both types of thinking, whether by means of words or images, involve the use of symbols.

Although symbolic thinking appeared later in evolution than direct perception, the habit of symbolic thinking is now so ingrained in us that it has become the sole and only way that we now perceive the world. It has become not our second, but our first nature, and that is why Ken Wilber has called this the **first** 'mode of knowing' (and direct knowing as the second mode of knowing — this is discussed further in chapter 3). We have completely forgotten how to see the world directly. We are now so used to symbolic thinking that we are unable to see things without the intervention of symbols, to see things in their 'suchness' or *tathathā*, 'as they are', (the 'direct seeing' of Zen). We are unable to see a flower without thinking of the word 'flower', unable to see the thing without thinking of the label. To the extent that we become obsessed with the label to the exclusion of the object. This is symbolism to the exclusion of the actual reality. We tend to forget that symbols are mere representations, not the thing. We mistake the symbol for the reality.

The 'I' is just such a label. It is the label for a particular body-mind complex, and it is mistakenly taken to be a separate entity by itself, over and above, and apart from the body-mind, whose label it is. This is how the fictitious entity is born — this is the genesis of separateness, scientifically explained. And it is this process which is repeatedly referred to by the sages, and which J. Krishnamurti calls 'fragmentation'.

There are some other factors which help to reinforce this illusion of a 'self'.

---

11. Weisz and Schopler, Morgan, King, *Introduction to Psychology*.

Free Will

Why do we behave the way we do? It is generally said that our behaviour is the result of genes and environment (or 'nature and nurture'). But the answer is not that simple. There is also a third very important variable which is often forgotten, and that is chance. Moreover, the environment influences the response of an organism in more than one way. The immediate, present environment acts as the stimulus to which the organism responds. But the past environment also influences the response indirectly by having modified the organism itself, by what is called 'conditioning'. This includes

(a) Culture — that is, what we are taught, which we can call 'taught conditioning' — a second-hand conditioning, and

(b) Experience — that is, what we learn on our own, which we may call 'learnt conditioning'.

Thus, how we behave is determined not by a simple combination of genes and environment, but by a very complex interaction of genes, environment and chance.

In any case, it is clear that the organism has little, or rather no choice in the matter — no 'free will' — because *it has no control over any of the factors mentioned earlier.*

However, there is a large element of **unpredictability** in the behaviour of the organism (because of the complex intermix of the above factors) which is traditionally explained as (in fact, mistaken for) 'free will'.

Religious tradition, on the other hand, does generally seem to favour the existence of free will — of choice of action between good and bad, meritorious and 'sinful'. But this is really only in deference to the average man's entrenched belief in a separate entity. It is only stating a relative reality, true as long as the belief in the separate entity exists. Because so long as this illusion persists, so will the illusion of free will. In fact, most religions, when they speak at the highest level of reality, at the level where Consciousness (or God) is all there is, do state the absence of free will quite unequivocally. This highest truth will be found stated at sometime or other, at some place or other in most religions, though it may not be stated everywhere, as it is not meant for universal consumption.

For example, it may surprise readers if we said that the *Bhagavad Gītā* does not support the existence of free will. But just consider the following verses from the *Bhagavad Gītā*, and compare them with what we have said above:

> Of actions which, in every way, are the doings of the Primal Nature's constituent-aspects, he, whose intellect is deluded by egotism, regards himself as their author.
> — III.27

> That the (various) acts which are being accomplished, are in every way accomplished by Nature (*prakṛti*): (he) who so perceives this, and also perceives the self as non-agent, he truly perceives. — XIII.29

> That (false) notion of self resting upon which thou art thinking, 'I will not fight', futile is this resolve of thine; thy inborn nature will (perforce) compel thee (to fight).
> — XVIII.59

> Constrained, O Son of Kuntī, by thy own inborn urge to act, what thou, through self-delusion dost not wish to do: even that thou wilt do in sheer helplessness. — XVIII.60

And in Christianity, Jesus says,

> Forgive them, Lord, for *they know not what they do*!

(For the religious implications of the fact of the absence of free will, see detailed discussion in 'Questions and Answers' at the end of this book).

This is what psychologist B.F. Skinner said:

> When we 'have an idea' or when 'an idea occurs to us', we tend to take credit for the idea as if we chose to produce it by an act of free will. In fact, . . . we 'have' ideas in the same sense that women 'have' babies — that is, we are merely a place in which the ideas happen.[12]

When a thinking organism considers or believes that it has 'free will', it begins to think of itself as something more than a mere body-mind apparatus.

Conditioning by Language

Our very language — its grammar and syntax, and the way we construct our sentences, conditions us into thinking of ourselves as distinct entities.

The linguistic relativity hypothesis of linguist Benjamin L. Whorf says that the way people use language determines how they see the world.[13]

When something happens through the agency of the body, we do not say "It was done", instead we say "**I** did it". Therefore we also think likewise. We mentally extrapolate backwards and unconsciously presume that there must be an 'I' who did it. Though all that has happened is the action, we assume that there must be a 'doer' of that action. In other words, our use of the active voice instead of the passive reinforces our entitification.

When something is perceived or known, we are absolutely conditioned to presume that it has to be known by a 'someone', that is, by a 'me' as an entity. Actually, the perceiving is a fact, but not the 'perceiver', who is an assumption.

The entity is thus just a conceptual extrapolation, a mental construct resulting from the way we speak.

---

12. *Introduction to Psychology,* p. 595.

13. Whorf, Benjamin L., *Language, Thought and Reality*, p. 230.

In this connection, it is interesting to note that one of the suggestions that Śrī Nisargadatta Mahārāj made to his followers was to make a habit of thinking in the passive voice instead of the active. We are already in the habit of using the passive voice for certain actions of the body, like for example, the beating of our heart. We say "My heart beats" and not "I beat my heart" which would sound ridiculous. But we reserve the active voice for those actions of which, we think, we are the 'doers'. In fact, we are no more the 'doers' of our so-called voluntary actions than we are of the beating of our hearts.

We have thus shown that it is symbolic thinking, reinforced by certain other factors, which gives man the ability to symbolise and conceptualise 'himself' as a separate entity over and above the body-mind. This explains how entitification occurs. That is, it reveals the mechanism of its occurrence. But it does not explain why it occurs. Why does man feel the need to believe in a separate 'soul', and why does he cling to this belief as firmly as he does? Later on (in chapter 7), we will learn that it is the fear of death and annihilation which gives him the incentive and reason to thus conceptualise. And so in his rejection of death, is born the idea of the separate soul or ego, which is considered to have existed as a separate entity even before the birth of that body-mind, and which will survive after its disintegration.

Thus is the idea of a separate, independent, autonomous entity born, and the story begins. . . .

Scientists are now researching into the way the brain thinks by means of PET (Positron Emission Tomography) scans and various other scientific methods including 'split-brain' experiments and other studies.[14] These studies show that the

14. Reported in 'An Infinitive Voyage' broadcast on 'Discovery' Channel on 6 November 1995, 10.30 p.m., IST and 'The Sunday Review' of *Times of India*, 10 March 1996, about phychologist V.S. Ramachandran of the University of California, speaking at the Society of Neuroscience meeting in San Diego in November 1995.

left cerebral hemisphere, the 'talking' half of the brain (the hemisphere which controls speech) takes unrelated events and attempts to relate them by concocting a 'story'. It thus tries to make sense out of the multiplicity of sensory signals and perceptual images that the brain is normally bombarded with. The left hemisphere's job is to create a model and maintain it at all costs. The right hemisphere, on the other hand, tries to detect anomalies. When anomalous information reaches a certain threshold, it forces the left hemisphere to revise the entire model and start from scratch. This is called a paradigm shift. The left brain tries to cling to the existing model, the right tries to force paradigm shifts.

It is the left part of the brain which is thus responsible for the illusion of a 'self' and the illusion of separateness from the rest of the universe. The belief in a separate 'self' is programmed into our brains right from the early formative years of childhood (by parents, religion and society), and it seems to fit in rather neatly with our linear, symbolic way of thinking. The left brain then builds further on this framework. It, by its very nature, tends to selectively pick up and remember events which would seem to support this belief, and selectively (unconsciously) edits those which point against it. By this constant 'filtering' of information, it thus maintains a 'consistent storyline'.

But there is a threshold level up to which this selective editing can be successfully carried out. This level is different in different people. Depending upon the level of this threshold, (which is, in simple words, the strength with which a person clings to his beliefs), even obvious inconsistencies pointed out by the right brain may be ignored. But when this threshold level is surpassed, something dramatic happens, which is described in chapter 4.

Moreover, the idea that Consciousness is one is finding support from science. Some experiments on laboratory animals like mice have shown that information available only to a particular group of the animals sometimes appears to be accessible to other animals of the same species well separated in space and time from the first group, almost as if the animals shared a common pool of information, or consciousness — something which has been called a 'Mindscape' (like 'landscape').[15]

And neurophysiologist Jacobo Grinberg-Zylberbaum was able to demonstrate a similar effect in humans by means of EEG recordings.[16] So did the 'ganzfeld' experiments.

Modern physics, too, is now reaching identical conclusions. The famous Aspect experiment of 1982 strongly indicated that our separateness from the world is an illusion.[17]

Also, consider the following statements, ('Mind' or 'Mind only' or 'Universal Mind' — with a capital 'M' — are terms used by some writers which are synonymous with what we have called Consciousness).

Erwin Schroedinger, who gave us quantum mechanics, says:

> . . . all consciousness is essentially *one* . . .
>
> Their (the individual minds') multiplicity is only apparent, in truth, there is only one Mind. . . .[18]
>
> . . . consciousness is a singular of which the plural is unknown; that there is only one thing and that which appears to be plurality is merely a series of different aspects of this one thing, produced by a deception; the same illusion is produced in a gallery of mirrors. . . .[19]

And Sir James Jeans says,

> When we view ourselves in space and time, our consciousnesses are obviously the separate individuals

---

15. Rucker, Rudy, *Infinity and the Mind*.
16. Goswami, Amit, *The Self-Aware Universe*, p. 132.
17. *Ibid.*, p. 257.
18. Schroedinger, Erwin, *What is Life? and Mind and Matter*, p. 139.
19. *Ibid.*, p. 95.

of a particle-picture, but when we pass beyond space and time, they may perhaps form ingredients of a single continuous stream of life. As it is with light and electricity, so it may be with life; the phenomena may be individuals carrying on separate existences in space and time, while in the deeper reality beyond space and time we may be all members of one body.[20]

This has been figuratively represented in *fig*.1.

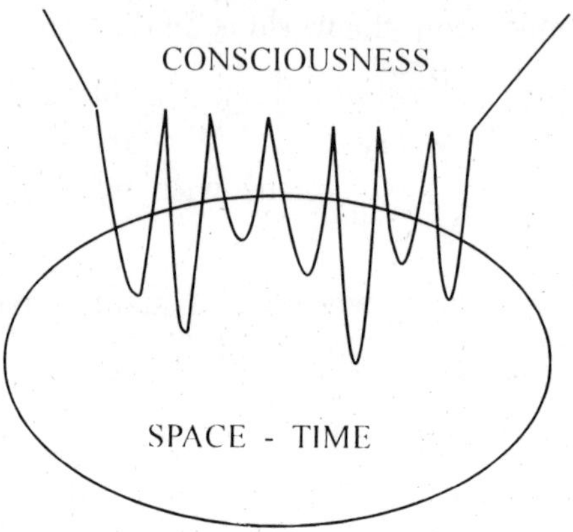

fig. 1

And again according to Schroedinger, this Reality beyond space and time is "essentially eternal and unchangeable and numerically *one* in all men, nay in all sensitive beings. . . . Inconceivable as it seems to ordinary reason, you — and all other conscious beings as such — are all in all."[21]

Thus we see that what the sages perceived with their intuitive vision, is now beginning to be corroborated by scientific observation — the illusory nature of the 'self', the absence of psychological separateness and the universality of consciousness.

The Upaniṣad says:

20. (Ed.) Commins, Saxe, and N. Linscott, Robert, *Man and the Universe, the Philosophers of Science*, p. 395.

21. Schroedinger, Erwin, *My View of the World*, p. 21.

He alone knows the truth who knows all living creatures as himself.

Consciousness — A Figurative Representation

Though there can be nothing like an 'inside' or 'outside' to Consciousness, yet for the purpose of this representation we will use the term 'inside' to indicate the reality relative to the common man's perception of consciousness (or awareness) as being merely a function of the brain, as something 'possessed' by his body. Also, since here there is no question of 'one' or 'two' or 'many', we cannot really say that there is 'one' Consciousness. However, we will be using this description of Consciousness with relation to its apparent appearance as 'many' to the average person:

'Within' the One Consciousness there are the myriad body-mind units. The 'one' unitary Consciousness operates through the brains of these units, which it uses as **instruments of sentience**. Thus we are all points of awareness, perception and expression of that One Universal Consciousness.

However, thinking animals like man (so far we know of no other) perceive an illusory separateness of the sentience, which is merely a result of their thinking.

Figuratively, we can let the blank of the page represent the original Consciousness, in which are the body-mind units (BM) (See *fig*. 2).

This reality is however perceived by the BM units as if each BM has 'its' own circumscribed consciousness or awareness. This apparent, illusory, circumscribed, limited *appearance* of the original consciousness is then called the 'soul,' 'self' or 'ego'[22] or 'me' (*fig*. 3).

---

22. The terms 'ego' and 'self' are used in this book in the philosophical, and not in the Freudian or psychoanalytic sense. They are used synonymously with 'soul' or 'me' to indicate the spurious, fictitious entity which is believed to exist distinct from the body-mind

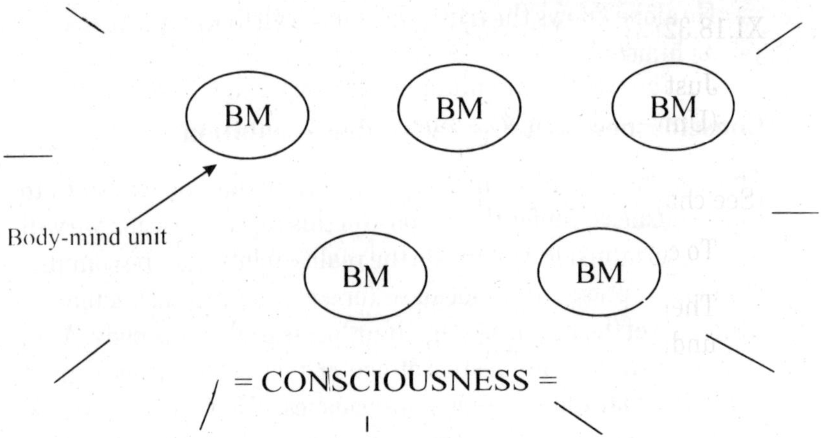

fig. 2: The Reality

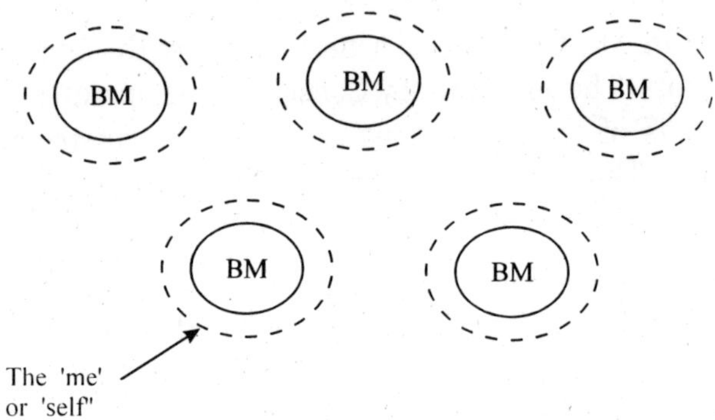

fig. 3 : Illusion (as we perceive it)

Just as the one Sun (cf. Consciousness) is the cause of multiple reflections (cf. individual 'souls') in various vessels of water (cf. body-minds). When the water dries up (cf. death), the reflection disappears or can be said to 'merge' with the original Sun (cf. 'soul' 'leaving' the body and 'merging' with the *param-ātman* or Oversoul). In actuality, however, the reflection never 'went' anywhere, for it was just an appearance, an illusion. Indeed, for that matter, did it at all 'come' from anywhere?

This analogy of a reflection is used in the *Jñāneśvarī* XIII.1094-7, XV.384-7 and the *Bhāgavat* (*Śrīmad Bhāgavatam,*

XI.18.32, XI.7.51). The *Bhagavad Gītā* gives a similar example:

> Just as the one sun illumines all the worlds, so does the (Universal) Subject animate all the fields (bodies).
>
> — XIII.33

(See chapter 7 for detailed discussion).

To conclude, in the words of King Janaka:

> There is here but one Self, which is of the nature of undivided Consciousness. There is nothing else![23]

---

23. *Śrī Vāsiṣṭha Saṅgraha*, II.17.

2

Suffering

THE problem of Suffering is the problem of Life, which concerns most people in this world. This is also the starting point from which the Buddha commenced his own investigations.

We can divide suffering into two types, which we will call unavoidable suffering (like physical pain, for example, which even animals experience, and which does not concern us here), and avoidable suffering (psychological suffering) which is unique to the human race (J. Krishnamurti: 'biological' or 'physical' suffering and 'psychological' suffering.[1]) The one is typified by the actual pain of the dentist's drill, and the other by the anxiety felt about the impending pain even before the pain actually occurs. Man is a thinking animal, and this is the price he pays for his intellectual development.

Of course, physical pain could also be avoided by means of pain-killers (or perhaps by simply avoiding the dentist altogether), but we are not discussing the matter from this (physical) aspect. We have called physical suffering 'unavoidable' only from the psychological point of view, to distinguish it from suffering which is purely psychological, and therefore unnecessary and avoidable.

---

1. Krishnamurti, J., *The Wholeness of Life*, p. 183.

Entitification And (its Relation to) Avoidable Suffering

Verbalised thought gives a person the power to think of the future and also the past in exact verbal terms. This is a great step, indeed a quantum jump, in evolution. It enables him to learn from the past, plan for the future, and to pass on his experiences to the next generation. However, this power is misused when he begins to think of the past with regret or of the future with anxiety. This causes avoidable or psychological suffering.

The basis for most such thinking is entitification. Entitification forms the basis for a whole body of Unnecessary Conditioning, the details of which will depend on the particular person's specific environment (culture, upbringing, etc.), but which is primarily based on the illusion of the existence of a separate 'me'. (For example 'I' must be successful, 'I' must be famous, 'I' must be well thought of, etc.).

This unnecessary conditioning, in turn, is the basis for a host of thoughts which are really not required for the healthy life of the individual, and which he would be better off without. These have been variously termed as 'Thinking Mind',[2] or 'Psychological' or 'Speculative' thoughts.[3] It is these thoughts which, then, are the cause of avoidable suffering. We could simply call them 'Unnecessary Thoughts', as distinct from 'Necessary Thoughts', ('Working Mind' of Sri Ramesh Balsekar, or 'Technical' or 'Technological Thoughts' of J. Krishnamurti), which are essential for the day-to-day functioning of the individual (like crossing the road, or performing professional or technical duties).

These unnecessary thoughts are fundamentally based on the primary illusion of the existence of an 'I' or 'me' as a separate

2. Balsekar, Ramesh, *Consciousness Speaks*.
3. Krishnamurti, J., *The Flight of the Eagle*, pp. 73-4; see also Krishnamurti, J., *The Wholeness of Life*, 71-5.

entity, separate from the 'other'—which is the rest of the world, and with separate interests. This 'I' is imagined to be distinct from, but inhabiting the body-mind complex. We somehow believe that there is a small man residing somewhere inside our skull, exactly like a child believes there is a small man inside the radio set. Śrī Ramaṇa Maharṣi maintained that the "I-thought" is the source of all other thoughts.[4] Wittgenstein said, "What is troubling us is the tendency to believe that the mind is a little man within." It is this unconscious assumption of being a separate entity that is the root cause of mental conflict in the average human being. It is this feeling of separateness which makes him feel that he is at cross-purposes with the rest of the universe.

Thus it is unnecessary thinking, based on the primary belief in the existence of this fictitious, spurious entity, the 'I', which is the cause of avoidable suffering.

We can summarise the entire process as follows:

> Higher functions of CNS → Conscious awareness → Language and Verbalised Thought → Illusion of a 'me' as a separate entity (Entitification) → Unnecessary Conditioning → Unnecessary Thinking → Psychological or Avoidable Suffering.

Whereas the average man is thus subject to psychological suffering, the hallmark of the Liberated person is that he is entirely free of it, because he does not suffer from the illusion of being a separate entity.

J. Krishnamurti has talked about 'me'-based suffering which is avoidable. "Suffering is the expression of the me. . . . So, there is an ending to sorrow when there is no me."

---

4. (ed.) Osborne, Arthur, *The Teachings of Bhagavan Sri Ramana Maharshi In His Own Words*, pp. 133-4, 138, 141-4.

The Average (Unenlightened) Person

All suffering is unpleasant, and this is no less true of psychological suffering. How, then, does the ordinary (unenlightened) person cope with psychological suffering?

The human mind has developed several mechanisms for this purpose. These are called mental mechanisms or defense mechanisms.[5]

These mechanisms are seen not just in maladjusted persons, but even in the average, normal person. "Everyone resorts to them from time to time. . . ."[6] Philosophically speaking, we could even say that the only perfectly normal and well-adjusted person is the Liberated One. All other persons can be to some extent considered as maladjusted.

Briefly then, the main mechanisms are:

Repression (Suppression) or 'motivated forgetting' is the process of 'forgetting' by 'pushing down' into the unconscious any unpleasant thoughts. As R.D. Laing put it, we forget and then we forget that we forgot. But anything repressed is not really forgotten — it remains in the unconscious. And these unconscious memories or urges continue to seek expression and may emerge in the form of neurotic symptoms.[7]

Repression is almost always accompanied by a focusing of the attention on something else — **substitution**.

In **sublimation** the energy is directed into some other activity combined invariably with an altruistic motive, such as religion.

---

5. *Savill's System of Clinical Medicine,* pp.1367-69, 14th Edn.; also refer Weisz and Schopler, Morgan, King, *Introduction to Psychology*, pp. 588-90.
6. Weisz and Schopler, Morgan, King, *Introduction to Psychology*, p. 591.
7. *Ibid*., p. 589.

J. Krishnamurti often spoke about 'suppression, substitution and sublimation.'

In a sense, we can see that sublimation is a special form of substitution, so that most of our mental mechanisms do involve some type of substitution. To put it simply, what we do consciously or unconsciously, is to replace a disturbing thought with one that is less disturbing (or even elevating, as in the case of sublimation). This is actually nothing but an attempt to **escape** from the original unpleasant thought. These mental mechanisms are ultimately nothing but tricks or ruses used by the mind to lull itself into a more congenial mood. The problem with them is that they have their limitations.

In the average person, the struggle between desires and their gratification results in mental conflict, which is accompanied by emotional tension. This is sought to be relieved by the mental processes described above. The root of desire is the **conditioning** which gives us a mental picture of the way we want things to be, as contrasted with the way things are. Say there is an event, the 'what is'. The mind has its own idea of 'what should be'. If the 'what is' conforms to it, the mind is happy. If not, the mind reacts to the **mismatch** between the 'what is' and the 'what should be'. If the reaction is unpleasant, there is a mental mechanism to cope with it. The limitation is that (a) the mental disturbance or agitation caused by the original mental reaction does not really go away. It is merely transferred to the level of the unconscious (it remains 'at the back of the mind'). But more important, (b) the conditioning which caused this disturbance remains.

This is not to say that it is wrong to have these mental mechanisms. Indeed there is no question of 'right' and 'wrong'. We are simply describing what happens in the case of the average person, as a natural consequence of his conditionings.

As the textbook of psychology says, when these mechanisms are used sparingly and without cost to others, they are nothing to worry about. If they allow us to feel more comfortable, as they often do, their value in reducing tension more than offsets the trivial self-deceptions they entail. It is only if a person comes to depend on them too much that these defense mechanisms can become harmful.[8]

But the point is that these mechanisms are not the ultimate solution to the problem of psychological suffering. The ultimate answer, the universal antidote, the panacea for psychological suffering can only lie in the dissolution of its root cause — entitification, for it is **this** which causes the unnecessary conditioning.

The Liberated One is devoid of such unnecessary conditioning. In other words, he has no concept of 'what should be'. So he only reacts appropriately to the 'what is', and that's that. He has no need for any of the mental mechanisms.

As J. Krishnamurti explained, conflict implies comparison, and comparison comes only when you compare 'what is' with 'what should be'. To live without comparison is to remove a tremendous burden. Then you are left with 'what is', and then there is freedom.[9]

*****

Tilak[10] has also divided suffering or pain into two types: 1. *śārīrika* (physical); and 2. *mānasika* (mental). This corresponds to our classification of suffering as unavoidable (or physical) and avoidable (or psychological). He has written that a similar classification is also made in the Vedas, with the addition of a third category of 'God-given' (*ādidaivika*) suffering.

Earlier we said that the mental state we ordinarily consider 'normal' may not be so normal after all. This idea is not new. Alan

---

8. Weisz and Schopler, Morgan, King, *Introduction to Psychology*, p. 591.
9. Krishnamurti, J., *The Wholeness of Life*, pp. 179-80.
10. Tilak, Bal Gangadhar, *Srimad Bhagavad Gita-Rahasya*, p. 130.

Watts, famous exponent of Zen mysticism, commented that "we are accepting a definition of sanity which is insane".

This idea even finds support from psychologists and psychoanalysts. Therapist and theorist R.D. Laing has described our so-called 'normal' condition as that of a "half-crazed creature more or less adjusted to a mad world".[11] Psychologists Putney and Putney wrote about "certain neuroses which are (considered) normal".[12]

Thus, writes Ken Wilber, what we generally call reality is nothing but "socially shared hallucinations" (Laing). We take these 'social fictions' and 'pseudo-events' for real only because "everyone believes everyone else believes them," thus resulting in *our* brand of reality, which is nothing but "an institutionalised nightmare which everyone is having at once."[13]

(See also chapter 5 : Liberation and Schizophrenia.)

---

11. Quoted by Wilber, Ken, *The Spectrum of Consciousness*, pp. 236-7.
12. *Ibid.*, p. 237.
13. *Ibid.*, p. 242.

3

Spiritual Knowledge and its Pursuit

In the preceding chapter, it was shown how entitification is the root cause of psychological (avoidable) suffering. It will therefore be clear that to be totally free of psychological suffering, entitification must disappear. That is to say, there must occur the dissolution of the 'I'-illusion (traditionally called *aharṁkāra*: 'I'-sense). In other words — **Enlightenment** must happen.

And since everyone would like to be free of avoidable suffering, it is important to know how Enlightenment occurs.

Indeed, the oriental religions attach great importance to the **spiritual pursuit** — the seeking of Enlightenment — and declare it to be the supreme goal of mankind. It is said to be the main aim and purpose of human life, and the ability to strive for Liberation is said to be the main feature which distinguishes and elevates man from beast.

Various ways and means are suggested, some extreme. In Hinduism, the spiritual seeker is called a *mumukṣu*, and several paths (*mārgas*) are described, like *bhakti, jñāna, karma*, etc. Each of these involves a variety of techniques. The path of *bhakti*, for example, includes no less than nine techniques (the *nava-vidhā bhakti*). That is not all. The seeker can also choose from a virtual plethora of specific practices and a range of elaborate systems like *rāja-yoga, haṭha-yoga, sahaja-yoga, tantra,* etc. To add to the confusion, there are various sects which lure the seeker with the promise of certain salvation. Very often, the spiritual aspirant is lost in this virtual maze of ways and methods.

Yet, although one and all are thus exhorted to strive for Enlightenment, it is also stated that of the many who may do so, very few actually attain it (*Bhagavad Gītā*, VII.3). And at least this last observation appears to be easily confirmed by the test of observation.

The Paradox of Spiritual Effort

Why is the 'success rate' of any and all of the spiritual techniques so abysmally low in practice (in spite of claims to the contrary by their respective adherents)?

Most people presume that this is because the techniques themselves are too difficult, or that the entire subject too abstruse, and quite beyond an average person's abilities — both physical and intellectual. But it is not so. The cause is much more basic, more fundamental than that.

Actually it is not very surprising that Enlightenment should occur so rarely. Enlightenment, it has already been explained, is the actual perception or realisation (not belief or mere intellectual understanding) that one is not a separate entity. Therefore, the very pursuit of this as a goal to be 'attained' by a 'me' will be counter-productive, because the very effort will reinforce the conviction in the existence of a 'me' as a separate entity. As this is the exact opposite of the result desired, the aspirant will be moving around in circles.

Śrī Ramaṇa Maharṣi said:

> The ego may take different and more subtle forms at different stages of one's practice but it is never destroyed. The attempt . . . is like a thief turning policeman to catch

. . . himself.[1]

And this will be true regardless of which method or technique is being used. In other words, (though this may appear to be a revolutionary statement), *all 'methods' are doomed to failure from the outset*! This is because the error is not in the **method** being used, but rather in the very basic **attitude** towards the method, and in the very comprehension of what constitutes the phenomenon of Enlightenment.

In fact, (though the average seeker may not see this), **the very idea** that a 'method' or 'technique' is required for Enlightenment, reveals a deep ignorance of what Enlightenment is all about. Most people fail to realise that Enlightenment is simply the **understanding** of the situation, and not a physical, mental or intellectual feat or achievement. (And Liberation is the automatic, natural result of Enlightenment.) And thus it is that the seeker makes a very fundamental error right at the point where he begins the search — he begins with the presumption that he is a separate entity — and the battle is lost before it is even begun!

For as long as it is the entity which wishes to eliminate itself, it cannot. And as long as there is any 'wishing' or any question of 'achievement', the entity **is** involved, and there can be no 'success' in the endeavour. By no amount of mental gymnastics or contortionism can the entity achieve its own dissolution.

It is only when there is a totally different type of seeing or perception, when there is no 'wish' to change, when there remains no question of 'achievement' or 'success', that it is seen very clearly that **there really never was an entity ever**.

As Jñāneśvar said to his father,

Like saying 'one's shadow will fight with one', you have

---

1. Osborne, Arthur, *The Teachings of Bhagavan Sri Ramana Maharshi In His Own Words*, p. 131.

> pointed (to) a non-existent *māyā* and an ego and declared that we must always be in *niṣṭha*. As the only result of fighting with an unreal shadow will be exhaustion, you will only have endless trouble, if you don't stay quiet in (abide in) *mauna* (silence), realising the unreality of *māyā*.[2]

Here *niṣṭhā* refers to spiritual effort,[3] and *mauna* refers, not to literal avoidance of speech, but to absence of unnecessary thinking, that is, silence of the mind.

The disappearance of (the illusion of) the entity cannot be 'achieved' because any achieving is done by the entity itself. It can only **happen**.

We shall now see what exactly is meant by the terms 'Spiritual Knowledge' and 'Ignorance'.

Ignorance

'Ignorance' or 'bondage' is the term traditionally used in the spiritual context to describe the condition of the average person who is under the illusion that the 'self' exists as a separate entity.

The word 'ignorance' (*avidyā, ajñāna*) used in this way does not refer to the lack of any specific knowledge or information, which is the usual meaning of the term. The actual meaning here is 'delusion', a wrong perspective, an improper or distorted way of seeing things because of which things are seen not **as they are**, but rather as they **appear to be** from a separate, individual point of view. We do not see things as they are. We either accept or reject, condemn or justify, identify with, compare, match with our own expectations. In other words, we do not see things as they are, but as how they would affect 'me'. If we could just see

2. Subedar, Manu, *Gita the Mother*, p. 314.
3. Tilak, Bal Gangadhar, *Srimad Bhagvad Gītā-Rahasya*, p. 435.

things without the intrusion of the 'me', that is, not from the viewpoint of a 'me' (indeed, not from any viewpoint at all), **that** would be seeing reality.

Another word used more or less synonymously is *māyā*, which is therefore often translated as 'illusion', 'delusion' or 'ignorance'. But to be exact, *māyā* represents the **cause** of the illusion, and therefore denotes the entire process by which symbolic thinking results in the 'me'-illusion (chapter 1). On the disappearance of *avidyā* and *māyā*, the world does not disappear (as is often misunderstood), but is merely seen as it is, without distortion, in its 'suchness' (*tathatā*).

Māyā

It is symbolic thinking or symbolic knowledge, (which we discussed in chapter 1, and which Ken Wilber calls the 'first mode of knowing' — see later), which is ultimately the cause of the illusion of the 'me' versus the 'other', and thereby the cause of our distorted way of seeing the world. And it is this symbolic thinking which is *māyā*. When we see the world through symbolic thought, we do not see the world, we see our concept of the world. Instead of Unity we see a 'me' and a myriad 'others'.

The word *māyā* itself is derived from the Sanskrit root *ma*. The English word 'measure' also has a similar origin.[4] It is by means of symbolic thinking that we are able to measure, divide, classify and label the one adual universe into conceptually different parts, and then distinguish between these apparent parts. Therefore we can also say that *māyā* divides the reality and causes dualism ('me' and the 'other'). Symbolic thinking is thus dualistic thinking, and *māyā* is dualism.

By this process of *māyā* (or dualism), the underlying unity or aduality is forgotten (*repressed*), and is *projected* as a

---

4. Wilber, Ken, *The Spectrum of Consciousness*, p. 107.

multiplicity of separate 'things.' Thus Dualism-Repression-Projection is the threefold process of *māyā*.[5]

In *Advaita* terminology, Repression is called *āvaraṇa* (covering or hiding), and Projection is *vikṣepa*. In the rope-snake example, the appearance of the snake in the rope is Projection, and the non-recognition of the rope is Repression. In the example of the pot, the unity of space is conceptually divided into the space inside the pot and that outside it. The unity of the original space goes unnoticed (repressed) and is projected as two (conceptually) separate spaces. The breaking of the pot **apparently** restores the *status quo ante*, though **actually** the unity of space had never been affected or altered by the existence of the pot. In the case of the individual, the basic universal consciousness is repressed and the apparently limited, circumscribed consciousness of the ego-entity is projected.

Thus by means of our symbolic thinking (verbalised thought or language), we, in the words of Benjamin Lee Whorf, "cut nature up, (and) organise it into concepts".[6]

But it is important to understand that symbolic thinking *per se* is not *māyā*. Symbolic thinking is very much necessary for our day-to-day functioning in life. It is responsible for all scientific advances and for transmission of knowledge from one person to another (communication).

The illusion of the ego is not caused by symbolic thinking *per se*, but by symbolic thinking with **symbols misinterpreted as reality**. *Māyā* is therefore symbolic thinking with symbols mistaken for reality.

Thus, we live not in a real world, but in a world of labels, of images. We cannot see a tree without thinking of the word 'tree', we cannot see a person except through our image of that person.

---

5. Wilber, Ken, *The Spectrum of Consciousness*, p. 118.

6. *Ibid.*, p. 134.

We classify, assess, demarcate, distinguish — and then we are so obsessed with the labels we have created, that we forget the reality behind them. For example, we do not see people as they are — we see them as Indians, Americans, Hindus, Muslims, Christians, 'ours', 'theirs', good, bad, and so on. And as we said before, the 'I' or 'me' is also just a label for a particular body-mind, but we mistake it for a real entity separate from the body-mind.

In other words, by means of *māyā*, we seemingly divide the One into the Many, and **then believe that to be the reality**!

It is not that the Liberated One does not have symbolic thinking — he does (in the form of necessary thinking — and such thinking is required for his functioning in temporal or 'everyday' reality). But he does not suffer from it. He uses the symbols but he sees through them. He is not taken in or fooled by them. He lives in the everyday world, acting as if it is real, but knowing that it is not fully so. The example given is that of a person seriously watching, and enjoying, a conjuror's act, knowing fully well that it is trickery.

Richard Feynman recalls how when he was a little boy, he asked his father to name a certain bird. His father told him what that bird was called in different languages. "But these names don't matter," the father said, "What is really important is to observe the bird carefully."

Both Hinduism and Christianity have the tradition that creation originated from the 'word' (*śabda*, Logos). This could be interpreted as referring to the fact that our mentally perceived universe with its past and future and all that this entails, began only with the spoken word and verbalised thought. Ken Wilber has also given the same interpretation to this belief, and writes that Logos is simply word-and-thought, the Supreme Divider, whereby the Godhead 'indivisibly divides' himself into all creation. 'Indivisibly divides' refers to the fact that this division is only an apparent, and not a real division. And *māyā* is precisely this —

the **apparent** 'creation' by measurement and distinctions performed by Logos the Supreme Divider.[7]

In other words, the **Word** gives rise to the **World as we see it**, which, if we refer to Chapter 1, is exactly what was said by the Linguistic Relativity Hypothesis of Benjamin Lee Whorf.

Knowledge — Conceptual, False and True

Used in the ordinary everyday sense, the word 'knowledge' implies 'temporal' knowledge or information. Such knowledge involves time (hence temporal) and memory. It can be taught and learnt. But, like the word 'ignorance', this word too is used in a different sense in the spiritual context. This will be discussed a little later.

However, the mere verbal knowledge of spirituality as learnt from the scriptures or from the *guru* is, in fact, a form of temporal knowledge which can be called '**conceptual knowledge**' because Enlightenment is still a concept for such a person, not a reality. (*Parokṣa jñāna*, indirect knowledge[8] where *parokṣa* means beyond sight, that is, not seen by oneself; or *para* (other) and *ukta* (spoken, uttered), meaning knowledge spoken by another, that is 'second-hand' knowledge or 'hearsay' knowledge).

Conceptual knowledge (that is, knowledge gained by *śravaṇa*, hearing), if properly and intelligently acted upon (*manana, nidhidhyāsana*), leads to the **intellectual understanding** of the situation, which, as we will describe in chapter 8, is often the precursor of the **intuitive understanding** which constitutes true awakening.

But in some cases, the individual, after gaining mere conceptual knowledge, feels that he has 'arrived', and gets the idea that he is Enlightened. This is the condition we have called

---

7. Wilber, Ken, *The Spectrum of Consciousness*, p. 114.

8. Tapasyananda, Swami, *Laghuvasudeva Mananam*, p. 137.

'false' knowledge. It is referred to in the *Aṣṭāvakra Saṁhitā* (XVI.10) and also by Jñāneśvar (*Amṛtānubhava*) and it is said to be a subtle form of 'ignorance':

> . . . if the *atman* which is of the very nature of knowledge, conceives of itself as knowledge, then that itself becomes its bondage.
>
> —*Amṛtānubhava* III.23, see also VII.6., III.6, 7, 10.

'False' knowledge does not transform the person's life, and does not lead to Liberation, for it does not change the motivation behind his actions (see next chapter). If at all, it may make him more vain, with a sort of subtle egoism which is more difficult to dislodge. Thus 'false' knowledge is a trap that the unwary can fall into, and may find it difficult to escape from.

The really Enlightened person never feels 'I am Enlightened' (though if the occasion demands, he may say so for convenience of speech). Believing that there is an entity who is Enlightened is the very antithesis of the phenomenon of Enlightenment, for Enlightenment is itself the intuitive perception of the **absence** of a separate entity.

The condition of the person in whom Enlightenment has occurred, has been compared by Jñāneśvar to that of a grain of salt which went to measure the depth of the ocean. But then it got dissolved in the water; so who was to know the depth of the ocean? (*Cāṅgdev Pāsaṣṭī* V.46).

And Sant Tukārām wrote:

> the surface of the water is not separate from the water;
> Just as gold gets a name by being made into an ornament,
> Tukā says, so are we.

'True' knowledge, which occurs with Enlightenment, is not really a form of knowledge in the sense of information or memory. That is, it is not temporal knowledge. It refers rather to the intuitive feel or understanding ('apperception') of the real situation (including the absence of the 'I' as a separate entity). It is a non-verbal, instantaneous insight, which cannot really be taught or learnt. It can only be roughly indicated or pointed out. That is why the teaching of a *guru* is compared to a finger pointing to the moon, not the moon itself. The word 'knowledge' is really not at all descriptive of the condition, which actually involves a sort of direct awareness, like the way we are aware of our own existence.

In *Advaita* terminology it is called *aparokṣa jñāna* — knowledge by direct experience.[9] The Buddha spoke of *vipassanā* meaning knowledge by seeing, clear perception.[10] It means to observe the reality in the right way, to observe it **as it is** — not as it appears to be, coloured by belief, by imagination.[11]

It must be emphasised that the word 'intuitive' is used in this book to denote a type of knowing which is instantaneous or rather timeless (a-temporal), and not as in 'woman's intuition' wherein it is used to denote a sort of 'sixth sense', a vague feeling, hunch or foreboding. It is the same type of knowing which Ken Wilber has called the 'second mode of knowing' and which has been also variously called insight, *prajñā*, etc.

The Two Modes of Knowing

From the preceding discussion, and also the discussion in the first chapter, it will be apparent that we have available to us two basic '**modes of knowing**':

(1) the **conventional** or **symbolic** mode, which Ken Wilber has called the 'first' mode of knowing, and has been variously termed map, or inferential, or **dualistic** knowledge (see 'Symbolic Thinking,' chapter 1 of this

---

9. Tapasyananda, Swami, *Laghuvasudeva Mananam*, p. 138.
10. Radhakrishnan, S., *Religion and Culture*, p.124.
11. Goenka, S.N., *The Gracious Flow of Dharma*, p. 7.

book). This is knowledge through symbolic or verbalised thought, or language. Although this appeared later in evolution than the other (direct) mode of knowing, it has been called the 'first' mode because that is the mode the average man now uses to the almost complete exclusion of the other mode.

(2) **direct** or **non-dual** knowledge, the 'second' mode of Ken Wilber—in Eddington's phrase, an "intimate knowledge of the reality behind the symbols of science". This non-dual awareness has been called '**apperception**' by psychologist and philosopher William James.[12] This is a type of knowing wherein the knower, the known, and the knowing are one inseparate process. And it is this type of knowing which the average man has more or less completely forgotten.

True knowledge is of this nature.

As Ken Wilber has shown, these two different forms of knowing are almost universally recognised. Taoism calls them conventional knowledge (knowledge of the universe as it is conventionally named and defined) as opposed to natural or unconventional knowledge (that is, a knowledge of the way the universe is in its actuality). These two forms of knowing are also clearly distinguished in Hinduism as the lower mode of knowing, termed *aparāvidyā* and the higher mode, called *parāvidyā*. In Christian theology Meister Eckhart has called them twilight knowledge and daybreak knowledge. Mahāyāna Buddhism calls them *vijñāna* and *prajñā*.[13]

In *Advaita* terminology however, the word *vijñāna* is generally used to indicate the essential nature of *Brahman*[14] and can be said to be, by implication, conveying the same meaning as

---

12. Wilber, Ken, *The Spectrum of Consciousness*, p. 160.

13. *Ibid.*, pp. 42-8.

14. Harshananda, Swami, *A Dictionary of Advaita*, p. 76.

the Buddhist *prajñā*.

At some places, in the ancient Hindu tradition, there are described three modes of visions by which humans approach reality:

māṁsa cakṣu — the worldly eye of ordinary, mortal experience (*māṁsa*, flesh);

divya cakṣu — the divine eye of intellect;

prajñā cakṣu — the penetrating eye of wisdom, the third eye of Śiva.

The first two clearly correspond to the symbolic mode, and the *prajña cakṣu* to the direct mode.

*****

With the advent of Enlightenment, both ignorance and conceptual knowledge are said to disappear.

> Just as the fire, in the process of burning the camphor, extinguishes itself, (leaving no residue, neither camphor nor fire), similarly doth take place the mutual destruction of Ignorance and (conceptual) Knowledge.
>
> — *Amṛtānubhava* IV.5

The true understanding is thus totally non-verbal, leaving no residue in the form of verbal understanding.

It requires a special kind of seeing — **insight**.

> But thou wilt not be able to behold Me with thine own eye. (Therefore) I give thee the eye Divine. Behold (now) my Divine and Transcendent *Yoga*.
>
> (*Bhagavad Gītā*, XI.8)

This and the subsequent verses from the *Bhagavad Gītā*, are traditionally understood to be a description of an actual physical vision seen by Arjuna. But it could also (and more plausibly) be understood to mean that Kṛṣṇa conferred **insight** on Arjuna, by which he could see (feel) the universality of Consciousness:

And Arjuna saw the form "Possessing many mouths and eyes. . ." (XI.10) and said:

> With manifold arms, mouths and eyes, (and) possessing countless forms, do I behold Thee in all directions. Neither end, nor middle, nor again any beginning do I behold of Thee, O Lord of the Universe, that dost possess every form (in the universe).
>
> — XI.16

The word *sākṣātkāra*, usually understood to mean a 'vision of God', also means "intuitive perception or knowledge".[15]

True Knowledge and the Guru

True knowledge is, of course, infinitely more important than conceptual knowledge. But the *guru* cannot grant true knowledge, for true knowledge, by its very nature, cannot be given or received: "The man who is experiencing reality from moment to moment has no means of communicating that reality." (J. Krishnamurti). He can only give conceptual knowledge. He can only teach in concepts about the state that is beyond concepts. Sāi Bābā of Śirḍī is reported to have said that the *guru's* instruction is also ignorance (because it is verbal, still in the realm of concepts). The *guru* uses ignorance to remove ignorance like a second thorn is used to remove the first — and then both thorns are thrown away (both ignorance and conceptual knowledge are discarded).[16]

The alternative is for the *guru* to remain silent like the legendary *guru* Dakṣiṇāmūrti.

---

15. *The Student's Sanskrit-English Dictionary*.
16. Osborne, Arthur, *The Incredible Sai Baba*.

Spiritual Suffering

This chapter would not be complete without a few words about the phenomenon of what may be called 'spiritual suffering'. From time immemorial, the pursuit of Enlightenment has been prescribed (whether rightly or wrongly), as a means to abolish psychological (unnecessary) suffering. The emphasis on this pursuit creates a sort of complex in those who take this injunction seriously (the 'seekers'), and their life becomes a seemingly unending series of spiritual efforts, interspersed with frustration at not having achieved what is considered to be the goal. The average seeker flits from one *guru* to another, from one technique to another, from one type of me-based effort to another, inevitably failing to find what he seeks — because of the very nature of his seeking. This apparent lack of 'success' in 'attaining' Enlightenment can eventually lead to a severe sense of guilt (because of the suspicion that this failure may be due to some inherent deficiency or shortcoming in the seeker himself), as well as an acute sense of frustration. Thus the psychological suffering actually increases. A typical example of the cure being worse than the disease.

> The fish in the Ocean was searching for the Ocean. . . . Stop searching, little fish. There isn't anything to look **for**. All you have to do is **look**.[17] (Emphasis added)

> *pāni vic mīn pyāsi* . . . The fish in the water is thirsty. . .
>
> — Kabīr

Enlightenment is, in fact, possible only when all ideas of personal volition disappear. This can happen through a comprehensive intellectual understanding of the situation, or through sheer exhaustion of spiritual effort, when one has tried every means and actually sees for oneself the utter futility of such effort. Then one is willing to discard all previous ideas and beliefs and start

---

17. Mello, Anthony de, *The Song of the Bird*, pp. 14-15.

afresh, with a clean slate, to find out for oneself. It is in such a mind that the phenomenon of Enlightenment is likely to happen, that the Sun of Understanding is likely to dawn:

kabīr tej anant kā, māno sūraj seni, (The splendour of the Absolute matches the brilliance of the Sun . . .)[18]

---

18. Singh, Dr. Jaidev and Singh, Dr. Vasudev, *Kabīr Vāṇī Pīyūṣa* (Hindi), Part II, p. 39.

4

Enlightenment

Synonyms: Realisation; self-realisation; awakening; *satori; jñāna, (gyāna)*.

ENLIGHTENMENT can be defined as the clear and deep intuitive perception ('apperception') or intuitive understanding (not just belief or intellectual comprehension) of the entire situation, that is, of the unity of Consciousness and of the absence of the 'me' or 'I' as a separate, autonomous entity.

> You look inside and find no-one there. And then, it is all over. Yet, Life goes on with a volition of its own.

Here the word 'understanding' must be taken in a negative sense, not as the acquisition of some new knowledge or information, but rather as the ending of the feeling of distinctness, the loss of the sensation of psychological 'otherness', the lack of the feeling of separateness of 'oneself' from the rest of the universe that characterises the thinking of the average man. Thus it is not really a positive feeling of 'oneness' but is rather the absence of a feeling of separateness.

A person may meditate and convince or hypnotise himself into feeling one with the world, but this is not Enlightenment. The Enlightened person feels no need to do any such thing, for he no longer feels any separateness from the universe in the first place.

The essence of the spiritual understanding is thus to **unlearn** the feeling of separateness, to lose it, and **not** to gain or learn or achieve a feeling of 'oneness,' which would be adding another artificiality, compounding the confusion.

- Original (Unity of) Consciousness + feeling of separateness = Average Man
- Original (Unity of) Consciousness + feeling of separateness + feeling of 'oneness' = most so-called 'spiritual' experiences, including *nirvikalpa samādhi*
- Original (Unity of) Consciousness (unmodified) = The sage

Also, it must be clearly understood that Enlightenment is the loss of the distorting sense of being a separate entity, but with full retention of all intellectual and mental faculties. All the adult capabilities and skills, intellectual and otherwise are retained upon Enlightenment. Hence, this is a **transformation** or **transcendence**, not a reversal or regression (which may occur in certain pathological states, and in which there is a loss of some mental and intellectual faculties). Ken Wilber has explained this in some detail in *The Atman Project*. The Enlightened person is also different from the newborn baby, who has no sense of being a separate entity because he is simply incapable of formed thought (and as we have shown in chapter 1, this feeling of separateness is a result of symbolic thinking). The infant is not Enlightened. He has no need to be, for he is not yet deluded. As the baby grows up, at some point of time the delusion of being a separate entity sets in, and then for the rest of his life, the person sees the world through this illusion, unless (and until) it disappears. The disappearance of this illusion is Enlightenment. To use terms similar to Ken Wilber's, the infant is 'pre-delusion', whereas the Enlightened person is 'trans-delusion'. He has seen through the delusion. (What holds true for the infant would also hold true for early evolutionary man.)

What do we mean by 'understanding the entire situation'?

Apperceiving that there is no separate 'me' implies at the same time the apperception that there are likewise no 'others'.

The state of *gyāna* is described by Ramaṇa Maharṣi as the state in which no other is seen, no other heard, no other known. (*Guru Vachaka Kovai*, V.1005).

In other words, "there is intuitive apperception that all events simply happen, without any egoic 'do-er' being involved" and that "all actions happen as part of the impersonal functioning of Totality". "The billions of sentient beings are merely the instruments . . . through which this impersonal process takes place."[1]

As a result of this, feelings of guilt or pride for one's 'own' actions, as well as feelings of blame towards others for 'their' actions, begin to disappear. This latter is beautifully exemplified by the Zen story of the empty boat: On a foggy day, a boatman found another boat dashing into him. He was about to swear at the other boatman, when he suddenly saw that the other boat was empty, whereupon he fell silent. There was no 'one' to swear at!

Jesus said "Love your enemies" and, at another place, "Forgive them . . . for they know not what they do." This makes eminent sense when viewed in the light of this understanding.

Enlightenment is more or less a **sudden** happening.

It may not all happen at one go. Instead there may be a series of small or big flashes of insight (little *satori* and great *satori*)[2] but each of these is sudden.

The sage Aṣṭāvakra, *guru* of King Janaka is said to have told him that Enlightenment could happen in the time it took him to

---

1. Balsekar, Ramesh (Conversations by air mail), *Consciousness Writes*, pp. 74, 78, 80.

2. Watts, Alan W., *The Way of Zen*.

mount a horse (in the time it took to place the second foot over the horse's back), that is, in an instant.

Kabīr said, "I became suddenly revealed in Benares."[3]

In a moment, in the twinkling of an eye, at the last trump . . . we shall be changed.[4] (I Corinthians 15:51-2)

The moment of Awakening must necessarily be sudden because the average man's condition and the Enlightened state are different **modes of consciousness**, (one centred on the restricted point of view of the imaginary individual, and the other centred on Totality). They could perhaps be called the Arjuna and Kṛṣṇa modes of Consciousness. (Śrī Nisargadatta once asked a visitor to read the *Bhagavad Gītā* from the standpoint of Kṛṣṇa rather than of Arjuna). The average person views everything from his limited, restricted individual viewpoint. He sees every event as 'how it will affect me'. The Enlightened person, on the other hand, sees things 'as they are', or in their 'suchness'.

> Events happen in life. The Enlightened person sees them happen. The average person sees them happen **to** a someone.

However, it must be understood that these are not simply two alternative viewpoints or different angles of viewing reality. The individual (dualistic) viewpoint is an illusory, make-believe, relative one, whereas the mystic's (adual) vision is not really a 'point of view' at all, it is the actual reality itself.

Thus Enlightenment is really what is called a 'paradigm shift', and like all paradigm shifts, it is sudden. It is not a gradual changing of scenario. It is rather a tearing up of the old, me-based world-view, and its replacement with a new Totalistic view. And this Totalistic view is really a 'no-view', in the sense that

---

3. Tagore, Rabindranath, *One Hundred Poems of Kabir*, XXIX.
4. Quoted by Wilber, Ken, *The Spectrum of Consciousness*, p. 346.

there is no real paradigm or pattern into which the brain tries to fit things any longer. Rather, the brain no longer feels the **necessity** for any pattern or paradigm, and things are merely seen as they are. (See 'Enlightenment as a Scientific Phenomenon' later.)

Whereas the average man's world-view can be likened to a circle with himself (the illusory 'me') as centre, the mystic's world-view is a circle "whose circumference is everywhere and whose centre is nowhere".

Enlightenment is eventually characterised by the following changes :

1. All spiritual efforts cease. The actual practice may (or may not) continue, but if it does, there is no idea that 'one' is 'doing' the practice, and with a particular motive ('effortless effort').

2. All spiritual seeking stops, all concern for further spiritual 'progress' ceases.

   The reason for the above two points is self-evident. Even a person who has had only a superficial intellectual understanding will be able to appreciate that there is really no 'one' to 'do' any effort, to 'achieve' any goal or progress. So the question "What should **I do**" asked by most seekers is a flawed question. That is why Śrī Nisargadatta Mahārāj used to ask, "Who is this 'one' who thinks he must do something — and to achieve what? Understanding is all!"

   In fact, these changes (the cessation of me-based spiritual effort and of spiritual seeking) occur with the deepening of the intellectual understanding itself, even **before** Enlightenment. And, it will be shown later that these changes are an essential *prerequisite*, indeed a *sine qua non*, for Enlightenment, because it is the shedding of me-based spiritual effort which removes the final obstacle to Enlightenment and thus creates conditions favourable for its spontaneous occurrence.

What happens **after** Enlightenment is that the basis of these changes, which was the understanding of the truth that **there is no I**, is now actually seen for oneself. What was a conviction becomes a direct reality. It is seen that all ideas of volition are illusory and that even earlier, there was no volition — only an illusion of volition. When there is the intuitive understanding, what had been earlier understood intellectually (that is, in the form of a concept), because of the teaching of some sage, now is actually seen for oneself, first-hand, without reference to any other authority, and non-verbally, non-conceptually. Earlier, one believed, understood and was convinced about the absence of the 'I', but now, the very idea of the possibility of its presence sounds utterly absurd, ridiculous, preposterous — even laughable, indeed hilarious!

3. All doubts (about spiritual matters) disappear.

4. There is a clear understanding of all that the sages have been saying.

   The sayings of the sages (and the Zen *koans*) appear mystical and paradoxical only to one who looks at them from an individualistic point of view. Doubts about spiritual matters, too, arise (and can never be fully resolved) only from the individual perspective.

5. **Concept** of God disappears. God becomes an actuality.

   'God', to the average man, means his concept of a personal God, but to the mystic, the word 'God' has the same meaning as *Brahman* or 'Consciousness' or 'Totality' (or whatever else one may wish to call it), **with which he now feels no separation**. (See chapter 10 for details.)

   In fact, all so-called 'holy' symbols are seen by him as

mere artefacts, for he now sees everything as holy.

It is said that when Nāmdev first saw Visobā Khecar, who was later to become his *guru*, the latter was sleeping with his feet resting on a hallowed *Śivaliṅga*. But, as the story goes, wherever Nāmdev shifted Visobā's feet, a *Śivaliṅga* sprouted at the new place. Literally true or not, the story exemplifies this same fact in a beautiful way.

A remarkably similar incident is related about Guru Nānak: A *Mullā* was once outraged to find Nānak sleeping with his feet towards Mecca, and reprimanded him. Nānak answered, "Then turn my feet in some direction where God does not dwell."[5]

As Mirzā Ghālib said :

... *(mujhe) vo jagaha batā, jahāṅ khudā nahīṅ!*
Show me that place where the Lord is not!

Thinking about God may actually become a distraction from the mystical state, an artificiality; and even a statement like *aham brahmāsmi* (I am *Brahman*) may become intolerable to the sage. To feel the need to assert that one is *Brahman*, means that one admits the implicit possibility that one may not, indeed, be *Brahman*. Even this purely semantic separation between 'I' and *Brahman* becomes unendurable.

When the understanding of the non-dual nature of noumenality and phenomenality is full and deep, even the *mahāvākya* like 'That Thou Art' becomes an unbearable abomination.[6]

---

5. Radhakrishnan, S., *Religion and Culture*, pp. 147-8.

6. Balsekar, Ramesh (Conversations by airmail) *Consciousness Writes*, p. 17.

It is not that such thoughts are excluded either. They simply fall away on their own. Alan Watts explains:

> As 'the fish swims in the water but is unmindful of the water, the bird flies in the wind but knows not the wind', so the true life of Zen has no need to drag in religion or spirituality as something over and above life itself.

De-conditioning

Post-enlightenment, the conditioning built up over the years does not disappear overnight. However, the process of de-conditioning starts. The end-point is Liberation — totally unconditioned living.

The process of Liberation is essentially a process of de-conditioning — not a process of learning something new (as the use of the word 'knowledge' may seem to suggest) but a process of unlearning — of faulty ways of thinking.

It is a gradual process, and may take a variable length of time depending on the original load of conditioning carried by the individual.

The de-conditioning affects only what we have termed 'unnecessary' conditioning, because only the conditioning which was based on the illusion of being a separate entity is reversed. 'Necessary' conditioning is unaffected, so the person does not become an imbecile or become ineffective in his professional work, whatever that may be. In fact, he will be more effective, for his working will not be affected by the overlay of anxiety about results, which actually detracts from efficiency, as even management experts tell us today.

In spite of the persistence of conditioning for some time after Enlightenment, Enlightenment eventually always leads to Liberation.

One reason for this is that since the 'me' concept is now

clearly seen for the illusion it is, all old me-based conditionings are re-evaluated in the light of this new perspective. This eventually leads to their reversal, that is, de-conditioning.

But an equally important reason is that now **no new conditionings are being formed,** whereas in the case of an unenlightened person, new conditionings are being added to (and old ones being reinforced) with every passing experience.

What actually happens to the thought processes after Enlightenment? After Awakening, it is seen for oneself that the separate entity, the 'I', (around which, as centre, one's entire life had been revolving), just does not exist and that therefore all thoughts based on the presumption of its existence, (all 'I'-based thoughts), are ill-conceived, irrelevant, invalid and void.

However, long years of conditioning ensure that the habitual thought patterns based on this fiction of an 'I' do continue. But now the chain of 'I'-based thoughts is halted or broken at some stage by the abrupt realisation that there is, in fact, no separate 'I'. With time, as the understanding matures, this cut-off occurs earlier and earlier, until finally it occurs at the very inception of the 'I'-based thought process. This is the state of Liberation. (This process is discussed in detail in chapter 8.)

This explains briefly how the **old** me-based conditionings are slowly reversed. But we also said that after Enlightenment, no **new** me-based conditionings are formed (nor old ones reinforced), unlike what happens in an unenlightened person. Why this is so will be clear from the following discussion on actions and their effects.

Motivated and Unmotivated Action and Their Effects

The average person is firmly convinced of the existence of his separate ego-entity, and his entire life revolves around this illusion. Most of his actions are therefore performed on the presumption that the 'me' exists as a separate entity (and therefore with the constant calculation about how the results would affect that 'me'). This is what the *Bhagavad Gītā* calls *kāmya karma* (*BG*, XVIII.2), that is 'desire-based' action. We could also call them 'me-centred' or 'me-motivated' action or for the sake of brevity, simply 'motivated action'. Thus, to put it simply, this is action done with a selfish motive.

'Unmotivated' action or *niṣkāma karma*, on the other hand, is action which is not self-centred. It must be explained that *niṣkāma* or 'unmotivated' action does not mean aimless or arbitrary action. *Niṣkāma* action can very well be result-oriented; only, it is not me-oriented. Such action has also been called 'pure' action or (by J. Krishnamurti) 'creative' action.

Unmotivated action does not mean that one denies the reality of the individual (as a body-mind unit) and his duties and liabilities. What is seen as illusory is only the existence of a separate ego-entity over and above this body-mind. Therefore this does not preclude activities like pursuing a profession, earning a living, supporting a family, and so on (and doing so with the maximum efficiency). But there is less anxiety about the results and one is less affected by life's stray successes and failures than earlier.

Niṣkāma karma may also be attempted by an unenlightened person, as a wilful choice, as suggested by the *Bhagavad Gītā* (see chapter 9 of this book: *karma-yoga*), but after Enlightenment it happens spontaneously, as a matter of course.

The effects of these two types of action are very different. Motivated action, being done on the false presumption of the existence of a separate 'me', reinforces this belief (in a separate 'me') and its attendant conditionings ('I' must be successful, 'I' must be famous, etc.). But when there is unmotivated action (which is what happens after Enlightenment), no fresh conditioning or reinforcing occurs. Instead, it helps the process of de-conditioning. And that is why such actions are said to be 'taintless' or even 'purifying', for they accelerate the process of de-conditioning that is Liberation:

> . . . . he (even while) performing actions, . . . incurs no defilement. . . . (and) is not fettered even when he acts.
> — *BG*, IV.21-2

> . . . it is by (such) action all along that Janaka and others achieved perfection — *BG*, III.20

After Enlightenment, since the me-illusion has disappeared, there will not be any more motivated (or self-centred) action. In the Hindu spiritual tradition, it is stated that after Enlightenment, no new *karma* occurs. *Karma* here refers to 'motivated action', that is, *kāmya karma*.

The word *kāmya* is often omitted, because, since only such action has a binding effect, it is felt that it alone need be considered as 'action' in the spiritual context, while unmotivated action, in the words of the *Bhagavad Gītā*, is not to be considered as 'action' at all:

> He who can in (apparent) action see (real) inaction, and who in (apparent) inaction sees (real) action, he amongst men is the man of discernment. . . .
> — *BG*, IV.18

> . . . such a person, although engaged in activity, does not do anything whatsoever — *BG*, IV.20

Unmotivated action does not bind the person further, (that is, it does not reinforce me-based conditioning). This is therefore 'taintless' action or 'sterile' action as far as the question of bondage is concerned, and therefore, though it is apparently action, it is as good as inaction in that (spiritual) context. On the other hand, actual physical inaction, if the mind is still centred in me-based thoughts, even though apparently inaction, is as bad as performing motivated ('tainted') action.

Hence the statement that after Enlightenment no new *karma* is formed should be taken to mean that after Enlightenment no more *kāmya karma* or motivated action occurs; and since it is such action that reinforces the illusion of a separate entity, which is 'bondage', no such reinforcement occurs in the case of an Enlightened person.

The tradition further goes on to state that although no new *karma* is formed after Enlightenment, the effects of old *karma*, termed *prārabdha*, have to work themselves out, and that these have therefore to be suffered by the Enlightened person.

This is exactly what we stated above: that after Enlightenment although no new conditionings are formed, the old conditionings (due to culture and the reinforcing effects of old me-based actions) do not disappear overnight, and take sometime to be reversed.

The word *karma* means action, but it is also used to imply the inevitable consequences of such action (which include conditioning).

Worldly Duties after Enlightenment — Action, not Inertia

There seems to be a fairly common misconception that after Enlightenment, a person would retire from active life, give up his usual work and lapse into a sort of inertia. This is a completely wrong idea, and Lokmānya Tilak wrote his famous commentary *Gītā Rahasya* mainly to refute this belief.

The Enlightened One, having understood (intuitively and deeply, not just intellectually), that there is no separate 'me', continues to do action **apparently as before**. Only, there is no more the earlier selfish motivation. It is the **attitude** towards the action that is totally changed, and not (necessarily) the action itself.

> Unattached to the fruits of actions, he who does what needs to be done, he is the one who has truly renounced, and who is a true *yogī*, and not he who relinquishes all action.
> —*BG*, VI.1

The knower has nothing to gain either by performing or by abstaining from action. Therefore, he performs action as (the need for) it arises.

— *Yoga Vāsiṣṭha* chapter 6, v.199

To me, it is just the same whether something is done or not. Why should I insist on not performing action? I perform whatever comes to me.

— *Yoga Vāsiṣṭha* chapter 6, v.216

For him, no purpose of any kind is to be served by action done, *nor is any purpose whatsoever served by action not done. . . .* —*BG*, III.18

Thus, contrary to popular notion, the Enlightened person may reveal **no gross change** in his external mode of life.

The legendary Kṛṣṇa and Janaka were kings, Kṛṣṇa an astute and cunning statesman as well. Janārdan Svāmī, *guru* of Eknāth, was a *killedār*, commander of a fort (a soldier), and Nisargadatta Mahārāj continued to sell *bidī*s in his small shop.

Miraculous power and marvellous activity:
Drawing water and hewing wood

— the Zen poet P'ang yun[7]

And the fact of his Enlightenment may go totally unnoticed even by those nearest to him. In the words of Zen, he becomes 'most ordinary'. Because it is the average man who is distorted, warped, confused and 'un-ordinary'. This is why the sage Fa-yung who was so holy that he used to receive offerings of flowers from the birds, received no such offerings after his *satori*, for his holiness no longer 'stood out like a sore thumb'!

Of such a man the Zen-rin says:

---

7. Watts, Alan W., *The Way of Zen*.

Entering the forest he moves not the grass;
Entering the water he makes not a ripple.

No one notices him because he does not notice himself.[8]

This is the quality of naturalness sought to be conveyed by the term *sahaja sthiti* which is used to describe the state of Liberation. It means 'natural state'.

Enlightenment as a Scientific Phenomenon

We had seen in chapter 1 how it is the left hemisphere which does the job of selecting from the abundance of sensory inputs that the brain is bombarded with, and how by its selective editing it tries to maintain a coherent belief system, a consistent storyline.

We saw that it is therefore this part of the brain which is responsible for the illusion of a 'self' and the illusion of separateness from the rest of the universe. This belief is programmed into our brains from early childhood. The left brain then consolidates on this. It selectively registers events which would seem to support this belief, and edits out those which point against it. By this constant 'filtering' of information, it maintains this fiction of a separate 'self'.

We also saw that the job of the right hemisphere is to point out inconsistencies in the storyline, and that there is a threshold level up to which the selective editing can be successfully carried out by the left brain. This level is different in different people. When the inconsistencies pointed out by the right brain reach that threshold, the left brain is forced to abandon the old model, and there is a paradigm shift.

Enlightenment is a paradigm shift — the most radical that there can be. The entire old, individualistic, 'me'-centred world-view is 'ripped up', and is replaced by a new world-view which is no more 'me'-based, but is instead universal in outlook —

---

8. Watts, Alan W., *The Way of Zen*.

where everything is seen not as from a centre, the 'me', but 'from no centre at all', as J. Krishnamurti has said.

That is why, (like all paradigm shifts), Enlightenment is **sudden** (though its effects will be gradual). A paradigm shift has to be sudden, because it is not a question of a slow transformation; rather it is a total scrapping of an old model and its replacement with a new one. Only in this case, there is no new 'model' in the real sense of the word. There is no more a 'storyline'. That is why things are seen 'as they are' and 'from no centre at all'. The brain has realised that there need not be a storyline. It no more burdens itself by constantly trying to 'fit things into' the picture.

The classic example to demonstrate the suddenness of a paradigm shift is the drawing of a transparent cube or a staircase (Fig. 4).

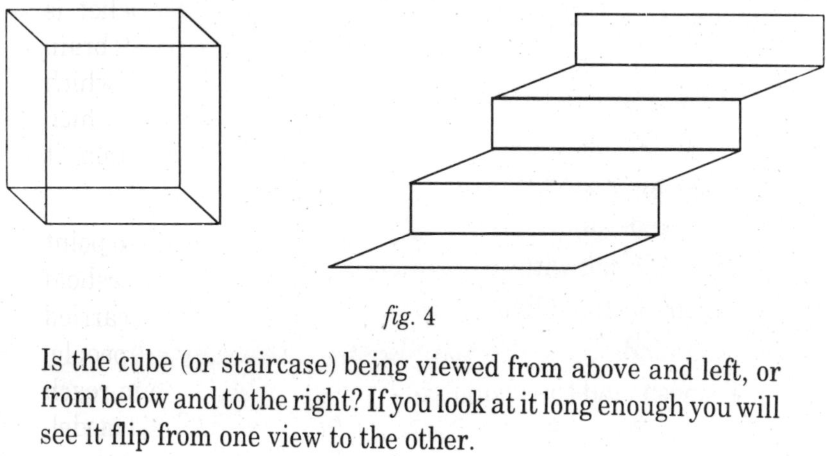

fig. 4

Is the cube (or staircase) being viewed from above and left, or from below and to the right? If you look at it long enough you will see it flip from one view to the other.

There are certain notable points about the flip:

1. It is sudden, almost timeless,
2. It has no intermediate stages, and
3. It happens by itself; you cannot **will** it to happen, or predict when it will happen.

As Anthony de Mello said, Enlightenment is merely a question of **recognition**, or **seeing** for the first time what we have been always looking at... and, "seeing is done in a flash".[9]

The traditional Advaitic illustration of the *rajju-sarpa* (rope-snake) delusion is a similar example. (A rope is mistaken for a snake in dim light, causing fear. It is then suddenly recognised for what it is.) Here too, the recognition is sudden, though the palpitations caused by the fear take time to wear off.

The above explanation also shows **how** Enlightenment occurs. When the right brain keeps pointing out inconsistencies in the existing world-view, these contradictions build up to a threshold where a paradigm shift becomes inevitable. The Zen '*koans*' and Śrī Ramaṇa Maharṣi's enquiry 'Who am I?' are also attempts at pointing out inconsistencies. Another example is given below from the *Rubaiyāt* of Omar Khayyām (v.80), where the poet points out a contradiction in a common belief:

> O Thou, who didst with
>   pitfall and with gin
> Beset the Road I was to
>   wander in,
> Thou wilt not with
>   Predestined Evil
>   round
> Enmesh, and then impute
>   my Fall to Sin!
>
> (If everything is pre-destined by God, including evil, how can I be blamed for 'sinning'? Both cannot be true).

It is also obvious from this explanation that the more tenaciously the brain clings to the old story-line, the more unlikely or

9. de Mello, Anthony, S.J., *One Minute Wisdom*.

difficult is the occurrence of the paradigm shift. That is why the first requirement is an open mind, that is, a mind open to other possibilities. The threshold for the paradigm shift will then be lower.

There are then two or three possible situations. One is when there is no firmly entrenched story-line, possible in the case of a young person, not too strongly conditioned culturally. In such a case, the threshold will be obviously very low. This is probably what happened in the case of Śrī Ramaṇa Maharṣi. He merely asked himself 'Who am I?' and everything was clear. Such cases are probably not too common.

The second situation is where strong cultural conditioning has already created a firm model world-view. Here the model is questioned only when gross inconsistencies are apparent and cannot be explained away or avoided. This can happen if, as in the case of the Buddha, everything — every method — is tried and fails, and the major inconsistency now obvious to the seeker is that this model **just does not work**, thus paving the way for a paradigm shift.

The third way is to have a comprehensive intellectual understanding of the actual situation, (as taught by Jñāneśvar and the *Nāth Panth* in general). This weakens the old world-view, and the constant pointing out of its contradictions, (say by the enquiry 'Who am I?'), builds up to the threshold for a paradigm shift.

(See chapter 8 and *Jñāna-Yoga* in chapter 9 for more details).

After Enlightenment, as performance-anxiety decreases, work efficiency increases. Life becomes 'lighter' or less burdensome as the incessant psychological demand for security (a 'consistent story-line') is diminished.

to bole te stavana, to dekhe te darśana,
advaiyā maza gamana, to cāle tenci.
to karī tetulī pūjā, to kalpī to japu māzhā,
to ase teci kapidhvajā, samādhi mājhī . . .
udakī kalloḷu, kāpurī parimaḷu, ratnī uzāḷu, ananyu jaisā.

— *Jñāneśvari*, XVIII.1180-3

Whatsoever he may speak, that is My praise,
Whatsoever he looks at, that is My form,
With his walking do I move, inseparably bound (to him) by non-duality.
Whatsoever he may be doing, that is itself My worship,
Whatever he thinks, that is My contemplation,
His very being itself, O Arjuna, is his absorption (meditation) in Me . . .
As the wave is to the water, the fragrance to the camphor, the lustre to the gem, so also is he inseparable from Me.

5

Liberation

Synonyms: *mokṣa; mukti; nirvāṇa*

THIS is the natural culmination of the process of de-conditioning initiated by Enlightenment.

The Liberated One is called a *jīvanmukta* or a *siddha*. The Buddhists call him an *arhat* or a *tathāgata*.

It may be noted right at the outset that the terms 'Enlightened One' or 'Liberated One' are used for convenience. They do **not** imply that there is an **entity** who is Enlightened or Liberated. They refer rather to a body-mind complex in which the phenomenon of Enlightenment or Liberation has occurred, and in which therefore the illusion of its being a separate entity has disappeared.

Liberation can be said to have occurred when the individual is totally devoid of unnecessary conditioning.

Let us now see what are the characteristics of the Liberated One:

1. Absence of Entitification

Complete absence of the 'I'-illusion (*ahaṁkāra* or I-sense) and a total lack of the feeling of separateness from the rest of the universe. In other words, absence of entitification.

We had already mentioned this in the last chapter, as also the fact that as a result of this, feelings of guilt or pride for one's 'own' actions, as well as feelings of blame towards others for 'their' actions, begin to disappear. The process is now complete with Liberation, and there is now a complete absence of such feelings.

Complete absence of self-image as well as image of other people.

Each of us carries a mental image of ourself (and of others) in our mind. This image is a product of past experiences, impressions, successes, failures, etc. It is this image which takes a beating when we are unsuccessful in some enterprise, or if we are insulted or criticised, and it is this same self-image which is boosted by what we consider 'our' stray successes. In fact, it is the self-image that we perceive as the fictitious, illusory, phantom 'me'. The 'me' is thus a mental image which we carry, and is nothing but a conglomerate of past psychological experiences etched in our minds as memory — 'nothing but a bag of edited memories'.[1]

Likewise, the average man's dealings with another person are based to a very large extent upon his image of that person, which is the residual impression left by past experiences involving that person.

The Liberated One carries no such image, either of himself or of others. He has no residual (emotional) impression regarding people (see point no. 6 later). He therefore deals with them on a moment to moment basis. This is not to say that he acts in an *ad hoc* manner, or that he is a simple, gullible person. It must be clarified that it is the emotional impressions which are absent, not the factual memory. For example, if he has been cheated by someone, he may not be bitter about it, and may bear him no ill-will or malice, but he will certainly remember the fact and will

---

1. Wilber, Ken, *The Spectrum of Consciousness*, p. 136.

not fail to take due precautions the next time he deals with that person. The Liberated One can therefore be extremely shrewd and calculating in worldly affairs, but his actions are not motivated by personal likes and dislikes. We can say that past experiences do not *emotionally* prejudice his view of the present.

2. Absence of Unnecessary Conditioning

It is important to understand that the state of Liberation is devoid of *unnecessary* conditioning only (that is, emotional or me-based conditioning).

From the medical (psychological) point of view, many of our ordinary activities and basic skills involve conditioned responses (e.g., driving a car). Skilled professional work also involves conditioning. Obviously, all these are not lost upon Liberation. We must therefore distinguish between these basic ('necessary') conditionings (which are of no interest from the spiritual point of view) and the unnecessary, bothersome and superfluous *emotional* conditionings which the ordinary person has and which lead to avoidable suffering.

The textbook of psychology too mentions these two types of conditionings:

> (The basic conditionings) .... have, by themselves, little significance in people's everyday affairs. What is important in human life are the emotional responses that become conditioned to certain stimuli.
>
> Many of our subjective feelings — from our violent emotions to the subtle nuances of our moods — are probably conditioned responses.... Since some emotional responses to stimuli are learned, perhaps they can be *un*learned. [2]

2. Weisz and Schopler, Morgan, King, *Introduction to Psychology*, p. 147.

And indeed it is this very process of unlearning which is the process of Liberation.

The Liberated One is then totally devoid of this type of conditioning, (the emotional, 'I'-based conditioning), and does not lose the basic (necessary) conditioning, without which indeed he would be unable to operate in daily life. However, as these basic conditionings are of no spiritual significance, we could say from the spiritual point of view, that he is totally unconditioned.

Some people believe that the state of Liberation is devoid of **all** conditioning, but we must understand that when sages (like Śrī Ramaṇa Maharṣi) say that there is no conditioning in that state, they are talking from the spiritual point of view, and referring to the spiritually relevant unnecessary (emotional) conditioning. Ramaṇa Maharṣi has clearly said that he is talking of a state in which the person 'could move about and act and speak',[3] and could even 'carry on trade or business',[4] and Śrī Nisargadatta Mahārāj is known to have done just that.

3. Total absence of Unnecessary Thinking, and hence of Avoidable Suffering

> Thought comes to an end, except in its right place. . . . (There is) complete silence, because thought has come to an end — except to function where it is absolutely necessary.[5]

The average man is a compulsive thinker. We are thinking during most of our waking state, and even when we are asleep and dreaming. In fact, ". . . it is hard *not* to think".[6] Thus, the

3. (ed.) Osborne, Arthur, *The Teachings of Bhagavan Sri Ramana Maharshi In His Own Words*, pp. 225-6.
4. *Ibid.*, p. 228.
5. Krishnamurti, J., *The Wholeness of Life*, pp. 116 & 144-5.
6. Weisz and Schopler, Morgan, King, *Introduction to Psychology*, p. 228.

ordinary person's mind is constantly thinking, verbalising, conceptualising, forming images. It is almost never silent.

Silence of the mind is the freedom of the mind from thoughts, but it does not mean the absence of all thought. Silence of the mind is the **absence** of **unnecessary thoughts.**

A Liberated person, when he is working or talking (or even planning), would have thoughts pertaining to the matter on hand (necessary thoughts). But when he is not doing anything, his mind would contain no thoughts — the 'fasting mind' of Zen.

> When I go for those long walks of mine, alone through the woods for one or two hours, it happens to me that not a single thought crosses my mind during all that time.[7]
>
> — J. Krishnamurti

This is a condition unknown to most of us, and hence we are unfamiliar with it. Though we do have a silent mind during dreamless sleep, we do not know what it is to have a silent mind when awake. In fact, most people are not even aware that such a state **can** exist. But this is in fact our natural, our original state, the *sahaja sthiti*.

There is a common misconception that the state of Liberation is one which is devoid of **all** thought. Sages sometimes do refer to it as a state "in which all thoughts cease to exist and the mind is killed".[8] But 'thoughts' here obviously refers to what we have called unnecessary thoughts and 'mind' to split-mind (Zen) or thinking mind (Śrī Balsekar). As we mentioned earlier, we are talking of a state in which the person 'could move about and act and speak,' and could 'carry on trade or business'. It should be fairly obvious that to do all this, necessary thoughts must exist. In fact, Śrī Ramaṇa Maharṣi has clearly said so:

---

7. Quoted by Carlos G. Valles S.J., *Unencumbered by Baggage*, p. 181.
8. (ed.) Osborne, Arthur, *The Teachings of Bhagavan Sri Ramana Maharshi In His Own Words*, p. 234.

Devotee: "Can we think without the mind?"

Śrī Ramaṇa Maharṣi: "**Thoughts can continue** like other activities. They do not disturb the Supreme Consciousness."[9]

And again:

sahaja samādhi . . . in this state . . .you are unaffected by what you do or say or **think**.[10] (Emphasis added)

He further states that

You have no worries, anxieties or cares . . .
— (that is, no unnecessary thoughts)

The fact is that what we have called 'necessary thoughts' are not really counted as thoughts at all in the spiritual context. This is discussed in detail later (See 'The Mind', this chapter).

A similar confusion is made between Liberation and trance-like meditative states (like *nirvikalpa samādhi*).

The state of the Liberated One is sometimes called *sahaja samādhi* (or *sahaja nirvikalpa samādhi*). This is often confused with *nirvikalpa samādhi* (or *kevala nirvikalpa samādhi*), which is a state brought about by intense meditation and in which **all** thought is suspended.[11]

(*Kevala*) *nirvikalpa samādhi* is essentially a temporary, trance-like state. It is a great mental feat, but of no particular relevance to the problem of psychological (avoidable) suffering,

---

9. (ed.) Osborne, Arthur, *The Teachings of Bhagavan Sri Ramana Maharshi In His Own Words*, p. 232.

10. *Ibid.*, p. 227.

11. Osborne, Arthur, *Ramana Maharshi and the Path of Self-Knowledge*, pp. 45 & 203, see also

    Osborne, Arthur, *The Teachings of Bhagavan Sri Ramana Maharshi In His Own Words*, pp. 224-7.

which is the problem of Life. *Sahaja samādhi*, on the other hand, is the state of a person who is totally devoid of unnecessary thinking, who is totally one with, at home with, the universe. His mind knows no conflict. He remains in that state whatever he may be doing. *Sahaja samādhi* is thus a **way of life**. Unfortunately, the word *samādhi* seems to suggest a trance-like state. That is why the term *sahaja sthiti* (*sahaja* state) is more appropriate.[12]

That the supreme state is a state of trance is an idea somehow deeply ingrained in the Hindu (and Buddhist) psyche. That is why most statues of the Buddha are in the position of trance-like meditation, and so are many pictures of sages in Hinduism (Jñāneśvar, for example). Thus, most of the confusion arises because the popular concept of the state of Liberation actually corresponds more closely to the state of *kevala nirvikalpa samādhi*.

Śrī Ramaṇa Maharśi clearly distinguished between the two:[13]

> Merging in Reality and remaining unaware of the world is *nirvikalpa samādhi*. Remaining in the primal, pure, natural state without effort is *sahaja nirvikalpa samādhi*.

This is the "state of *samādhi* while retaining full possession of human faculties".[14]

In answer to the question "What is *samādhi*?" Śrī Ramaṇa Maharṣi said "In *yoga* the term is used to indicate some kind of trance. . . . But the *samādhi* I speak to you of is different. It is *sahaja samādhi*. In this state you remain calm and composed

---

12. (ed.) Osborne, Arthur, *The Teachings of Bhagavan Sri Ramana Maharshi In His Own Words*, p. 226.
13. *Ibid.*, p. 225.
14. *Ibid.*, p. 224.

during activity."[15] But such people may "carry on trade or business or rule a kingdom".[16]

In Mahāyāna Buddhism, the Bodhisattva is one who sees the Godhead everywhere and does not have to retire into solitude and trance in order to 'find' it. The Bodhisattva's mystic vision is identical with whatever he happens to be doing at the moment.[17]

We have thus shown that the *sahaja sthiti* is different from trance-like states (or *nirvikalpa samādhi*). But there may still be those who believe that it is the trance-like state, and not *sahaja sthiti*, which is the highest state.

This is what some Buddhists believe. According to them, the Buddha deliberately refrained from coming to the final term of Enlightenment in order to help others on the way.[18] This idea originates from the belief that in the highest state, the person is incapable of performing such functions.

However, it should be clear that a temporary state, which is the result of particular practices or techniques (and therefore dependent upon them), could not be the natural, original, perennial, highest state.

Śrī Ramaṇa also answered this question similarly:[19]

> Q. (Devotee): . . . they say that the highest state is withdrawal from all sense activities, thoughts and experience; in fact, cessation of activity.

---

15. (ed.) Osborne, Arthur, *The Teachings of Bhagavan Sri Ramana Maharshi In His Own Words*, p. 227.
16. *Ibid.*, p. 228.
17. Wilber, Ken, *The Spectrum of Consciousness*, pp. 298-9.
18. Radhakrishnan, S., *Religion and Culture*, p. 113.
19. (ed.) Osborne, Arthur, *The Teachings of Bhagavan Sri Ramana Maharshi In His Own Words*, pp. 226-7.

A. (Ramaṇa Maharṣi): . . . it would (then) be a state which, however exalted, comes and goes and would therefore not be the natural and normal state, so how could it represent the eternal presence of the Supreme Self, which persists through all states, and survives them? It is true that there is such a state and that in case of some people it may be necessary to go through it. It may be a temporary phase of the quest or it may persist to the end of a man's life . . . but in any case you cannot call it the highest state.

It should be fairly obvious that the highest state cannot be **dependent** on anything—concentration, bodily posture, activity, speech, or even thinking (or **not** thinking).

(Also see Appendix — *nirvikalpa samādhi* and *sahaja sthiti*.)

4. Time and its Perception

The way the sage perceives time is different from the way the average man does. The average man sees time as something inflexible, inexorably passing in a linear fashion from past to present, and from present to future. But it should not be too difficult to see that in actuality, all there exists, is the Present. The past and future exist only in our minds (memory and imagination respectively), and that too as thoughts in the **present**. Actually it is our (present) memory of the past and our (present) imagination of the future which **create an illusion** of sequential time.

This happens because our thought proceeds in a linear fashion. We can think of only one thing at a time. Memory serves to link the successive, sequential bits of thought to create an effect (in fact, an illusion) of continuity. Here memory takes the place of the phenomenon of 'persistence of vision' which enables us to see a motion picture as a continuous movie rather than as a series of still slides.

Thus, we come to see that **time itself (as we know it) may be a product of our thinking**, its apparent linear flow being a result of the way we think.

Ken Wilber writes that even modern physics has destroyed forever the old Newtonian notion of serial time, and has replaced it with the absolute Here-Now. Schroedinger said "Mind is always Now. There is really no before and after for Mind."

The Liberated One sees through this illusion of Time. Therefore in his case the sense of continuity of time is lost (it is seen for the illusion it is). That is, there is no sense of 'psychological' time as opposed to 'physical' or 'chronological' time (J. Krishnamurti):

> It . . . means the ending of time. . . . Time coming to a stop totally . . . (psychologically speaking).[20]

As a result, the continuity of events is broken, and their emotional impact is marginal. (Zen saying: 'There is winter and there is spring, but winter does not *become* spring'.)

The illusion of a separate 'I' and the sense of continuity of time are inter-related and inter-dependent. One feeds on the other. Each gives substance to the other. The past and the future are seen in relation to this 'I', as 'my' past and future. And it is the conceptual continuity from the past to the future which gives body or substance to the image of the 'I'. Thus, the average person sees life as a linear movement through time — with the 'I' (or individual) as the centre. In this view, the individual's progress can be traced through time, and 'he' 'has' a past and a future. The Liberated One, on the other hand, sees life as a horizontal spread in the present moment, the successive moments being psychologically unconnected. This view is not seen as from a centre — an 'I', but rather in its totality.

---

20. Krishnamurti, J., *The Wholeness of Life*, pp 121-2, 173 and see also Krishnamurti, J., *Questions and Answers*, pp. 72-3.

Indeed, even this succession of moments may be seen by the mystic as illusory, the Reality being seen as an Eternal Now — there being no past moments or future moments, only a timeless 'Now-moment'. (Meister Eckhart[21]). (Also see later: 'Boredom'.)

That is why such a person is said to be **'living in the present'**. However, it should be clear that he does not do this by a volitional act, (as one may do by trying to 'concentrate on the work in hand'). To the Liberated One, 'living in the present' happens as a matter of course — that is his natural way of life. Whereas the ordinary person's mind is constantly occupied with the past and the future, the mind of the Liberated One does not wander unnecessarily into these. Therefore, his mind remains in the present, the *eka kṣaṇa* — the 'Eternal **Now**' — quite naturally, effortlessly, 'by default', so to speak.

As he is wholly in the present, he is **totally absorbed** in whatever he may be doing at the moment — a fact regularly observed about sages (Śrī Ramaṇa Maharṣi and Svāmī Ānandāṣram of Chitrapur, for example).

He savours the present fully, undistracted by extraneous thoughts. That is why the Liberated One is sometimes described as a *mahābhogī* (enjoyer *par excellence*) as well as a *mahāyogī*. The average person thinks and acts with what, in Zen terminology, is called a 'split mind' — one part of the mind standing aside and anxiously 'looking over the shoulder' of the other. The Liberated One does not suffer from any such distortion of the mind. His is the 'whole mind' of Zen.

> I enter fully into each experience, and I come out clean from each of them too. I put the whole of me into all I do, and . . . out of all I do. Nothing sticks to the mind, and may be that is why it remains clean.[22] (Anthony de Mello)

---

21. Wilber, Ken, *The Spectrum of Consciousness*, pp. 91-4.
22. Carlos G. Valles S.J., *Unencumbered by Baggage*, pp. 181-2.

The philosophy of Anthony de Mello as described by his biographer Carlos Valles:

> Live every experience to the full, so that it leaves no residue in the mind. No leftover, no remainder, no scraps. Account without carry over. Journey without luggage. No living on credit, but cash down each time. In and out; fully in and fully out . . . the lotus and the water.[23]

> Some for the Glories of This
> World; and some
> Sigh for the Prophet's
> Paradise to come;
>
> Ah, take the Cash, and
> let the Credit go,
> Nor heed the rumble of a
> distant Drum!
>
> — *Rubaiyāt of Omar Khayyam*, v.13 — in English verse by Edward Fitzgerald

Anthony says,

> A free mind carries no encumbrance. A free mind lives life moment to moment, and this is the secret to enjoy it to the full.[24]

On the other hand, let us see how the sense of psychological time ruins the peace of mind of the average person. Such a person suffers from attachment to a past experience on one side and anxiety over a coming event on the other.

And as far as happiness is concerned, he is always looking to the future for it. He is busy planning for it, pursuing it, busy trying to make it happen. He is so involved in planning future

23. Carlos G. Valles S.J., *Unencumbered by Baggage*, p. 182.

24. *Ibid.*, p. 182.

happiness that he completely misses the joy of the moment — the sunlight, the chirping of the birds, the gentle swaying of the trees, the flapping of a bird's wings. And finally, when that future happiness really materialises, he cannot fully enjoy it, for half his mind is now occupied in working out how to prolong it or repeat it in the coming future. In the end he spends so much time chasing future happiness that it becomes difficult for him to distinguish the **pursuit** of happiness from happiness itself.

A businessman on a fishing vacation, seeing a fisherman lazing away, asked him if he had no work to do. The latter replied that he had already caught his day's stock of fish. The businessman was aghast. He said, "Show some enterprise. Catch some more. In fact, if I were you, I would expand the business, buy a large trawler, start exporting."

"What then?" asked the fisherman.

"You could make a lot of money."

"What then?"

"Then you could afford to relax once in a while like I am doing now."

"But that's what I was doing anyway," said the fisherman.

In short, the average man lives so much in the future (and the past), that ironically enough, he has no time for the present.

BOREDOM

Boredom is the sense of *ennui* caused by the absence of sensory stimulation in the form of entertainment or titillation. There is a sense of the dreary hours passing by with nothing to do.

This sensation of 'time passing by' is our sense of psychological time. And **psychological time is measured only against thought**. It is thought which 'counts' the passage of chronological time to give us the sensation of its passing —

which is psychological time. It is thought which 'marks time' and tells us that time is passing.

That is why an animal has no such sensation, and is therefore never bored in the human sense — nor for that matter is a baby or a Liberated person (who will have no thoughts when he is not working — the 'fasting mind'). When there is no thought, *there is nothing against which the passage of time can be measured.*

(Of course, there would be necessary thoughts when he is working, but the question of being bored arises only when one has nothing to do, not when one is working. Here 'working' would also include mental work like planning or conceiving, if that is in his line of work.)

5. Emotions

Emotions, when they do occur, are fleeting, and they leave no mark — 'like a line traced on water'.(Svāmī Ānandāṣram.[25])

Here it should be mentioned that the common perception of a saint is that he is a man of perfect equanimity, immune to emotions like anger, etc. This is simply not true. There may be many unenlightened people who have near-perfect equanimity, but we must distinguish between *saintly* people, and saints, who are Seers of the Truth.

> All these are noble men, but the man of knowledge is my very self. — *BG*, VII-18

Similarly, Jesus said of John the Baptist that he was the best of those born of women but the least in the Kingdom of Heaven was greater than he. (*Matthew*, III: 2; *Luke*, III.10-14)

Several saints are known to have had flaring tempers (Śrī Sāi Bābā of Śirḍī, for example). The difference between the

25. (Ed. and pub. by) Hattiangadi, Dr. G.S., *Fifty Years of Bliss*, p. 57.

anger of a saint and that of a common person is that

(1) the saint's anger is not based on selfish motivation, and

(2) it is very short-lived, and there is absolutely no residual impression left on his mind the next moment.

The basic temperament or the traits of the person may not change upon Liberation.

> Man, **even when possessed of knowledge**, acts conformably to his inner nature. Creatures follow out their inborn nature. What can coercion avail (there)?
>
> — *BG*,III.33

This explains why different saints have been known to have had different temperaments, from mild (Śrī Ramaṇa Maharṣi) to quick-tempered (Sāi Bābā of Śirḍī, Nisargadatta Mahārāj), solitude-loving (J. Krishnamurti, known for his long solitary walks) or gregarious (Fr. Anthony de Mello), literary (J. Krishnamurti) or poetic (Jñāneśvar), intellectual (Svāmī Vivekānanda) or devotional (Eknāth), monastic (Śrī Ādi Śaṅkara) or fully immersed in worldly life (Śrī Kr̥ṣṇa); he may love to teach (the Buddha taught for many decades) or prefer to remain silent (like the legendary Dakṣiṇāmūrthy), he may continue to do ritualistic worship (Svāmī Ānandāṣram of Chitrapur) or have nothing to do with it (J. Krishnamurti).

But whatever the basic temperament of a sage, his reaction to events is always absolutely objective, and the emotional aspect, if any, is minimal and momentary. We could say that he has the maximum of **emotional maturity**.

Earlier, science considered mainly 'IQ' or Intelligence Quotient (developed by Alfred Binet and Theodore Simon) to assess human intelligence. But it is often found that people with similar IQs and with comparable opportunities and education, often fare differently in life. 'Emotional Intelligence' is now being given importance after a book by this name by Daniel

Goleman became a best-seller recently. Goleman's thesis is that their 'EQs' (Emotional Quotients) were different.

Emotional Quotient should ultimately be a measure of emotional maturity, and a Liberated One would score a perfect 100 on this scale.

6. No Unnecessary (Emotional or Psychological) Memory

Because emotions, as we said above, (when they do occur) leave no mark, the Liberated One does not carry the unnecessary burden of past emotional experiences as memory. This does **not** mean that he has no memory of the past. The factual memory does exist.

> Normally the brain is registering almost everything . . . like a tape (recorder). (But in that state it does not register anything) except that which is absolutely necessary . . . to operate in daily life — as a technician, a writer and so on — but . . . there is no registration **psychologically**.[26] (Emphasis added)

> There is the non-registering of any psychological reactions. . . . Someone insults you, someone flatters you, someone calls you this or that — no registration.[27]

Also, there is no *attachment* to the past, and he sees the present, the actuality, as it is, without the mind forming comparisons, conclusions, opinions (except when viewing in a technical sense, for example, as a doctor or as an engineer).

> It's curious what happens to me, but I've observed it again and again. I often pass through the old . . . grounds where I lived and worked so many years with the intensity you all know, so that those grounds and every corner in them are full of memories of all kinds for me.

---

26. Krishnamurti, J., *The Wholeness of Life*, p. 144.

27. *Ibid.*, p. 213.

> I know all this, and I remember all this, and yet the fact is that whenever I pass through those grounds . . . I feel absolutely nothing by way of emotion, attachment, romance or nostalgic feeling. . . . The reason must be that I lived that experience to the full, and it has left no residue within me. (Anthony de Mello[28])

7. Because the Liberated One has no unnecessary memory, and no attachment to the past, and because his mind is always in the present, there is a **freshness** and **novelty** in his view of the world at every moment, somewhat like that of an avid tourist seeing many wondrous sights for the very first time.

As J. Krishnamurti said:

> It means to be totally free. . . . No attachments, no gods, no future, no past. . . . So that throughout life you are not attached to **anything**. . . . So that **each day** is a **new day**.[29] (Emphasis added)

This state in which all things are seen as new has been referred to as **'de-automisation'**. The object is seen as if for the first time, without the dulling effect of the habituation which has resulted from previous perceptual experience of the same kind — that is, the perceptual world always appears new. This has also been demonstrated in EEG studies of Zen meditators, in which there was absence of habituation to a click stimulus as found in ordinary people.[30]

8. True Virtue

Traditionally it is taught that a person must be 'pure' in thought,

---

28. Carlos G. Valles S.J., *Unencumbered by Baggage*, p. 183.
29. Krishnamurti, J., *The Last Talks*, pp. 92-3.
30. Kretschmer, W., "Meditative Techniques in Psychotherapy", in *Altered States of Consciousness*, ed. by C.T. Tart, and Huxley, Aldous, *The Doors of Perception*.

word and deed before he can aspire for Enlightenment. Hence supreme importance is given to so-called self-control or mind-control as a preliminary step on the 'journey' to Enlightenment.

However, the *Bhagavad Gītā* says:

> Sense-objects recede from the body's owner when he ceases to feed upon them, but **leave behind his relish** for them; even this relish ceases after the vision of the Supreme. (Emphasis added) —*BG*, II.59

The meaning is clear. No amount of self-control can lead to true detachment, that is, inner detachment. True detachment cannot be cultivated. It occurs **after** the 'vision of the Supreme', that is, after Enlightenment. **True virtue is a result of Enlightenment, not its cause**.

The virtue of the saint is not cultivated, it is a spontaneous virtue. The virtuosity of an unenlightened person is *sattva-guṇa*, but *guṇa* nevertheless, whereas a *jīvanmukta* is beyond the three *guṇa*s (*guṇātīta* or *nistraiguṇya*, *BG*, XIV.25, II.45). This means that he is not just virtuous, but he is beyond the attributes of virtue and vice, beyond morality. He is not 'good' for any reason; he is what he is, spontaneously, without choice.

Our virtuosity depends upon our doing unto others as we would have them do unto us. In other words, the average man's virtue, like his vice, is also me-based. The saint, on the other hand, has lost his 'me' and simply does not see anyone as the 'other'. (See *Bhāgavat*, XI.7.11).

Śrī Nisargadatta Mahārāj too taught that true virtue can only occur after Enlightenment. All virtue prior to Enlightenment is 'cultivated' virtue. This means that what the common man calls 'virtue', occurs naturally to the Enlightened person, whereas the unenlightened person has to work at it.

To put it in a nutshell, when the 'me' is good, there is ordinary virtue, but when there is no 'me' at all, then that is true virtue.

The related point that emerges from this is that self-improvement by itself may not have much to do with Enlightenment.[31] Efforts at self-improvement, though commendable in themselves, constitute activities in one plane of life, whereas Enlightenment is a total transcendence of that plane into a different dimension altogether. Such efforts attempt the betterment of the 'me', and while they may admittedly contribute to the making of a better 'me', expecting that they lead to Enlightenment is unrealistic, because Enlightenment occurs not when the 'me' is bettered to perfection (as some may well believe), but instead when the 'me' is seen as false and disappears altogether. Thus while self-improvement may be a highly desirable goal socially and morally, it may not add up to much in the context of Enlightenment, unless it is combined with the **understanding** that is primarily required for Enlightenment. As Jñāneśvar has said, **the only remedy to heal a wound caused in a dream is to awaken** (*Jñāneśvarī*, XV.254).

And this point has been noted in other religious literature as well. The *Divani Shamsi Tabriz* says:

> The man of God is beyond infidelity and religion,
> To the man of God right and wrong are alike. (VIII)

Although Christianity as practised today greatly emphasises the leading of a virtuous life (like all organised religions), Dr. S. Radhakrishnan has noted this difference between the teachings of Jesus and John the Baptist:

> John speaks to us of salvation through moral life. He tells us what to **do**, not what to **be**. Jesus insists on inner transformation. John symbolises the man of external piety, Jesus the man of inner understanding. (*Luke*, XVII, 20) John asks us to become better, Jesus asks us

---

31. Alan Watts has elaborated this beautifully in *What is Enlightenment*, pp. 22-3.

> to become different, new. John the Baptist was puzzled when he heard that Jesus and his disciples ate and drank and did not fast. They plucked the ears of corn on the *sābbath* day.[32] (Emphasis added)

In fact, Jesus himself commented on this:

> John is still a man born of woman; he has not experienced rebirth.

This is not to say that cultivating virtue has no **social** value and should be given up — it only means that the **spiritual** understanding is of a different dimension altogether, which totally transcends the entire issue of virtue and vice.

Śrī Ramaṇa Maharṣi, too, clearly stated that although it is said one should cultivate one virtue after another and thus prepare for ultimate realisation, but "for those who follow the *jñāna mārga*, Self-enquiry is quite enough for acquiring all the divine qualities; **they need not do anything else**."[33] (Emphasis added).

In short, developing so-called 'purity' (strange though it may sound) is not a precondition to Enlightenment. In fact, it is the other way around. An unenlightened person can never hope to be really 'pure' — rather, it is Enlightenment alone which can make a person totally 'pure'. This is because the root cause of the 'impurity' is the 'me'. When that disappears, 'purity' naturally follows.

> No amount of perfume could mask the stench from Nasruddin's sickly ass. Till finally someone said — get rid of the ass, you fool.

---

32. Radhakrishnan, S., *Religion and Culture*, pp. 13-14.
33. (ed.) Osborne, Arthur, *The Teachings of Bhagavan Sri Ramana Maharshi In His Own Words*, p. 162.

9. True Detachment

As mentioned earlier, the Liberated One is a *mahābhogī*, an 'enjoyer' *par excellence*.[34] He always enters into the spirit of things, with unreserved enjoyment of the moment, with unalloyed pleasure.

> He is the real Sādhu, who . . . keeps the spirit of union in the midst of all enjoyments . . (Kabīr)

Paradoxically, he is also truly detached. His pleasure is not dependent on the external source to the extent that its removal would cause distress. If it is there, he enjoys it. If not, he does not miss it. True detachment is **inner** detachment:

> Inwardly (*manasā*) renouncing all actions, ...
>
> — *BG*,V.13

It does not preclude actual enjoyment of an object. On the other hand, those who renounce things externally, may find that these very things prey on their minds, so that there is (external) renunciation, but not true detachment.

> He who, repressing the organs of actions, continues recalling in mind their objects, deludes himself . . .
>
> — *BG*, III-6

The whole point is that actual (external) renunciation is often performed, but is of no avail without inner detachment, and if there is true inner detachment, then there is no reason for physical renunciation. In fact, this point is the subject of a beautiful debate between Jñāneśvar and his father.[35] Jñāneśvar has herein described the state of the *gyānī* as being "like a kite's shadow, which while touching anything, is not attached to it".

If at all a Liberated person appears to 'renounce' certain actions or objects, it must be understood that these have not

---

34. *Śrī Vāsiṣṭha Saṅgraha*, XXIX, 43-8.

35. Subedar, Manu, *Gita the Mother*, pp. 311-16.

been forcibly renounced, but have rather spontaneously dropped away, because he no more feels the need for them.

10. Dreamless Sleep

After the occurrence of Enlightenment, a remarkable development is that dreams begin to intrude less and less upon sleep, till finally (upon Liberation), they cease altogether.

This point has also been noted in the Buddhist scriptures, which state that an *arhat* does not dream.

> An *arhat* has no residuary thought that needs to rise up in the form of a dream.[36]

J. Krishnamurti often remarked that he did not dream.[37]

What are dreams and why do we dream? Dreams are a form of thinking that occur usually during a stage of sleep called Paradoxical Sleep or REM (rapid eye movement) sleep. Freud believed that dreams are our unconscious urges and conflicts which find expression during sleep when our conscious suppression of these is absent.[38]

It is believed that during sleep the brain discharges its pent-up electric potentials which have built up during the day. This flow of electricity in the brain serves to restore the brain to its resting equilibrium. This has been likened to the 'rezeroing' of electronic analog computers which is required after their prolonged use.[39] And one simple explanation of why people

---

36. Weeraperuma, Susunaga, *J. Krishnamurti as I Knew Him*, p. 89. (The words quoted were spoken by Adikaram, Weeraperuma's mentor).
37. *Ibid.*; and see also Krishnamurti, J., *The Flight of the Eagle*, p. 27 and Carlos G. Valles S.J.,*Unencumbered by Baggage*, pp. 181-2.
38. Weisz and Schopler, Morgan, King, *Introduction to Psychology*, pp. 55-6, 684.
39. Guyton, Arthur C., *Textbook of Medical Physiology*, pp. 673-4.

dream is that dreams are the images perceived when the brain discharges these pent-up electric potentials.

It seems logical to postulate that the potentials which build up are mainly caused by unnecessary thinking. If that is so, then it would also seem logical that a Liberated person's brain would always be more or less at equilibrium, and hence very little such discharge would occur in his case.

Of course, it is possible that dreams may occur and may not be remembered. But it is probably the remembered dreams that are indicative of a restive mind, and which are really significant.

According to the *Textbook of Physiology*, there are two different types of sleep:

SLOW WAVE SLEEP

It is so-called because in this type of sleep the brain waves are very slow. This sleep is exceedingly restful. (This corresponds to the *suṣupti* or 'dreamless sleep' of spiritual literature.)

Though slow wave sleep is frequently called 'dreamless sleep', dreams actually do occur very often in such sleep. The difference between such dreams and those occurring during REM sleep is that those of REM sleep are remembered whereas those of slow wave sleep usually are not. That is, during slow wave sleep the process of consolidation of the dreams in memory does not occur.

REM SLEEP

(So-called because in this type of sleep the eyes undergo rapid eye movements.) Dreams occur in this type of sleep, and the dreams which occur are impressed in memory and therefore remembered upon waking. It is thus this type of sleep which is generally associated with dreaming.

The electroencephalogram shows a desynchronised pattern of beta waves similar to those that occur during wakefulness.

Therefore, this type of sleep is also frequently called **desynchronised sleep, or paradoxical sleep** because it is a paradox that a person can be still asleep despite marked activity in the brain.

In summary, the slow wave variety is the deep, restful type of sleep, whereas REM sleep is not so restful, and it is usually associated with remembered dreams. REM sleep is a type of sleep in which the brain is quite active. However, the brain activity is not channeled in the proper direction for persons to be aware of their surroundings and therefore to be awake.[40]

From the above description we could infer that it is during slow wave sleep that the brain really rests, and which is probably the real sleep, and since there are no remembered dreams during this type of sleep, it is to this type of sleep that the Buddhist scriptures and J. Krishnamurti are obviously referring.

The fact that there is no consolidation of dreams in memory (even if they do occur) is closely reminiscent of the fact, already discussed, that the Liberated One has no emotional registration of events as (unnecessary) memory even in the waking state.

REM sleep, as seen from the above description, is hardly a rest for the brain, and is probably an anomalous variant evolved as a result of unnecessary thinking.

The remembered dreams of REM sleep are probably associated with the emotionally charged unnecessary thinking, whereas the dreams seen during slow wave sleep may be related to the mild build-up of neuronal potentials associated with the innocuous technical or necessary thinking which may have occurred during the preceding waking hours.

And perhaps if even these small unresolved potentials could be equalised or equilibrated before sleeping, dreams could be dispensed with altogether. It is interesting to note that J.

---

40. Guyton, Arthur C., *Textbook of Medical Physiology*, pp. 671-2.

Krishnamurti said that he actually sort of 'went over' the day mentally before going to bed every night — to 'finish with it once for all', and he believed that this was why he had no dreams. A process of 'tying loose ends' to mop up any residuary thought before sleeping.

11. The Mind

What we mean by 'mind' is basically thoughts and memories, conscious and unconscious.

But, before we proceed, we must understand that we are using the word 'mind' in the medical sense. The Sanskrit *manas*, though often translated as 'mind', actually has a different connotation.[41] In Vedānta, different aspects of the mental faculties have been given different terms, like *manas, antaḥkaraṇa, manomaya-kośa, vijñānamaya-kośa*, etc. Secondly, the basic or background **awareness** of the **Now** (the present moment) which is ever-present, even during sleep, is **not** a **content** of the mind. It is rather That **which is aware of the mind** — in other words — it is *prajñā* or the Reality, the 'screen' upon which thoughts are projected. It is **That** which is our real Self. It is sometimes termed *turīya* — see later. (An animal will have only a scaled-down version of this awareness, that is, a limited awareness of the **Now** — how limited will depend on its level in the scale of evolution.)

CONTENTS OF THE MIND

In an average person, we can classify the contents of the mind as:

1. Hidden conditionings and memories (unconscious).
2. Technical thoughts (necessary thoughts) whenever required.

---

41. Harshananda, Swami, *A Dictionary of Advaita,* Ramakrishna Math, p. 49. Also see Glossary.

3. Unnecessary thoughts of past and future.

Thus, the average person's mind contains, (apart from the unconscious), both necessary and unnecessary thoughts. That is, it is split between the two, his attention divided — a 'split' mind.

The Liberated person's mind, when he is working, contains necessary thoughts only, and whatever he does has his undivided attention — the 'whole' mind. When he is not doing anything, his mind will be empty of all thoughts — the 'fasting mind' of Zen.

In the case of the Liberated person, we have already seen that unnecessary thinking is absent. We will also be showing that the unconscious is absent in his case. Finally, from the spiritual point of view, as we will presently demonstrate, necessary thoughts are often not counted as 'thought' at all, so that, in that sense, the Liberated One's mind can be said to be 'dead' (as Śrī Ramaṇa Maharṣi often observed).

THE UNCONSCIOUS OR SUBCONSCIOUS

This contains memories and motives of which we are not consciously aware — hidden motives. In other words, hidden conditionings. As the Liberated person has no unnecessary registration of events as memory, and no unnecessary conditionings, (no emotional conditionings, only technical conditionings), the unconscious as we understand it would be almost absent, or insignificant in his case.

> I want to ask the experts if there is such a thing as the unconscious, because I don't think it has played any important part in my life at all.[42]

Ken Wilber too agrees that at the 'Level of Mind', (which is synonymous with what we have termed Liberation), there is no

---

42. Krishnamurti, J., *The Wholeness of Life*, p. 80.

more any unconscious.[43] This is because (as we had explained in chapter 2) the Liberated One does not have to take recourse to the mental (defence) mechanisms. And it is by the mechanism of repression that thoughts are pushed into the unconscious. Therefore, as there is no more any repression there is no more any unconscious.

This fact may be a sensational revelation to the psychoanalyst, but it is not surprising if one considers that the very goal which the psychoanalyst attempts, of bringing the unconscious into the conscious, has already occurred on its own, spontaneously, in the case of the Liberated One during the process of Liberation, which, as we said earlier, is nothing but a process of *de-conditioning*. (Also see chapter 8 : 'The spontaneous processes'.)

TECHNICAL OR NECESSARY THOUGHTS

These are non-me-based thoughts relating to a person's work, profession, or daily life. Also some speculative thoughts like planning for (but not worrying about) the future may be essential for a person in his professional capacity or even as a householder. (And it should be generally clear by now that a Liberated person may continue to be both). Such thoughts too will be classified as 'Working Mind' (Balsekar) or 'technological' thoughts (Krishnamurti), or as we have done here, simply as 'necessary' thoughts.

It must be understood that necessary or technical thoughts too are a form of symbolic thinking or symbolic knowledge (the first mode of knowledge), as is probably all human thinking. But this is *necessary* symbolic thinking comprising harmonious cortical activity of the brain — innocuous and harmless to the person in the context of psychological suffering. Indeed, it is such thinking that has led to advances in all fields of human endeavour

---

43. Wilber, Ken, *The Atman Project*, pp. 161-2.

including the sciences, and it is also this type of knowledge which is necessary for communication between human beings. This (first or symbolic) mode of knowing therefore causes delusion **only** if we confuse its symbols or concepts with the reality itself.

As we have said before, there is no unnecessary thinking in the Liberated state, but necessary thinking does occur whenever required. If even such thoughts did not exist in a Liberated person, then, in the words of Śrī Ramaṇa Maharṣi, that state would be "no different from deep sleep", or it would mean "being inert like a stone", which it certainly is not.[44]

However, as necessary thoughts are directly pertaining to some activity, they may, in a sense, be considered to be a part of the activity itself, and in that (philosophical or spiritual) sense they may not be counted as 'thoughts' at all. It is obviously from this point of view that Śrī Ramaṇa Maharṣi has said, at times, that the Liberated person has 'no thoughts'. He has clarified at other places (see above and p. 76) that (certain types of) thoughts can occur. This seeming contradiction between the sage's statements at different times is easily resolved if it is remembered that in the former case he is referring to me-based (unnecessary) thinking, and in the latter, to necessary thinking.

Thus, one must understand that the word 'thought' as used in spiritual literature generally refers to unnecessary thinking. Necessary thoughts are not counted as 'thought' in this context. The same is the implication of the statement that the 'mind is dead.'

Ken Wilber, too, has made it clear that the words 'thought' and 'mind' (*manas*) are used differently in spiritual literature.

In Buddhism, *manas* refers to the "psychological agent that introduces the subject *vs.* object dualism",[45] "our persistent and

44. (ed.) Osborne, Arthur, *The Teachings of Bhagavan Sri Ramana Maharshi In His Own Words*, p. 226.

45. Wilber, Ken, *The Spectrum of Consciousness*, p. 111.

irreducible feeling of existing as an isolated self"[46] — in other words, dualistic or me-based or unnecessary thinking.

He has also explained that the word 'thought' used in the spiritual context does not refer to the thinking involved, for example, in "solving a math problem", (that is, necessary thought), but rather "to the very root process whereby we create distinctions and dualisms" (which is me-based or unnecessary thought).[47]

Unfortunately, such use of the word 'thought' has been misunderstood, leading to the common but erroneous belief that the state of Liberation is devoid of **all** thought, and that the occurrence of any thought is a distraction, and is incompatible with that state.

The truth is that thinking will not disturb the *sahaja sthiti* because *there is no longer the concept or idea that one is the thinker*. The 'thinker' has long since vanished.

Wei Wu Wei[48] defined *wu-nien* as "What thinking is when there is no thinker."[49]

And Śrī Ramaṇa Maharṣi affirms : "Thoughts can continue . . . they do not disturb the Supreme Consciousness"[50]

Just as the sky remains unaffected by the clouds which drift across it, so too does the serene expanse of the 'original mind' remain unaffected by the thoughts which pass across it.

In fact, in the ultimate analysis, thinking (which is symbolic

---

46. Wilber, Ken, *The Spectrum of Consciousness*, p. 175.
47. *Ibid.*, p. 110.
48 Wei Wu Wei, author of *Open Secret*, Hong Univ. Press, 1965 was actually an Irishman named Terrence Gray (Balsekar, Ramesh, *Consciousness Speaks*).
49. Quoted by Wilber, Ken, *The Spectrum of Consciousness*, p. 342.
50. Osborne, Arthur, *The Teachings of Bhagavan Sri Ramana Maharshi In His Own Words*, p. 232.

knowledge or *vijñāna*) is not different from the thought-free state (the second mode of knowing or *prajñā*), because it is *prajñā* which allows the thoughts to be perceived. *Prajñā* is ever-present. It is **that which is perceiving the thoughts.**

Thus the mystic who has seen through the trick of dualism can be said to be thought-free even when he is thinking.

12. States of Consciousness

The average man is familiar with three states:[51]

1. Waking, when he is almost never without thought; and, during sleep,
2. Dreaming, which is associated with thoughts, (corresponding to the state of REM sleep), and
3. Dreamless sleep, (*suṣupti*), the only thought-free state that he knows (corresponding to the state of 'slow wave' sleep).

(Here 'thought' refers to unnecessary thinking, and 'dreams' refer to remembered dreams.)

He does not know the thought-free state when awake, which is really his original, natural state, and which the Liberated One has regained or returned to.

In the case of the Liberated One, both his sleep as well as his waking state are thought-free (not counting 'technical thoughts').

This thought-free waking state is thus the *fourth* state of consciousness, and is therefore called *turīya* (the 'fourth').

---

51. Harshananda, Swami, *A Dictionary of Advaita*, Ramakrishna Math, p. 26.

To summarise:

Waking	*Sleeping*
1. Waking state of average person : Thoughts present	2. Dreaming: Thoughts present
4. Waking state of Liberated person (*turīya* or *jāgr̥t suṣupti*): Thought-free (not counting technical thoughts)	3. Dreamless sleep (*suṣupti*): Thought-free

The average person experiences the states 1, 2 and 3, the Liberated One only 3 and 4.

4 and 3 are analogous in that both are thought-free states (and that is why 4 is also called *jāgr̥t suṣupti* which means 'waking deep-sleep').

Similarly it can be seen that 1 and 2 are also analogous, both being states involving (unnecessary) thinking. It is mainly in this context that it is said that the waking state of the average person is no different from the dreaming state of sleep:

> There is no difference between the dream, and the waking states. . . . Both are the product of the mind.[52]

This statement is echoed by the textbook of physiology which states that in REM sleep the brain activity (as detected by the EEG) is similar to that present during the waking state.[53]

Sometimes the word *turīya* is used to mean the *sahaja sthiti* itself. And sometimes it is used to refer to the ever-present, basic or background awareness which underlies the three states of waking, dreaming and dreamless sleep, in short, *prajñā*.

52. (ed.) Osborne, Arthur, *The Teachings of Bhagavan Sri Ramana Maharshi In His Own Words*, p. 237.

53. Guyton, Arthur C., *Textbook of Medical Physiology*, p. 671-2.

Incidentally, how can it be shown that such basic awareness exists even during sleep? Śrī Ramaṇa Maharṣi used to answer this question by asking 'How do you know that you existed during deep sleep?' (We are certain that we did not cease to exist when we slept). Also, 'How do you wake up from deep sleep when someone calls out your name loudly?' (See Appendix: *turīya.*)

The Liberated One, the Animal and the Child (Difference Between Pre and Trans)

The Liberated One is, in many ways, comparable to a very young child or even an animal, in the sense that he can remain without thought, without concept of (psychological) time, living spontaneously in the present, reacting to the moment. But he is different from them in the sense that he **can** use thought where necessary, he **can** be consciously aware of the world around, he **can** feel the sense of wonder and joy, beatitude and benediction which the animal cannot.

Thus, although the post-Enlightenment stages are in some respects similar to the early developmental stages, the two are in actual fact very different. The early stages are characterised by an **inability** to perform certain functions, like symbolic thinking (and therefore the absence of its consequences, both good and 'bad'—like psychological suffering). The mature adult stage is marked by the **inability** to rise beyond or break through the limits set by these very abilities, which are now well developed, and which, ironically, themselves trap the individual within their confines. The Liberated One has transcended both these limitations. He retains all the abilities of the mature adult, and can also rise beyond the limitations imposed by them. He 'straddles both the worlds like a colossus'.

The newborn baby has no sense of being a separate entity because he is not yet developed to the point where he can conceive of any such thing. The newborn knows no space or time. His awareness is thus spaceless and timeless. It is what Ken

Wilber has called pre-spatial and pre-temporal.[54] All of the developmental stages of evolution prior to language are basically timeless — either completely atemporal, like the newborn, or pre-linear time, like the child before he learns language. But the mystic union is **trans-temporal**, timeless as in 'beyond time'. It is no longer confined to the strait-jacket of linear time, yet it all the while retains knowledge of (and 'potential access to') this conventional world.

And, as Ken Wilber has said, this is true for every other central characteristic of the mystic *versus* the infantile state. The infant is pre-subject/object differentiation, which means the infant cannot distinguish subject from object. But the Liberated state (*sahaja sthiti*) is trans-subject/object, which means that it transcends subject and object (see later in this chapter), while remaining perfectly aware of that conventional duality.

In short, the infantile state is pre-temporal, pre-spatial, pre-verbal and pre-personal. The Liberated state, on the other hand, is trans-temporal, trans-spatial, trans-verbal and trans-personal.[55]

Thus, the animal (and the human baby) has no capacity for formed thought. The average man has it, but misuses it to such an extent that it makes him miserable, whereas the Liberated One has the best of both worlds!

Liberation and Schizophrenia

Some psychiatrists are of the opinion that schizophrenia and mysticism have a lot in common.[56] Nothing could be further from the truth. The sage (or mystic) is the most sane, most (psychologically) normal person on earth. He is totally in touch

---

54. Wilber, Ken, *The Atman Project*, p. 8.
55. *Ibid.*, p. 78.
56. *Ibid.*, p. 151.

with reality — not only the mystical reality, but also the day-to-day temporal reality (*vyāvahārika satya*) which he alone sees in its suchness. The common man sees things not as they are, but coloured to various extents by his ideas. He can therefore be said to be mildly schizophrenic, if we define schizophrenia as being out of touch with reality. The frank schizophrenic, who is labelled as such, represents the extreme other end of the spectrum. Thus we see that Liberation is not akin to schizophrenia. Instead, they represent the two opposite ends of the spectrum. But as our definitions of normality are mainly statistical, the sage, who is a rarity, loses out, and the ubiquitous common man ends up being considered 'normal'. R.D. Laing has said

> True sanity entails in one way or another the dissolution of the normal ego, that false self competently adjusted to our alienated social reality. . . ."[57]

Would the Enlightened (or Liberated) One Reveal the Fact of his Enlightenment?

There is a saying in Zen: "The one who knows, does not say. The one who says, does not know."[58]

This is true as a rule. The Enlightened One does not announce the fact of his Enlightenment from the rooftops to all and sundry, for he requires no fame, adulation or publicity. But he **may** reveal the fact, if the occasion requires it, because, neither does he suffer from a false sense of humility, which is nothing but an inverted sense of pride. He is quite unselfconscious. He may therefore reveal it as a simple matter of fact to those who may be interested to know.

But as Enlightenment itself is a rare event, and as such revelation is further made only on selected occasions, it may be

---

57. Quoted in Wilber, Ken, *The Atman Project*, p. 159.
58. Mello, Anthony de, *The Song of the Bird*, p. 39.

said with a fair degree of accuracy that generally those who declare that they are Enlightened, are not so.

Conversely, it may be taken as a fairly accurate rule of thumb that a person who *denies* that he is Enlightened is generally telling the truth. For there is little reason for an Enlightened person to lie and say he is not.

Why do the Masters Sometimes Say that Actually Speaking, Everyone is Already Enlightened?

"... everyone is in fact Self-realised."
(Śrī Ramaṇa Maharṣi)[59]

The average person believes that 'he' is a separate entity over and above, and apart from the body-mind complex. In reality no such entity exists, and we have defined Enlightenment as the (intuitive) understanding of this very truth. But when the average person hears about this, his immediate reaction is to think of (and pursue) Enlightenment as something to be achieved **by** or **for** the **entity** that he believes himself to be. The original (erroneous) idea that he is a separate entity, is further qualified by yet another idea that he is an 'unenlightened' entity. **This is a double fallacy**. That is why he may become even more miserable than another person who is not bothered about Enlightenment at all (see 'Spiritual Suffering', chapter 3). It is to clear this double fallacy that the Master tries to point out that there are no unenlightened beings or entities, because there are no separate entities at all in the first place (see Buddha's answer, chapter 6).

The truth is that there are no entities — either Enlightened or unenlightened. There **is** the fact of Enlightenment, but this occurs not 'to' an 'entity', it occurs **in** a body-mind complex or unit.

59. (ed.) Osborne, Arthur, *The Teachings of Bhagavan Sri Ramana Maharshi In His Own Words*, p. 19.

The statement 'all are already Enlightened' implies that if (as the average man thinks), Enlightenment is considered to be the disappearance of the entity, then it already exists, because there **are** no entities — there never were any.

(But of course if Enlightenment is defined as the disappearance of the **illusion** of the entity in a body-mind unit, as we have defined it, then all body-mind units could not be considered as Enlightened.)

We are Already ***Brahman*!**

1. In other words, if a person believes that the meaning of Enlightenment is to **become** the Reality (or *Brahman*) (or to be united with that Reality or *Brahman*), then he is labouring under a delusion, for **we are already that Reality**. (In fact, that is why we call it the Reality — that which we really are). If Enlightenment is understood thus, then indeed we must all be said to be already Enlightened.

   Actually, we can only become something which right now we are not; we cannot become that which we already are. Enlightenment simply means **realising** that we are, and have always been, *Brahman*.

2. Also, if someone has to **think** that he is *Brahman*, that too will be an artificiality, perhaps worse than 'forgetting' that one is *Brahman*. The famous assertion '*aham brahmāsmi*' (I am *Brahman*) is a simple statement of fact, not a *mantra* to be repeated *ad nauseam* to hypnotise oneself into believing that one is indeed *Brahman*.

   O mind, thou hast suffered thinking, 'I am a *jīva*'; do not fall into worse delusion by believing 'I am *Brahman*'; in the Transcendental State there is no one (no individual) answering to the name 'I.' (Śrī Ramaṇa Maharṣi)

   — *Guru Ramaṇa Vacana Mālā*, 148

3. Finally, when we talk of 'knowing' That or 'knowing' *Brahman*, the word 'know' is used to mean simply **be**-ing That, as in the direct or non-dual (second) mode of knowing in which the knower **is** the known (see chapter 3), and not 'know' as in temporal knowledge or information and memory, that is the indirect, dualistic or symbolic (first) mode. Thus to **be** That is to **know** That. And in that sense, since we already **are** *Brahman*, it means we already **know** *Brahman*.

Thus in short, the ego-entity cannot be annihilated because it never even existed; we cannot **know** *Brahman* in the sense of learning, information or memory—we can only know It by **being** It; and we cannot **become** *Brahman* because we are already It. And that is why, to prevent the common man from entertaining a double delusion, the Masters tell him that (since he considers Enlightenment to be the destruction of the ego-entity and 'merging' into *Brahman*, then by this definition) he is already Enlightened.

However, the fact that he has to be told this, shows that the illusion of being a separate entity still exists, and hence by our definition, Enlightenment has not occurred in this case (in this body-mind).

fig. 5 From 'GARFIELD' by Jim Davis, Courtesy PAWS INC.

People who have climbed onto the 'self-realisation' bandwagon are like Odie, the dog. In spite of already being *Brahman*, they are reading complicated manuals on how to be (or become) *Brahman*. Moreover, they read them upside down (misinterpret them), resort to elaborate, complex, intricate manoeuvres, and end up with weird results like Odie's upside-down bark. And yet, in the final analysis, even the weird results are not so weird, and the would-be 'awakened souls' remain *Brahman* in spite of themselves, for the upside down "ARF" is only **conceptually** upside down. It really reads the same anyway, for who ever heard of an upside down **sound**?

To put it another way, Zen or realisation is simply **being what you are**. But this sounds absurd, because you are anyway what you are, and in that case everyone is already living the true life of Zen (which is in fact exactly what the sages have been saying). The difference, then, between a sage, (that is, a person who knows he is living the true life of Zen), and another who considers himself a 'spiritual aspirant' (who considers that there is something still to be 'achieved' by him spiritually), is that the former is content in being simply what he is (spiritually), whereas the latter is making hectic efforts to become something different from that which he is, and which he **thinks** is how the real life of Zen should be. What Chuang Tzu has called, "To wear out your brain trying to make things into One without realizing that they are already One. . . ."[60]

Once this is understood and thoroughly absorbed, spiritual efforts fall away, and so do all ideas of so-called spiritual progress. But this does not mean that the person stops effort wilfully because he wants to 'become natural'. In fact, that would again be trying to be something which he is not (because what he is right now, is a person-trying-to-achieve-spiritual-progress). Rather, the understanding includes the apperception of the fact that what he is right now is itself the true life of Zen, and that includes his attempts at being what he is not, (until they fall away of their own, as a result of this very understanding).

This fact, as Ken Wilber has said in a slightly different

60. Quoted by Wilber, Ken, *The Spectrum of Consciousness*, p. 79.

context, is extremely difficult for most individuals to grasp, and the difficulty arises not because it is too complex to understand, but rather because it is too simple, "so that we miss it at the very point where we begin to think about it".[61]

The way we fail to see our own nose.

As Mirzā Ghālib said:

jabki tujha bin nahīn koi moujūd,
to yeh haṅgāmā, ai khudā, kyā hai?

When there exists nothing apart from You, O Lord,
What then is all this racket about?

The 'I' of the Liberated One — Subject and Object

The Liberated One does not think of himself as a separate entity, an 'I'. When he refers to himself, he may use the passive voice, or he may refer to himself in the third person. J. Krishnamurti often referred to himself as 'the speaker'.

But the Liberated One **may** use the word 'I.' When he does so, what does it mean?

1. It may be used simply for convenience of speech, to indicate 'himself' not as an entity but as that particular body-mind apparatus. This is the commonest usage.

2. Subject-object adualism — the Observer *is* the Observed

Nisargadatta Mahārāj once remarked (with reference to his illness) "I am the pain"!

When pain (or anger, or any other sensation) is felt, there is certainly the experiencing of the sensation, but there is really no 'I' who is experiencing the sensation, that is, there is experience-**ing** but there is no experience-**er**. In other words, there is no 'I' **separate** from the sensation who feels the pain or anger.

61. Wilber, Ken, *The Spectrum of Consciousness*, p. 122.

Therefore, "I am (not different from) the pain".

This would appear to be mere quibbling over words, but it is a point of great significance, for the moment we conceive of an 'I' **separate** from the sensation, the process of acceptance or rejection starts. A pleasurable sensation is desired again for the 'I'; a disagreeable sensation is wished away. If there is the feeling that 'I' am angry, it is followed by the feeling that 'I' should not be angry (guilt) or perhaps the feeling that it was perfectly correct for 'me' to be angry (justification). But the fact is that one cannot escape (psychologically) from the sensation because one **is** the sensation, or rather, there is no 'one': the sensation is all there is.

In the case of the average person, the one single, indivisible, complete, self-sufficient fact of perceiving is conceptually extrapolated backwards (or inwards) to an 'I' who is doing the perceiving and forwards (or outwards) to an object which is being perceived. Thus the single act of perceiving is conceptually split into an apparent **subject** who perceives and an apparently separate **object** which is being perceived.

> When there is anger, there is no I, but a second later thought creates the I and says: 'I have been angry' and brings in the idea that I should not be angry. So there is anger and then the I who should not be angry; the division brings conflict. When there is no division between the observer and the observed, and therefore only the thing that is, which is anger, then what takes place? . . . When anger occurs and there is no observer, no division, it blossoms and then ends — like a flower, it blooms, withers and dies away. But as long as one is fighting it, as long as one is resisting it, or rationalising it, one gives life to it. When the observer is the observed, then anger blossoms, grows and naturally dies — therefore there is no psychological conflict in it.[62]

62. Krishnamurti, J., *The Wholeness of Life*, p. 142.

The Liberated One sees all this very clearly. He does not see any separation between the seer and the seen, the perceiver and the perceived, the knower and the known — in short, between subject and object. This is not to say that he feels that 'he' (in here) is the same as the object (out there). It means that he sees or feels no separate 'he' and no separate object — only the fact of perception, the act of perceiving.

Ken Wilber has explained that when the subject *vs.* object dualism vanishes, the subject and object don't vanish, but the gap between them does — or rather it is understood to have never existed in the first place.[63]

And modern science, too, agrees. Quantum mechanics and relativity have shown that the observer cannot be separated from the observed, that event and observer are not separable.

Erwin Schroedinger said "Subject and object are only one. The barrier between them . . . *does not exist.*"[64] (Italics added)

And Werner Heisenberg stated that the common division of the world into subject and object is no longer adequate and leads us into difficulties.[65]

Jñāneśvar has described it thus:

> The inside of a ball of string is not different from its outside. Know that in the same fashion is this triad (the seer, the seen and the seeing) without the quality of 'threeness' (*tinpaṇe viṇ tripuṭi*)
>
> — *Cāṅgdev Pāsaṣṭī*, v.19

> The wind merges with its own movement in the lap of the sky,

---

63. Wilber, Ken, *The Spectrum of Consciousness*, p. 277
64. Schroedinger, Erwin, *What is Life? and Mind and Matter*, p. 137.
65. Heisenberg, Werner, *The Physicist's Conception of Nature*, p. 24.

> The sun loses its individuality when all is light at the end of the world,
> Similarly, on beholding Śiva-Śakti (upon Enlightenment),
> the (distinction between the) seen and the seeing both disappear.
>
> —*Amṛtānubhav*, I.48, 49

> (Just as) two cymbals produce the one note,
> Two flowers but one perfume,
> The lips are two but speech is one,
> The eyes two but sight one. . . .
>
> —*Amṛtānubhav*, I.18, 19

In the classic Hindu pose of sitting meditation (*dhyāna*), the hand is held with the index finger and thumb opposed. This signifies subject-object adualism, which is one of the points the meditator is supposed to dwell upon — Is the finger feeling the thumb, or the thumb feeling the finger? (Actually, both are concepts. Only the feeling of touch—the sensation itself—is real.)

We had earlier seen how Time as we know it is an illusion, this fact being attested to both by the mystic (by direct perception), as well as by modern science (by inference). Now we see that even Space is so. We have not entered into these questions in great detail because this book is more about the practical and medical (psychological) aspect rather the physics and chemistry of the matter. Moreover, an excellent discussion on this already exists.[66]

Thus, we can see that if the entire frame-work of Time and Space, upon which our everyday lives are so totally and inextricably based, is itself illusory, then it would seem logical that our lives themselves, to which we attach such all-encompassing importance, are themselves an illusion, a myth, a hoax.

---

66. Wilber, Ken, *The Spectrum of Consciousness*.

In fact, *saṁsāra* or our everyday life as we see it — the whole thing is a 'tissue of interconnected lies', a fabrication. If only we can see through any one aspect of it, then the entire structure comes crumbling down like a house of cards. Śrī Nisargadatta Mahārāj said the same thing. And Śrī Jñāneśvar compared this to a *dhotī* (an Indian lower garment), in which on pulling one end, the entire garment falls apart.

The moral is that we can take any starting point, and the conclusion reached will be identical. The starting point may be that Consciousness is one, (as we have done), or it may be *bhakti*, in the ultimate surrender of which the one who surrenders himself disappears, or it may be quantum mechanics, or subject-object adualism; whatever it is, if we go deep enough, we reach the Unity of Consciousness.

Throughout, we have discussed (and will continue to discuss) Enlightenment and Liberation as if they are sequential, temporal events or processes occurring in Time and Space to body-mind units. However, in the ultimate analysis, as we have just seen, (in the ultimate Reality as seen by the mystic) there is neither Space nor Time, both being aspects of the phenomenal manifestation of the one timeless, spaceless Reality. All events and objects in Space-Time are simultaneous, apparent 'happenings' (or appearances) in the 'Now-moment'. As such, although Enlightenment and Liberation are discussed as if they are developments in Time, it should be understood that such elaborations are ultimately only relatively or apparently true, within the limits of the phenomenal, relative (and not ultimate) Newtonian reality in which individual body-mind units have a 'birth', a 'death', and 'lives' or life-histories 'in between'. That is why Śrī Ramaṇa Maharṣi said that ultimately, "there is neither creation nor destruction". Nothing has happened !

3. The Liberated person may sometimes also use the word 'I' in its broadest sense to indicate the Universal Consciousness, or 'All-that-is', with which he now feels no separation. The subtle point to be noted here is that he does not *identify* with the Universal Consciousness, that is, he does not feel that 'he' (as the entity) is the Universal Consciousness. He rather feels that there is no separate 'he' apart from the Universal Consciousness. This is the 'I' referred to in the *Bhagavad Gītā*:

> By Me . . . is all this world of living things permeated. . . .
> — IX.4

> I am the soul . . . abiding within the heart of all the beings; I am their origin, middle and also their end.
> — X.20

And Arjuna says:

> . . . Thou art Thyself the All. Thou pervadest the All, and art hence the All. — XI.40

In short, Andrew Lang was not far off the mark when he wrote this cricketing witticism (parody notwithstanding) on the *Gītā*:

> If the wild bowler thinks he bowls,
> Or if the batsman thinks he's bowled,
> They know not, poor misguided souls,
> They too, shall perish unconsoled.
> I am the batsman and the bat,
> I am the bowler and the ball,
> The umpire, the pavilion cat,
> The pitch, the stumps and all.

. . . indeed, it is precisely so!

On the Idea That the World Disappears after Enlightenment

Sometimes the view is expressed that after Enlightenment or Liberation the material world vanishes totally or ceases to be perceived.

This is the result of a misinterpretation of certain mystic statements made by the sages.

For example, the state of *gyāna* was described by Ramaṇa Maharṣi as "the state in which no other is seen, no other heard, no other known". (*Guru Vachaka Kovai*, v.1005)

Here 'no other seen' means that no one is seen **as 'other'**, the sage having lost the dualism of 'me' *vs.* the 'other'.

On the disappearance of *avidyā* and *māyā*, the world does not disappear but is merely seen as it is (*yathābhūtam*), without distortion, in its 'suchness' or 'thusness' (*tathatā* as the Buddhists call it), and not as it is labelled, classified, not through the screen of symbolic thought. Eckhart called it "isness", the Taoists call it *tzu jan*, the Hindus *sahaja*.[67]

The entire manifestation including the perceiver is seen as a 'seamless' whole, that which is perceived being seen as completely **'inseparate'** from That which is perceiving it.

Also, the sage knows that the manifestation that is seen is just an appearance of the underlying one Reality. Not that he does not see the manifestation at all. But he gives it just the significance it deserves, neither less, nor more.

As Ken Wilber has observed, the non-dual awareness of the sage does not mean that in his perception the "universe melts down into one huge monistic lump of clay" or that it becomes a "luminous mush of undifferentiated jelly". To the sage, too, the universe exists exactly as we perceive it — but not necessarily as we name and divide it.[68]

(See also Questions and Answers — 'The world as illusion' at the end of this book.)

All-knowing and All-powerful?

Many people believe that the Liberated person is 'all-knowing' and 'all-powerful'.

67. Wilber, Ken, *The Spectrum of Consciousness*, p. 229.

68. *Ibid.*, p. 161.

The Liberated person does not feel any separation from the Universal Consciousness, but this does not make him all-knowing. It should be clearly understood that the occurrence of Enlightenment or Liberation does not increase the person's worldly knowledge (temporal or secular knowledge). The confusion arises because of the use of the same word 'knowledge' for both the conditions (secular knowledge as well as Enlightenment), and also because the common people relate the Liberated person to God, who is supposed to be 'all-knowing'. It is further reinforced by the occurrence of 'miracles' in the vicinity of the Liberated person (see Appendix).

It is true that the Enlightened person may have a much keener insight into worldly affairs because he sees things very clearly, in a totally objective way, and therefore his impressions may be more in tune with reality. The average person's judgement is often clouded by conditionings and bias.

> A clear, illusion-free view of life's 'interpatterned threads' is one part of what many mean by the concept of wisdom.[69]

But many people believe that the Liberated One is an expert in all matters. He is hence often asked questions on matters unrelated to spirituality. These he may or may not answer. If he does answer, he will do so to the best of his ability relying on his worldly knowledge (like any average person), and the accuracy of the answer will necessarily depend on his education and information. In such matters his opinion has no more value than that of any other objective, unbiased and sensible person. And the opinion of an expert in the particular field is likely to be more correct.

People often claim that so-and-so saint is 'very powerful'. This statement is a contradiction in terms, for there is no such

---

69. Weisz and Schopler, Morgan, King, *Introduction to Psychology*, p. 497.

thing as 'so-and-so' saint. The saint is a saint precisely because he has lost his (illusion of) separateness from the Universal Consciousness. The saint **is**, when the person (as a separate psychological entity) **is not**. The Liberated person is not really a separate 'person' at all (psychologically). Rather, he is inseparate from the Universal Consciousness, and so there is no separate 'one' to be all-powerful. If there were, he would not be considered Liberated at all.

> I have no corporeal existence,
> but Universal Benevolence is my divine body.
> I have no physical power,
> but Uprightness is my strength.
> I have no religious clairvoyance
> beyond what is bestowed by Wisdom.
> I have no power of miracle
> other than the attainment of quiet happiness.
> — *Oracle of Sumiyoshi*

The Liberated One is not a superman or a god. He is simply the most natural, the most uncomplicated of human beings. Śrī Ramaṇa Maharṣi said,

> The state we call realisation is simply being oneself, not **knowing** anything or **becoming** anything.[70]

Actually, the Liberated person is most ordinary, utterly natural, *sahaja*; it is to us un-ordinary people that he appears extra-ordinary. Kabīr said,

> *sahaja sahaja sab koi kahai, sahaja na cīnhai koi,*
> *jinhi sahajai sāhib milai, sahaja kahījai soi.*

> Everyone talks of *sahaja*, the natural state, but no-one recognises or knows what it is, He who realises the Lord

70. (ed.) Osborne, Arthur, *The Teachings of Bhagavan Sri Ramana Maharshi In His Own Words*, p. 198.

> naturally, spontaneously, without effort (*sahajai*), **he** is to be called *sahaja* (the natural one).[71]

As Alan Watts says[72]

> The Zen masters are quite human. . . . The perfection of Zen is to be perfectly and simply human . . . (it is) the ordinary run of men . . . (who) are, in one way or another, at odds with their own humanity, and are attempting to be angels or demons. . . .
>
> The wild geese do not intend to cast their reflection,
> The water has no mind to receive their image.

Not magic, mystery, power, miracles, meditation . . . but naturalness, spontaneity, simplicity, and **compassion** . . .

Psychological Suffering and Liberation

We started our discussion with the fact of psychological suffering, and we will now see what happens to such suffering during the spiritual evolution of the individual which we have just described.

We had seen in chapter 3 that it is me-based spiritual effort which, when unsuccessful (as it inevitably must be), causes what we called spiritual suffering. We also saw in chapter 4 that such effort spontaneously falls away after the intellectual understanding, even before Enlightenment. It will therefore be easily seen that the intellectual understanding itself puts an end to such suffering.

The intellectual understanding is eventually followed by Enlightenment. Post-Enlightenment, the earliest type of psychological suffering to disappear is the one caused by unnecessary thinking based directly on the premise of the

---

71. Singh, Dr. Jaidev and Singh, Dr.Vasudev, *Kabir Vani Piyush* (Hindi), part II, p. 98.

72. Watts, Alan W., *The Way of Zen.*

existence of the separate ego-entity. Unnecessary thinking directly related to the misconceived I-notion drops away easily after Enlightenment, when this illusion is clearly seen for what it is.

Examples: Ideas of 'name and fame', power, prestige, and so on.

Psychological suffering related to ideas which are not ego-based but 'body-based', that is, concerning the material body or physical organism, do not disappear with Enlightenment alone. But as the process of de-conditioning proceeds to the stage where even the distinction between body and the environment becomes blurred (that is, subject-object duality becomes weak), as well as the idea of psychological time, such ideas, too, weaken, and eventually disappear. And with their disappearance, the corresponding psychological suffering also disappears. That is, these ideas (and the related suffering) begin to disappear when the sense of being a separate 'person' to whom things happen in Time disappears.

Example: Thinking related to bodily needs, and real material needs — like housing, clothing, livelihood, and so on (different from purely psychological needs like fame and prestige). Even so, planning about such matters will necessarily continue, but the (unnecessary) anxiety and worrying disappear.

Finally, there are the ideas related to the basic biological urges like hunger, thirst, sex, etc. These are the last to disappear. But what must be clearly understood is that it is **not the urges themselves which disappear, but the unnecessary thinking about them**. The urges have no reason to disappear, for they are basic instincts. Most people have a very mistaken picture of the Liberated One as a sort of a sexless vegetable, or one who keeps his instincts totally suppressed, or one for whom sex is taboo.

But, as J. Krishnamurti said, it is not sex that is the problem, it is **thinking** about sex.

AWARENESS

The reader who is not interested in technical details may skip this section entitled 'Awareness' without loss of continuity.

Anatomy and Neuro-physiology

To recapitulate what we had mentioned in the note at the beginning of this book, we are using the word 'consciousness' (with the small 'c') for the individual consciousness, and the word 'Consciousness' (capital 'C') to denote the collective or Universal Consciousness. The word 'awareness' is specifically used to denote the active aspect of consciousness, or consciousness 'in action'.

To the mystic, it is obvious and self-evident that the original Consciousness is not physically located or contained **inside** the body. (Nor is it outside the body). It is the body which is an object in Consciousness. Indeed, the entire phenomenal universe is an object in Consciousness, and in this phenomenal manifestation, it only appears as if the (individual) consciousness is a function of the brain which is located in the physical body. Thus, it only **appears** to us as if the consciousness arises in the body, and **as if** it begins with the birth of that body, and ends with its death. Just as in a dream, the dream-consciousness appears to originate in the brain of the body seen in the dream, so also the one Consciousness appears to us phenomenally as the individual consciousness when it is operating through the individual brain, in **apparent** isolation from other brains. But in reality, Consciousness is original, primordial, and the birth and death of the body are events that apparently occur in conceptual Space-Time within that Consciousness. Consciousness has no origin or end, for these ideas relate to Time, whereas Consciousness is beyond concepts of Space and Time. Such descriptions cannot apply to it.

This is not merely mysticism. A similar view has also been expressed by quantum physicist Schroedinger, who said that the localisation of the personality, of the conscious mind, inside the body is only symbolic, just an aid for practical use.[73]

Is Then the Awareness in the Body, or is the Body Really in Awareness?

Of course, the rationalist would say that the former is obviously true, for if not for the body, where is the question of awareness? On the other hand, the mystic sees the body as an object in Awareness. This is as obviously true, for if it were not, we would not be aware of the body.

The problem is that whereas a computer could be said to be aware of its environment in a certain sense, the body is not only aware of its environment, but is also aware of **itself**. (This property of the human brain is called 'self-reference'.) Hence, both statements cannot be disproved. It is like asking whether the chicken came first or the egg.

Is it possible that both statements are true? If light can exist both as a wave and as a particle (or a wavicle), if an electron can exist at several different places at once, this will not sound so strange to a quantum physicist. As Haldane said, "the universe is not only queerer than we suppose, it is queerer than we can suppose." To give a simplistic explanation, we could say that both are true from different angles of perspective or view, or at different levels of reality. But that will leave us wide open to the next question — which level of reality is higher, or more real? It would be tempting for us to say that it is the mystical view which is higher. But the final truth is that no view can be said to be higher, or rather 'no-view' is the highest reality. In fact, in the final reality this question would not arise, for the very question 'which is in which?' arises because of our limited, dualistic, symbolic-thinking. As Śrī Ramaṇa Maharṣi said:

There is neither creation nor destruction, neither destiny

73. Schroedinger, Erwin, *What is Life? and Mind and Matter*, p. 133.

nor free will; Neither path nor achievement; this is the final truth.[74]

Nevertheless, it must be conceded that within the limited reference of Space-Time, it certainly appears to us as if the awareness has its origin in the body, or is a function of the body. And we will now pursue this discussion at the level of that relative reality.

As Śaṅkarācārya explained to the enquiring king who had just observed the illustrious sage rush up a tree to avoid a mad elephant, "Yes, the elephant is illusory. But then so am I, so are you, and so is the tree. Your seeing me run up the tree too was an illusion."

We will therefore try to see **where** in the body the awareness originates (or appears to originate).

As far as the cerebral cortex is concerned, we know that the left hemisphere is associated with language and verbal symbolism, the right with non-verbal experiences.

As we had postulated earlier (chapter 6), **Enlightenment happens at the level of the cortex**. It occurs when the right cortical hemisphere (R-H) forces the left hemisphere (L-H) to abandon, not just the old 'story-line', but to abandon the very need for having any story-line at all (which is really its need for psychological security — the brain seeks security in a consistent story-line).

However, the source or seat of the timeless awareness of the Liberated State, that is, *prajñā*, cannot be in the cortex, which is the thinking part of the brain. The pure, non-dual awareness of *prajñā* is upstream of all conceptualisation. We will have to look for it deeper down.

Ken Wilber, too, agrees that *prajñā* (which he calls 'organismic' awareness) is not a function of the cortex. He writes that though the R-H is said to be the seat of 'intuitive' knowledge

74. Quoted by Wilber, Ken, *The Spectrum of Consciousness*, p. 196.

(while the L-H is the seat of logical and analytic knowledge), the 'intuitive' knowledge of the R-H is merely to see 'patterned wholes' and is not to be confused with *prajñā*.[75]

The seat of the basic, primordial, undifferentiated awareness, *prajñā*, which is the basic awareness or 'sense-of-being' present to some extent in all sentient beings with at least a fair degree of neural development, has to be some gray matter[76] which is present even in relatively lower forms of animals say like reptiles, and which, in humans, should be situated rather deep inside the brain, both anatomically and neuro-physiologically. It has to be earlier in evolution than that part of the brain responsible for symbolic thinking which is the cortex, but has to be more advanced than the primitive portions controlling the basic functions like heart beat and respiration (which are the medulla, pons and the mesencephalon) as also those involved in muscular coordination, equilibrium and balance (namely the cerebellum). Probably the only part of the brain which fits these requirements is the **thalamus**.

It is probably the thalamus which is referred to by the ancient Indian mystics as the seat of awareness inside the skull. Perhaps the 'thousand-petalled lotus' of *yoga* also refers to the thalamus with its myriad neuronal connections radiating from it. Some people have associated these references with the pineal gland, but it is now fairly well understood that the pineal gland has no such function. It is the thalamus which acts as a relay station for impulses on the pathway to the cortex, and is known to be involved in an important way with the sense of cortical awareness.[77]

---

75. Wilber, Ken, *The Spectrum of Consciousness*, p. 342-3.

76. Gray Matter consists of nerve cells or neurons, whereas 'white matter' contains mainly their connecting fibres.

77. Guyton, Arthur C., *Textbook of Medical Physiology*, pp. 652, 668, 558, 564.

The study of the EEG (brain waves) correlates closely with this hypothesis. It is to be expected that the average person's brain would show a more or less asynchronous pattern, especially during 'unnecessary' thinking, whereas when the thalamic influence predominates, the pattern should be more synchronised. This is seen as beta and alpha wave patterns respectively.

Let us now see briefly how the known facts about these waves fit in with our theory.

Alpha waves are rhythmic waves found in normal adults in a quiet resting state of cerebration. Alpha waves will *not* occur in the cortex without connections with the thalamus. Also, stimulation of the thalamus often results in alpha waves. Therefore, it is assumed that the alpha waves result from **spontaneous activity** in the generalised thalamo-cortical system. They represent synchronous activation of literally millions of cortical neurons during each wave.

Beta waves are asynchronous and occur during specific mental activity or during tension.

Theta waves occur in stages 2 and 3 of slow wave sleep.

(A fourth type, called Delta waves occur strictly in the cortex independently of activities in lower regions of the brain. They occur in stage 4 or very deep "slow wave" sleep).[78]

Thus we could say that the waves signify the following:

Alpha : Synchronous (harmonious) thalamo-cortical activity, (thalamus, with cortex quiescent or having necessary thoughts).

Beta: Asynchronous cortical activity (cortex active and excited, especially with unnecessary thinking), thalamic activity masked.

---

78. Guyton, Arthur C., *Textbook of Medical Physiology*, pp. 669-72.

Theta: Only thalamus, (cortex 'asleep').

The mystic probably fluctuates between (1) alpha — when awake and working or thinking (necessary thoughts), or when asleep with unremembered dreams; and (2) theta — when awake with 'fasting' mind, or asleep (dreamless sleep).

Studies of Zen meditators have also shown similar findings.

> EEG studies of Zen meditators confirm that the state of consciousness achieved by *Zazen* (Zen meditation) is a neurophysiological reality with appearance of alpha-rhythm characteristic of relaxed wakefulness. In Zen meditation, however, this shows increase in amplitude and decrease of frequency succeeded in many cases by theta rhythm.[79]

Sleep

It had been mentioned earlier ('States of Consciousness'), that the waking and dreaming states (of the average person) are both similar, (and our ancients too have always stated this) and we see that the brain activity shows **beta waves in both the waking state and in REM sleep**.

In fact, the textbook states:

> . . . (In REM sleep) the electroencephalogram shows a desynchronised pattern of beta waves similar to those that occur during wakefulness. Therefore, this type of sleep is also frequently called desynchronised sleep, . . . or paradoxical sleep because it is a paradox that a person can be still asleep despite marked activity in the brain.
>
> In summary, REM sleep is a type of sleep in which the brain is quite active. However, the brain activity is not

---

79. Kretschmer, W., "Meditative Techniques in Psychotherapy", in *Altered States of Consciousness*, ed. by C.T. Tart.

channelled in the proper direction for persons to be aware of their surroundings and therefore to be awake.[80]

As mentioned earlier ('Dreamless Sleep'), it is during slow wave sleep that the brain really rests, and which is probably the real sleep. In REM sleep the brain is as active as it is in the waking state, and does not rest. REM sleep is probably an anomalous variant evolved as a result of unnecessary thinking.

We could now try to understand how the awareness operates in the case of the mystic and in the case of the average man.

Awareness of the Mystic (the Liberated One)

Pure or basic thalamic awareness, (we have used these terms rather differently than the medical text-books), our natural, *sahaja* state, devoid of (or 'upstream of') thought and conceptualisation, without concepts of space and time. This is present in all individuals at all times, but is seen in its purest form in the mystic when in a wakeful, relaxed, resting state. It underlies all the states of awareness (like waking and sleep) and is referred to as *turīya* in Hindu spiritual literature. This is the *prajñā* of Buddhism, and the 'organismic' awareness of Ken Wilber. It would be represented by a predominantly theta wave pattern on the EEG.

When active or working, to the basic thalamic awareness is superadded the cortical activity involving what we have called 'necessary thinking'. This is seen in the mystic while at work. This is the brain working in harmony with itself — thalamic awareness with harmonious cortical activity. *Prajña* with harmonious *vijñāna*. The EEG would show an alpha rhythm.

Average Man's Awareness

Thalamic awareness *apparently* distorted by disharmonious cortical activity (unnecessary thinking) superimposed upon it

80. Guyton, Arthur C., *Textbook of Medical Physiology*, p. 671-2.

on the surface of the brain. This is cortical activity with thalamic awareness apparently repressed, allowing the cortex to run away with its ideas. The hold of the thalamus on reality or actuality, on the present, is apparently lost. It is marked by excessive, unnecessary cortical cerebration — what we have called 'unnecessary' thoughts. This is *prajñā* (apparently) distorted by disharmonious *vijñāna*. It should correspond to the beta pattern on the EEG.

Somewhere in-between will lie the awareness described as existential awareness by Ken Wilber, and which we have identified as the awareness of the **early post-Enlightenment period**, marked by the presence of space-time perception, but with diminishing unnecessary thinking.

Compassion

We did say earlier that the sage is compassionate (p. 118) but we did not say why. We have not discussed this so far because compassion is not really a property or virtue of the sage. Compassion is a property of the one Consciousness, and as such, is always potentially there. But in the average individual, compassion is (partly or fully) blocked or masked by his sense of separateness, which makes him think of the different body-minds as 'others'. It is thus the feeling of 'othership' which blocks compassion in the average man. In fact one could say that the capacity for compassion is inversely proportional to the degree of the feeling of otherness in any individual, and whenever compassion is felt, it is because of the residual feeling of oneness left in that individual. The very words 'COM-passion' or 'SYM-pathy' seem to suggest this. A sage, on the other hand, sees no one as 'other'. To him therefore compassion occurs naturally – as naturally as anyone would feel for oneself. Thus the sage is not merely compassionate. Rather, being completely inseparate from Consciousness, he is compassion incarnate.

6

The Guru

ALTHOUGH Enlightenment can happen without any external help, often the key is provided by another person, usually Enlightened. This person is then called the *guru*.

Is the Guru Essential for Enlightenment?

Most spiritual traditions consider that a *guru* is essential for Enlightenment, but views have also been expressed to the contrary, notably by J. Krishnamurti.

While there can be no doubt that in most cases in which Enlightenment occurs, the spark is provided (to the ripe recipient) by another Enlightened person, it is also true that in the case of most average 'seekers', the existence of a *guru* proves to be of little benefit, and sometimes, ironically enough, even proves to be a hindrance, at times the final obstacle, to Enlightenment.

For one thing, the seeker, being 'ignorant', is unable to judge who is the proper *guru*, and may well land up with an unenlightened *guru*, a person who is himself living in delusion — an instance of the blind leading the blind. And this is what often does happen.

But paradoxically, when the seeker has reached a level of understanding when he can really select a proper, Enlightened *guru*, he will have already reached beyond the need for any *guru*.

Moreover, even if a seeker has an Enlightened *guru*, he may fail to make the proper use of his teaching in one of several ways:

1. He may devote himself largely to the worship of the *guru*'s physical form, rather than pay attention to what he is saying — a custom unfortunately widely prevalent in India.
2. Forgetting the basic purpose of having a *guru*, he may merely get used to relying upon him for psychological support for the material problems of life.
3. He may believe the teaching to be a sort of an automatic formula to Enlightenment, and memorise it and keep repeating it verbally, mechanically — another practice which is very common in India.
4. He may fail to comprehend the teaching, and misinterpret it in the light of his own fixed ideas, beliefs and preconceived notions, by clinging to them tenaciously. Man is often found to be as possessive about his ideas as of his physical belongings.
5. He may partly understand the teaching, but, forming a mental picture or image of the Reality from the *guru*'s description, become addicted to conceptualising or intellectualising about it.

Thus, most average seekers, even after hearing a genuine *guru*'s teaching, fail to actually act upon it, and, at the end of the day, are no nearer to the Understanding than before.

To summarise, having a truly Enlightened *guru* is a matter of rare good fortune, but even this can be totally useless, or may even prove to be an impediment, depending on the ripeness and aptitude (or the lack of it) of the disciple, and what use he makes of the teaching. Most people ignore the teaching and idolise the teacher, which really gets them nowhere, (for what they are doing is merely substituting one idol for another). Or they misuse the teaching in such a way that, rather than helping them, it becomes an obstacle to understanding the Truth. The fact that there are so many *guru*s each with so many more disciples, and very little to show for it in terms of Enlightened people, bears witness to this.

The true disciple must use the *guru*'s teaching as a stepping stone to higher things, to go **beyond** the very need for a guru.

The truly Enlightened *guru*, however, **never sees the disciple as a separate entity**.

In the *Diamond Sūtra*, after speaking of compassion, the Buddha explains that in reality there are no others to be compassionate to. The Lord Buddha continues:

> Do not think, Subhūti, that the Tathāgata (i.e., the Buddha) would consider within himself; I will deliver human beings. That would be a degrading thought. Why? Because there are really no sentient beings to be delivered by the Tathāgata. Should there be any sentient beings to be delivered by the Tathāgata, it would mean that the Tathāgata was cherishing within his mind arbitrary conceptions of phenomena such as one's own self, other selves, living beings and a universal self. Even when the Tathāgata refers to himself, he is not holding within his mind any such arbitrary thought. Only terrestrial human beings think of selfhood as being a personal possession. Subhuti, even the expression 'terrestrial beings' as used by the Tathāgata does not mean that there are any such beings. It is only used as a figure of speech.[1]

---

1. Goddard, Dwight, *A Buddhist Bible*, quoted in *Buddhism and Christianity in the Light of Hinduism* by Arthur Osborne, p. 114 and also in *The Teachings of Bhagavan Sri Ramana Maharshi in His Own Words*, (ed.) Arthur Osborne, (5th edn.), p. 228.

If there are no 'Others' then Why Does the Arhat Teach?

Indeed, some do not. People then say that these teach 'in silence'. In fact, they are silent not because they have nothing to say, but rather because they see that there is no 'one' to say anything, and no 'others' to say it to.

But the Liberated One who does teach, does so for the reasons given below:

1. Although he sees that there are no separate entities, he also sees that the delusion of being separate entities is the cause of much suffering in the world, and such suffering is avoidable. He sees that though there are no entities who suffer, no 'sufferers', there is **suffering**. Compassion therefore makes him speak out.

2. There may be some 'ripe' persons for whom a few words of guidance may make all the difference.

   "Teach 'not-ripe' person, waste of words. Not teach ripe person: waste of person."

3. The Liberated person does not teach as a form of self-fulfilment. He does not receive sustenance or gratification from teaching. His teaching is more in the nature of a spontaneous outpouring in response to the demands and needs of his disciples, or of the occasion.

J. Krishnamurti said:

> . . . I do not depend on you as a group who come to listen to the speaker. The speaker is not attached to a particular group nor is it necessary for him to have a gathering. . . . (But) I think when one sees something true and beautiful, one wants to tell people about it, out of affection, out of compassion, out of love. And if there are those who are not interested, that is all right, but those who are interested can perhaps gather together. Can you ask the

flower why it grows, why it has perfume? It is for the same reason the speaker talks.[2]

Why does the bird sing?. . . Not because he has a statement, but because he has a song. (Anthony de Mello)[3]

4. Another reason why the Liberated one speaks out is to 'repay' what could be called the 'Debt of Speech' (that is, of conceptual knowledge).

   Conceptual (verbal) knowledge received from the *guru* paves the way for true knowledge. This is the 'debt' or obligation which is owed to Speech. After Enlightenment, it is sought to be 'repaid' by expressing the truth in words for the benefit of mankind. In other words, the Enlightened One feels an obligation or compunction to express or record his own feelings and observations in words. He does this not exactly for the benefit of 'others', because he sees that there are no others, but rather in the manner of a true scientist performing an experiment and recording his results. He puts on record his own corroboration of the conclusions of earlier sages, which conclusions may have helped him to realise that state which is beyond speech.

   However, he is quite clearly aware that this 'debt' can never be fully 'repaid', because this Truth can never be fully described in words.

5. All things tend to equilibrium. Although it is said that any system, left to itself, tends to disorder, yet even the seeming disorder in the Universe is the result of this very tendency to equilibrium. The word 'cosmos' means

---

2. Krishnamurti, J., *Questions and Answers*, pp. 87-8.
3. Mello, Anthony de, *The Song of the Bird*, pp. 4-5.

> 'order' in Greek, the opposite of chaos. The illusion of the 'me' may be seen as an anomaly in the functioning of the Universe. Only humans suffer from it, and humans occupy an infinitesimal speck of Space-Time in the cosmos. Nature would therefore seek to correct this anomaly. The insight and the teaching of the sages is the corrective mechanism.

Ramaṇa Maharṣi said the word *upadeśa* literally means 'restoring an object to its proper place'.[4]

Can the Guru Grant Enlightenment?

It was mentioned earlier that 'true' knowledge, which occurs with Enlightenment, is not really a form of knowledge in the sense of information or memory, that is to say, it is not temporal knowledge. It is rather an instantaneous, intuitive insight, which cannot be taught or learnt. It can only be roughly indicated or pointed out.

The *guru* cannot therefore grant true knowledge, for true knowledge, by its very nature, cannot be given or received. He can only give conceptual knowledge.

The Guru and Conceptual Knowledge

The sage 'sees' the Truth or Reality for himself, but what he sees (or feels or knows) is something non-verbal. To communicate this experience to others, he has to express this non-verbal 'knowledge' in words, in the form of verbal (that is, conceptual) knowledge. This, different sages may do differently, and with different degrees of excellence. Some may do it poetically, some with graphic descriptions, some in enigmatic statements, and still others may prefer to keep quiet, for in any case the description

---

4. (ed.) Osborne, Arthur, *The Teachings of Bhagavan Sri Ramana Maharshi In His Own Words*, p. 113.

is not the thing. As Fr. Anthony said, no one ever became drunk on the word **wine**.[5]

The fact is that one can convey the impression but not the actual feeling. It is difficult to describe even an ordinary emotion or a colour (or a taste or a tune) in words. Some may do it better and with more fidelity than others but it is never the same as seeing or feeling for oneself. Imagine different persons describing a beautiful scene to a blind man. Though the scene is the same, different persons will describe it differently. Also, the fact remains that no amount of description can give the actual 'feel' of the scene to the blind man. As Śrī Ramaṇa Maharṣi said,

> He (the Liberated One) cannot describe that state. He can only **be** That.[6] (Emphasis added)

What, Then, is the Use of Conceptual Knowledge?

Conceptual knowledge is merely to be used as the starting point for the seeker's own investigation. Conceptual knowledge (that is, knowledge gained by *śravaṇa*, hearing), if properly and intelligently acted upon (*manana* — reflection, and *nididhyāsana* — cogitation), leads to the **intellectual understanding** of the situation, which creates conditions favourable for the spontaneous occurrence of the **intuitive understanding** which constitutes true Awakening.

So ultimately the disciple **has** to think out his salvation for himself. The Buddha's last words were "O monks, . . . work out your deliverance with earnestness."[7]

Svamī Vivekānanda said:

---

5. Mello, Anthony de, *The Song of the Bird*, p. 3.
6. Osborne, Arthur, *The Teachings of Bhagavan Sri Ramana Maharshi In His Own Words*, p. 198.
7. Radhakrishnan, S., *Religion and Culture*, p. 122.

> Work out your own religion,
> Work out your own salvation.

The conceptual knowledge derived from the *guru* (or scriptures) must be put to use by applying it in one's own case, to see in one's own particular instance how the me-based thoughts arise, based on the fiction of the illusory 'me'. The use of conceptual knowledge is to replace 'wrong' concepts (which are a major obstacle to Enlightenment) by 'right' concepts (which are only a minor obstacle). 'Right concepts' constitute the intellectual understanding. However, the seeker must be eventually prepared to give even these up, if true knowledge (the intuitive understanding) is to occur. If intellectual understanding becomes an end in itself, it will not lead to Enlightenment; it will merely make the person a spiritual scholar.

One Zen master was said to have been in the habit of hitting the questioner on the head with his staff, when asked to demonstrate the Reality. That was his way of drawing the disciple away from sterile intellectual discussions and pointless theorising about the Reality, of drawing him directly, (albeit painfully) into the actuality, the reality of the present moment.

This then is a practical investigation into the way one's own mind works. This is thus a process in which thought is used to end (me-based) thought — a thorn to remove a thorn.

As Paul Brunton was told by the 'Sage who never speaks':

> You have thought yourself into your present ignorance; now think yourself back into wisdom . . . . Thought is like a bullock-cart which carries a man into the darkness of a mountain tunnel. Turn it backwards, and you will be carried back to the light again. . . . This backward turning of thought is the highest *yoga*.[8]

Ramaṇa Maharṣi said "Go back the way you came." He called

8. Brunton, Paul, *A Search in Secret India*, p. 113.

this Self-enquiry or 'turning the mind inwards'.[9]

The *Jñāneśvarī* says:

āpale pāyavarī, cālije āpule pāṭhīvarī

On our own feet must we walk back the way we came

—*Jn*, VI., 390

Christ asked his followers to 'return to the mother's womb and be born again'.

(This subject will be tackled in detail in chapter 8).

And all of a sudden, a ripe disciple may 'see' the truth in a flash.

Thus ultimately, the *guru* can only provide 'food for thought'. He can only plant the seed of Truth in the heart of the disciple. If the ground is fertile, it will sprout, grow, flower forth and bear fruit, like in Christ's parable about the farmer and his seeds. As J. Krishnamurti said,

> It is that seed that is flowering in me. . . . That seed which has been planted by my awareness, alertness, and intense listening, *that* seed will flower."[10]

mogarā phulalā . . .
ivalesey ropa lāviyaley dvārī,
tayācā velu gelā gaganāvairi

the *mogarā* (jasmine) has blossomed . . .
the tiny seedling planted at my doorstep (by the *guru*)
has grown into a creeper reaching beyond the sky.

— Jñāneśvar

But the seed needs space to grow. Space free of fixed beliefs,

9. Osborne, Arthur, *The Teachings of Bhagavan Sri Ramana Maharshi In His Own Words*, 5th edn., pp. 66, 132.

10. Jayakar, Pupul, *Fire in the Mind*, p. 95.

preconceived notions and ideas. It needs the open space of an open mind.

The Guru as Teacher

Although all Liberated persons can 'see' the Reality, leading the 'way' to see it is difficult for there is no such 'cut and dried' way or method. As a teacher, the Liberated One may be good, bad or indifferent. Teaching, after all, is a skill and art unrelated to the fact of Enlightenment. Teaching involves communication skills which not all may possess to the same degree. Of two scientists with comparable knowledge, one may be a very good teacher, and another not so good.

The Attitude of the Guru

As ultimately the seeker must think out his own salvation, the effective teacher must **make the disciple think for himself**. This is all-important.

Thus, it will be seen that the teacher fulfils two functions:

1. He gives conceptual knowledge, that is a verbal description of the truth. (The theoretical aspect.)
2. He makes the disciple think (and eventually see) for himself. (The practical aspect.) This is more important (for conceptual knowledge can be had from the scriptures as well).

Also, the teacher must offer not authority, but helpful guidance.

> Together we are going to seek, find, discover the right answer.[11]

As two friends sitting in the park on a bench in the

---

11. Krishnamurti, J., *Questions and Answers.*

dipping light; . . . Let us talk it over as two friends . . .

(J. Krishnamurti)[12]

If the *guru* asks for blind faith and belief, then he is not likely to be helpful as far as Enlightenment is concerned. Psychological support or psychological security is perhaps all that such a *guru* could offer to his disciple.

Must the Guru Himself be Enlightened?

There are teachers who profess to teach on the authority of their *guru* or the scriptures alone (without having seen the truth themselves). But, as Fr. Anthony remarked, can a kiss be transmitted through a messenger?

This is not to say that such a teacher will not be useful at all. However, as explained above, the teacher fulfils two functions — giving conceptual knowledge, and making the disciple think for himself. Not having seen the truth himself, the unenlightened teacher is tremendously disadvantaged in fulfilling the first function, which he can only do in a 'second-hand' manner. As to making the disciple think, the question may be asked why such a teacher has not done so in his own case.

Therefore an unenlightened teacher, to be effective, must have had *at least the intellectual understanding*. Such a teacher must also be capable of thinking out his own salvation, and that means we are talking about a person who has had the intellectual understanding **and is en route to his own Enlightenment**. This can therefore be taken to be an exceptional case, and not the rule. In most other cases, the unenlightened *guru* would be of limited help, and would run the real risk of misleading his disciples.

(For role of the *guru*, see chapter 8, pp. 171, 187.)

12. Quoted in article 'J. Krishnamurti's teachings — relevance to mental health' by A. Venkoba Rao, in *Indian Journal of Psychiatry*, Oct. 1995, 37(4), p. 155.

What should be the Attitude of the Disciple?

The disciple must keep aside his preconçeived notions, ideas and beliefs — his mental baggage, and know how to **listen**. He must listen without the intervention of his mind — direct listening. Not trying to remember, to grasp, to opine, compare, evaluate — just listen. He must let the words have their own effect.

> The words of the scholar are to be understood. The words of the Master are not to be understood. They are to be listened to as one listens to the wind in the trees and the sound of the river and the song of the bird.[13]

> . . . don't bring in the mind for a moment. When the brain is absolutely quiet, . . . *That is real listening.*
>
> (J. Krishnamurti)[14]

What must he do After Listening?

After listening must come reflection, and finally application (Self-enquiry). This will be discussed in chapter 8.

What will be his Attitude to the Guru After His (the Disciple's) Enlightenment?

After his own Enlightenment, the disciple too realises that he was never a separate (psychological) entity, and he no longer sees the *guru* (or anyone else) as separate from himself — "and all that is left is for both to have a hearty laugh together"

But he does feel an overwhelming sense of gratitude towards the **persona**[15] (and not the person) of the *guru*, who has served as a conduit for the occurrence of his Enlightenment, who has

13. Mello, Anthony de, *The Song of the Bird*, p. 5.
14. Jayakar, Pupul, *Fire in the Mind*, p. 203.
15. *Persona*: aspect of personality as shown to or perceived by others Literally (Latin): Mask worn by actor on stage.

been instrumental in lighting the flame of understanding in his heart. This sense of gratitude has often led to the disciple's eulogising the *guru* in no uncertain terms.

However, this has been generally misinterpreted as an acknowledgement of the authority of the *guru*.

Authority

Authority has actually never been given much importance in either Hinduism or in Buddhism.

Towards the end of the *Bhagavad Gītā*, Kṛṣṇa tells Arjuna (XVIII.63):

> . . . ponder over (all) this well and fully, and (thereafter) **do as thou willest**. (Emphasis added)

The *Bṛhadāraṇyaka Upaniṣad* (II.4-5) tells us that we can have *ātma-darśana* through *śravaṇa, manana,* and *nididhyāsana* (listening, contemplation, and cogitation)[16]

The Buddha said *ātma dīpobhava* (Be a lamp unto yourself)[17] and asked us to accept his words only after examining them and not merely out of regard for him: *parīkṣya bhikṣavo grāhyam madvaco na tu gauravāt*.[18]

J. Krishnamurti said:

> There is no authority here. I happen to sit on a platform for convenience so that everybody can see, but that little height does not give me any authority whatsoever.[19]

Blind acceptance of the truth as it is verbally enunciated by the

16. Radhakrishnan, S., *Religion and Culture*, p. 23.
17. Diwakar, R.R., Bhagwan Buddha, 1980, 78-86, quoted in *Indian Journal of Psychiatry article.*
18. Radhakrishnan, S., *Religion and Culture*, p. 15.
19. Krishnamurti, J., *Questions and Answers*.

guru or the scriptures is of no use. We will remain unchanged, merely parroting the truth as quoted by someone but never seeing it for ourselves.

> A truth that comes from outside always bears the stamp of uncertainty (Scientist and social philosopher, Rudolf Steiner).

What is required is *viveka* — **discrimination**, not *andah-śraddhā*, blind faith.

> One must begin with doubt — completely doubting — then you end up with certainty. But if you start with certainty, then you end up in uncertainty and chaos.[20]

Excessive adulation of the teacher may even take the form of actual worship of his physical form, as mentioned earlier. What is then lost sight of is the fact that, as J. Krishnamurti often said, it is not the speaker who is important, but his message; not the teacher, but the teaching.

> When Krishnamurti dies, which is inevitable, you will set about forming rules in your minds, because the individual, Krishnamurti, had represented to you the Truth. So you will build a temple, . . . have ceremonies, . . . and create philosophies . . . you will be caught . . . in that temple and you will have to have another Teacher come and extricate you from that temple. But the human mind is such that you will build another temple round him, and so it will go on.[21]

Selecting a Guru

The basic problem seems to be that one usually requires a *guru* who is himself Enlightened to guide one on the spiritual path.

---

20. Krishnamurti, J., *The Wholeness of Life*, p. 172.
21. Krishnamurti, J., *The Last Talks*, p. xii.

But to really know who is Enlightened, one has to be Enlightened oneself! What is the answer to this *impasse*?

It was shown earlier that the *guru*, even though himself Enlightened, can only guide or point the way. The aspirant has to work out his own 'salvation'.

> God and the *Guru* will only show the way to release; they will not by themselves take the soul to the state of release. (Śrī Ramaṇa Maharṣi)[22]

To be effective, then, the *guru* must stimulate original thinking in the seeker. That is, he must make the disciple **think for himself**. This is most important, and even an Enlightened *guru* will be ineffective if he cannot do so. Teaching, as said before, is ultimately an art unrelated to the fact of Enlightenment. An Enlightened person may not have it. If an Enlightened *guru* was a guarantee of the disciple's Enlightenment, then every single disciple of a sage should have been Enlightened, and there should have been many, many Enlightened people on earth.

So the only advice that can be given to the sincere seeker is that he should stop searching for the proper *guru* and start thinking for himself. If a genuine *guru* comes along, well and good. His aim should be, not to search endlessly for the 'right' *guru* (which is an impossible task), but rather to prepare himself in such a way that he can make the best use of the right *guru* when he does appear. And it will often be found to be the case that Life provides a *guru* at the right moment — to the ripe disciple.

Moreover, as mentioned before, Enlightenment **can** occur even without a *guru*. Indeed, it **will** occur of its own, without any external help, or even without any effort on our part whatsoever, (for that is our natural state), provided we only stop obstructing

---

22. Mahadevan, Dr. T.M.P., *Who Am I? (Nān Yār)* of Sri Ramana Maharshi, 12th edn., 1969, p. 9.

it with our fixed ideas and beliefs. (See chapter 8.)

Gospel

A very important rule that the genuinely sincere seeker may do well to follow, is to consider nothing as gospel.

There are two kinds of statements which people consider as gospel.

1. Scriptures.
2. Those directly spoken by an Enlightened or Liberated person.

1. Scriptures

S. Radhakrishnan has said, "Spiritual truth is a far greater thing than the scriptures."[23]

Although the scriptures are usually considered the 'word of God', there may be several slips in their actual application.

(A) UNFAITHFUL REPRODUCTION AND INTERPOLATIONS

What was originally said by the speaker was not usually written down instantly. The Christian Gospels, for example, are believed to have been written at least a half century after the death of Jesus.[24]

Hindu history is well-known for its long oral tradition when very little was noted down. Tilak[25] puts the date of the events of the Mahābhārata war around 1500 BC. But it is his opinion that the text (which includes the *Bhagavad Gītā*) was first put down in writing only around 900 BC, and appeared in its present form

23. Radhakrishnan, S., *Religion and Culture*, p. 24.
24. Craveri, Marcello, *The Life of Jesus — An Assessment through Modern Historical Evidence*, Panther History.
25. Tilak, Bāl Gaṅgādhar, *Orion*, p. 39.

around 400 BC, that is, about a thousand years later.[26] Over this period, it also grew in volume to several times the size of the original composition. Some people believe that in the process the *Bhagavad Gītā* was also added to. To the extent that there is one body of opinion which considers that the original *Bhagavad Gītā* consisted of a mere seven verses, the rest being later additions.[27]

Jñāneśvar composed the *Jñāneśvarī* in about AD 1290. But it was corrupted over the years so much so that it had to be re-written by Eknāth in AD 1584, less than 300 years later.[28]

Every book or scripture suffers as it is printed and reprinted, edited and translated, as it is passed on from generation to generation.

(B) INTERPRETATIONS

The same text is often interpreted differently by different commentators. Ādi Śaṅkarācārya taught that the *Bhagavad Gītā* considered *jñāna-yoga* as superior to *karma-yoga*, whereas Tilak vehemently stated that it does just the opposite.

2. The Words of a Master

Presuming that the words of contemporary persons who are accepted as Enlightened or Liberated have been accurately recorded and faithfully reproduced, these should be more reliable in guiding the sincere seeker. But even these cannot be taken as gospel, for the following reasons:

The words have usually been said in a particular context, and to a particular listener or listeners. Ramaṇa Maharṣi:

---

26. (Eng. Tr.) Sukthankar, Bhalchandra Sitaram, *Srimad Bhagavad Gita-Rahasya*, by Bal Gangadhar Tilak , 6th edn., 1986, pp. 771, 781, 796.

27. *Ibid.*, p. 10.

28. (Eng. Tr.) Bhagwat, R.K., *Bhāvārtha-Dīpikā: Jñāneśvarī*, p. 673.

"What is said is adapted to the temperament of the listener".[29]

Moreover, although the Enlightened person knows the Reality intuitively, when asked to put it in words, he is automatically limited by his temporal knowledge, his proficiency in the language, the extent of his vocabulary, his education and background. That is why different Masters enunciate the same principle differently.

Also, the Master may talk at different levels of reality. For example, this was said by Śrī Ramaṇa Maharṣi in English: "Only one consciousness, equally distributed everywhere. You, through illusion, give it unequal distribution." Then immediately he said, apparently correcting himself, "No distribution, no everywhere."[30]

Because of all the above reasons, there may even be apparent contradictions or inconsistencies in the statements made by the same Master at different times. For example, the whole of the *Bhagavad Gītā* is all about exhorting Arjuna to fight. Yet, towards the end, Kṛṣṇa says:

> Futile is this resolve of thine not to fight, (for) thy inborn nature will (perforce) compel thee to (to fight).
>
> — XVIII.59

Ramaṇa Maharṣi is known to have said that the ultimate truth is that there is no creation and no destruction — nothing has happened. Yet he gave detailed instructions regarding Self-enquiry and so on to enquiring seekers.

The sincere seeker must appreciate that the *guru* and the scriptures can only provide clues or pointers, but the seeker **must** finally venture out on his own and chart his own course. The *guru* can show him how to open his eyes, but the seeker must

29. Osborne, Arthur, *The Teachings of Bhagavan Sri Ramana Maharshi In His Own Words*, p. 108.

30. Godman, David's article in *Mountain Path*, 1993.

see for himself. The *guru* cannot see for him. The *guru* and the scripture act merely as signposts. They are not the destination.

> The *guru*'s teaching is like a finger pointing at the moon.
>
> Do not suck the finger . . . .
>
> — Fr. Anthony de Mello

At the end, the *śiṣya* realises that he is not separate (psychologically) from the rest of Consciousness, and that he and the *guru* are also not separate. . . .

> just as gold and the golden ornament
> both abide in the one element gold,
> or the moon and the moonlight both exist in the moon;
> The separate (concepts of) camphor and its fragrance,
> is (really) only camphor;
> Sweetness and jaggery are both the jaggery itself;
> Similarly, in the pretence of *guru* and *śiṣya*,
> He alone rejoices, even though they appear as two.
>
> — *Amr̥tānubhav*, II.62-64)

the whole thing was a charade. . . .

7

Death and After
(Death, the Soul, and Rebirth)

FROM what has been said so far, it should be fairly obvious that there is nothing that remains after death. The body disintegrates, the mind ceases to function with the death of the brain, and the 'I' was just an illusion in the mind. Nothing happens because there is none to whom it can happen. What was born was an illusion in the mind, and with the death of the mind, the illusion has ended. Only, in the case of the Enlightened person, it ends even before death. What existed was not the ego, soul or self, but the **illusion** that such a thing exists. In fact, there lies the point — that it is an illusion. If the ego or self (or soul) did, in fact, exist, then there would be no question of realising that it is an illusion, which is what Self-realisation is all about.

How did this belief in a 'soul' originate?

Man occupies a unique place in the world of living things, for he is the only animal who is **aware of his own mortality**, who knows that he must himself, some day, die. This places him in a "position of unique despair which no other organism on earth needs to endure".[1] This is a terrible burden of knowledge to bear. No animal can easily reconcile itself to such an idea. While the lower animals live in blissful ignorance of their mortality, man

---

1. Asimov, Isaac, *Ghosts*, from Introduction.

knows, but refuses to believe. Though he is not aware if he existed before his birth, he rejects the possibility that, now that he has been born, there will be a day when 'he' will be no more. In that sense the birth of the illusion of the ego is a 'one-way street'. Once born, it refuses to die. Once imbued with the idea that one is a separate entity, it is very difficult to get rid of this idea. But actually speaking, if we come to think of it, the idea is quite preposterous. Consider the example offered by Fr. Anthony De Mello: (Emphasis added)[2]

> It would be correct to say that:
>
> Pages + print + cover + pictures = book.
>
> But would it be right to say that :
>
> Pages + print + cover + pictures + **book** = book?

The Buddhist monk Nāgasena explained much the same thing to his King Milinda in the following way: he dismantled the king's chariot part by part and asked him at each step "Are these horses the chariot?", "Are these wheels the chariot?", and so on till nothing of the chariot was left. He finally asked "Where then is the chariot, O noble Milinda?"

The 'self' or 'soul' is that elusive something which, we want to believe, exists, over and above the body and mind, and which, we wishfully think, will continue to exist after the body and mind are no more. We picture it as some sort of unique distillate of our individuality, which will live to see another day, long after our bodies have returned to dust.

And thus man, in fleeing death, identifies with "the seemingly undying idea of himself".[3] It is this 'idea of himself' which is the 'self' or 'soul'.

---

2. Carlos G. Valles S.J.,*Unencumbered by Baggage*, p. 88-90.
3. Wilber, Ken, *The Spectrum of Consciousness*, p. 125.

What is the Truth?

The truth of the matter, even according to Freud, is that the peculiar structure of the human ego results from its incapacity to accept reality, specifically the supreme reality of death.[4]

So we see that man's very *ability to think* makes him susceptible to the **fear of extinction**, and this leads to **denial of death**, and inevitably, to the invention of an 'after-life'. Not only does man find solace in the idea that he will somehow live for ever, it is also extremely comforting to believe that one's departed near and dear ones are also alive and well, albeit in some other world.

Organised Religion

Life, by its very nature, is full of change and is highly unpredictable, and man's ability for forethought naturally gives him a feeling of insecurity about the future. He finds security in several devices, the most ancient of which is religion. Only humans have religion because only humans can think, and religion is a psychological device. Religion thus caters to a very basic, very fundamental need of mankind — the need for psychological security.

Organised religions invariably support man in his belief in an after-life, thus strengthening this belief—putting the 'stamp of authority' on it, so to speak.

But then why did organised religions support belief in an after-life? They probably did so because it was convenient to them for several reasons. Like, for example:

(1) LAW AND ORDER

Man by nature is a disorderly creature. Left to himself there would be anarchy in society. In the modern world, law and order is maintained by strict policing aided by modern communications

4. Quoted by Brown, N.O., *Life Against Death*, p. 159.

technology. In olden days, this was difficult, and man was left more cr less to his own devices. The only way law and order could be effectively maintained was by religious injunctions. The idea of reward and punishment from an all-seeing, all-knowing God, from whom no action was hidden, was an effective deterrent. However, as such rewards and punishments were not always so easily demonstrable in actual life, where often the good remained oppressed and the wicked rarely brought to grief, an 'after-life' had to be invented to make the logic more convincing.

(2) WAR

The instinct of self-preservation is the strongest instinct in any animal including man. It requires a very strong commitment to an ideal or ideology to make a soldier disregard that instinct and risk his very life for 'the cause'. In earlier days, when nation states were in a state of flux, and nationalism not as potent a force as it is today, soldiers were exhorted to give their life up for religion. In exchange for this supreme sacrifice, the soldier was lured by the promise of heaven in his after-life.

If the soul does not exist, what is it that really happens after death?

The truth is that for the 'one' who is asking the question, there is no life after death. From the point of view of our (apparently) separate individual awareness, to the question 'What will **I** experience after death?' the answer in one word is: **Oblivion**. (That is, the same as what 'you' experienced before you were born or conceived).

The individual point of awareness and perception that a person constitutes, as just one of many such points, will be extinguished. And the entity, of course, was only an illusion.

From the point of view of humanity and the universe, life will go on. As the psychological **separateness** of the 'one' from the rest of humanity was an illusion, in that sense it may be said that the consciousness of the 'one' who dies 'merges' with the 'Universal Consciousness'. But this is just a different way of expressing the same idea. Thus it is the **Universal Consciousness** which manifests ('incarnates') in the form of different sentient, living beings, and which could be said, in a manner of speaking, to 'reincarnate' from one body to another. The illusory separate entity or 'soul' cannot reincarnate because it really never existed at all in the first place. Indeed, if we consider that we are all points of awareness, perception and expression of that one Universal Consciousness, then in that sense, *we are all reincarnations of each other*.

The relationship between the one (Universal) *ātman* or Universal Consciousness, and the individual life-forms, is best illustrated by the example of electricity and its individual manifestations.

The 'I' as Universal Consciousness (which is the 'I' referred to by Lord Kṛṣṇa in the *Bhagavad Gītā*), was never born and will never die because it always existed and will always exist — in fact, it is beyond the concepts of Space and Time, and therefore, beyond the duality of Existence and Non-existence.

The 'I' as the (illusory) individual self, which is the 'I' referred to by most questioners, also was never born and will never die, for it never even existed. This is the meaning of the verse:

> For the non-existent there is no coming into existence, nor passing out of existence for the existent.
>
> — *BG*, II.16

The *ātman* referred to in the *Bhagavad Gītā* which 'fire cannot burn, and wind cannot dry', and which 'changes bodies' like a person changing garments, is the Universal Consciousness which animates all bodies, not an individual 'soul'. See the verses immediately preceding:

> Know **That** to be indestructible by which all this is pervaded. (Emphasis added) — II.17

> These perishable bodies are said to belong to that eternal body-owner, the indestructible one. — II.18

The *ātman* (meaning the Universal Consciousness or 'All-that-is') is already 'immortal', but the whole problem is that the fictitious, superimposed, phantom 'I' desires immortality for **itself as a separate entity**.

The question remains, if this is true, why have the Masters not stated this unequivocally? Indeed many of them have even spoken of soul, rebirth and so on.

This is because this stark truth is not to be told casually to one who has been brought up on the comforting belief of the existence of the 'one' as a separate entity, and whose every action in life is based on this premise. To the extent that even his search for 'Enlightenment' (which is the understanding of the fact that there is no separate 'I') is itself undertaken, paradoxically enough, with the idea of an 'I' seeking 'Enlightenment' as an attainment. (If one can see the paradox in this, it is all that is required.)

> The teaching varies according to the understanding of the listener. (Ramaṇa Maharṣi)[5]

> These . . . , the knowers of the part (truth), one who knows the whole (truth) should not unsettle.
> — *Bhagavad Gītā*, III.29

> How can a child which can with great difficulty suck the mother's breast, take heavy food? Therefore, O Dhanurdhara, no heavy food should be given to such a child. — *Jñāneśvarī*, III.172

Arthur Osborne wrote about Śrī Ramaṇa Maharṣi,[6]

---

5. Osborne, Arthur, *The Teachings of Bhagavan Sri Ramana Maharshi In His Own Words*, p. 25.

6. In *Mountain Path*, Dec. 95, pp. 82-4.

Bhagavān (the *maharṣi*), like the Buddha (was) unwilling to speak about the afterlife. He even said explicitly:

> But people do not like even to hear of this truth, whereas they are eager to know what lies beyond, about heaven and hell and reincarnation. Because people love mystery and not the truth, religions cater to them so as to eventually bring them round to the Self.

This is a very significant statement from Śrī Ramaṇa Maharṣi — 'People do not like to hear the truth, they love mystery and not the truth'. And **that** is why religions and sages cater to them and tell them what they want to hear, hoping to eventually bring them round to face the real facts.

Sāi Bābā of Śirḍī is reported to have said:

> I give people what they want, so that they may begin to want what I want to give them.

But this does not mean that the sages have never revealed this fact. Indeed, the Buddhist view is that there is nowhere a permanent self or *ātman* to be found. This is known as the *anatta* doctrine, or the doctrine of 'no-self' (Sanskrit *an-ātma*). Consider the Buddha's statement in the *Diamond Sūtra*, (see chapter 6 of this book) where the Buddha explains that in reality there are no sentient beings to be delivered by the *tathāgata*. Ideas such as one's own self, other selves, living beings and a universal self are merely "arbitrary conceptions".

He continues:

> Subhūti, even the expression 'terrestrial beings' as used by the *tathāgata* does not mean that there are any such beings. It is only used as a figure of speech.[7]

---

7. Goddard, Dwight, *A Buddhist Bible*, quoted in *Buddhism and Christianity in the Light of Hinduism* by Arthur Osborne, p. 114 and also in *The Teachings of Bhagavan Sri Ramana Maharshi in His Own Words* by Arthur Osborne, (5th edn.), p. 228.

And Alan Watts writes:

> It is fundamental to every school of Buddhism that there is no ego, no enduring entity which is the constant subject of our changing experiences.

He further explains that the ego exists in an abstract sense alone, somewhat like the illusory circle of fire made by a whirling torch, or the path of a bird through the sky.[8]

Apart from the Buddha, other sages too have definitely, at sometime or the other, asserted this undiluted truth.

Śrī Ramaṇa Maharṣi said:

> There is only one Consciousness and this, when it identifies itself with the body, projects itself through the eyes and sees the surrounding objects.[9]

Arthur Osborne wrote:

> Śrī Bhagavān (Ramaṇa Maharṣi) declared that there is only *ātman*, while the Buddha declared that there is no *ātman*; but . . . Śrī Bhagavān used the word '*ātman*' to mean the universal Self, . . . whereas the Buddha used it to mean the individual soul.

And

> Śrī Bhagavān also taught (like the Buddha) that *there is no individual being*, not only in the sense that it will not endure after death but that *it is not* (*even*) *now*. . .

> Teachers who have directed their followers on a more gradual path, shielding their eyes from the blinding simplicity of ultimate Truth, have affirmed the survival

8. Watts, Alan W., *The Way of Zen*.
9. Osborne, Arthur, *The Teachings of Bhagavan Sri Ramana Maharshi In His Own Words*, p. 20.

> of the soul after this life. However, the contradiction, like all spiritual contradictions, is only apparent. (Emphasis added)[10]

And this is what Fr. Anthony De Mello said in reply to the question "What happens when I die?":

> "**There is no I**,... Nobody dies. **There is no death**." (emphasis added)[11]

And Śrī Nisargadatta Mahārāj said:

> Forms get created and forms get destroyed. Who is born? And who dies? And who is to be reborn?
>
> Consciousness, as something non-objective, cannot be 'born', cannot 'die' and certainly cannot be 'reborn'.[12]

J. Krishnamurti:

> You can believe that you will be reincarnated. That's a very comfortable idea, but it's not a fact.[13]

Most people believe that the *Bhagavad Gītā* supports the idea of the existence of a separate individual soul. Some verses have already been quoted earlier in this chapter to show that it really does just the opposite. Almost throughout the poem, it is constantly emphasised that there is only one Universal Consciousness or *ātman*, which appears by illusion as the animating influence in the different living 'beings'.

> Of mine own Self a portion . . . it is, which, in the world of the living, appears to be the individual soul.
>
> —XV.7

---

10. In *Mountain Path*, Dec. 95, p. 84.
11. Carlos G. Valles S.J.,*Unencumbered by Baggage*, p. 94.
12. Balsekar, Ramesh S., *Pointers from Nisargadatta Maharaj*, p. 125.
13. Krishnamurti, J., *The Last Talks*, p. 92.

Jñāneśvar has explained this as follows:

> I, who am the cause of sentience in that which is inert, and of self-awareness in the body, **appear to be** the individual soul in this phenomenal world. (Emphasis added) —*Jñāneśvarī*, XV.345

Further, the *Jñāneśvarī* continues:

> You should view Me in this phenomenal world just as the moon reflected in the water is really outside the water, or just as a crystal placed on vermilion, would appear red though it is not. —XV.348-9

The verse XV.8 of the *Bhagavad Gītā* which mentions the "Master leaving the body carrying with it the senses, like the wind carries the fragrance of a flower" is explained thus:

> like the connecting thread of the dancing doll 'takes away' (figuratively speaking) all the doll's movements (when snapped), or just as the sun, when it sets, 'takes away' everyone's vision. —*Jñāneśvarī*, XV.365-6

That is, 'takes away' in a purely **figurative sense**.

Also *Jñāneśvarī*:

> When the body is animated (by Me, or because of Me), people say 'The soul has come (into the body).' Similarly, the senses (of their own inherent nature) interact with their objects, and this is termed the 'enjoyment' (by the soul). Finally, when the body, of its own (by its own nature), becomes infirm and drops down, people loudly lament that the '*jīva* has gone'. —XV.373-5

> The star-studded firmament is seen reflected in the ocean, yet it is obvious that it has not fallen into the sea. The sky remains in its place — its appearance in the sea is unreal (an illusion). In the same way, the encasement (apparent appearance) of the 'individual soul' in the

> body is also an illusion (*ābhās*). . . and this the men of knowledge do perceive. —XV.384-90

Tilak, too, has written[14] that although the word *aṁśa* used in the *Bhagavad Gītā* in the above-mentioned verse (XV.7) means 'particle' or 'part of' (fragment, portion), yet, in this particular context it should be understood in a different way, since the *Bhagavad Gītā* has already stated that the Absolute is not something gross, but is in fact imperceptible and attributeless, and therefore is not divisible or partitionable (*achedya*). Indeed, it is immutable (*avikārya*). What is meant here is not 'part of a whole', but 'part of' in a figurative sense as described in the *Jñāneśvarī*.

Tilak writes that though the word *aṁśa* is used "in common parlance" to indicate the relationship between the two (God or the Absolute and the so-called individual soul or *jīva*), yet the word *aṁśa* or 'part' should not be taken to mean 'an independent piece which has been cut out' or as 'one of the grains taken out of the numerous grains in a pomegranate'.

Clement of Alexandria expressed the same idea as "the Spirit of God indivisibly divided to all".[15]

And quantum physicist Schroedinger stated:

> this life of yours which you are living is not merely a piece of the entire existence, but is in a certain sense the whole . . . .[16]

Śrī Ramaṇa Maharṣi said:[17] "God is not separate from you or the cosmos." When asked how we were to understand the line in the

14. (Eng. Tr.) Sukthankar, Bhalchandra Sitaram, *Srimad Bhagavad Gita-Rahasya* by Bal Gangadhar Tilak, 6th edn., 1986, pp. 339-40.
15. Wilber, Ken, *The Spectrum of Consciousness*, p. 89-90.
16. Schroedinger, Erwin, *My View of the World*, p. 21.
17. Osborne, Arthur, *The Teachings of Bhagavan Sri Ramana Maharshi In His Own Words*, p. 48.

Gītā: 'This whole cosmos forms a particle of me', he answered:

> It does not mean that a small particle of God separates from Him and forms the universe. . . . the fact is that *Brahman* is all and remains indivisible.

Responding to a questioner's statement that God is infinite whereas he (the questioner) is finite, the Maharṣi said:

> Infinity and perfection do not admit of parts. If a finite being is apart from Infinity, the perfection of Infinity is marred. Thus your statement is a contradiction in terms.[18]

In fact, the entire 13th chapter of the *Bhagavad Gītā* is devoted to this very question, and the view of the author of the *Gītā* is quite unambiguously set forth:

> It is clearly stated here that the *ātman* exists . . .
>
> **Undivided** amongst the beings, and withal **as though divided**. (Emphasis added) —XIII.16

It further states:

> The Knowers of the Truth consider this body, O Son of Kuntī, as the 'field' (*kṣetra*); and him who knows (is aware of) this field as the 'Subject' (*kṣetrajña*, lit. one who knows the field). —XIII.1
>
> Furthermore, know Me to be the (One) Subject within all the fields, O Scion of Bharata. This knowledge of the (true) relation between the field and the Subject, is what I consider (true) knowledge. —XIII.2

The *Jñāneśvarī* explains this as follows:

> Just as the sun, though reflected in the water, is not wetted by it, because it only **appears** to be in the water.

---

18. Osborne, Arthur, *The Teachings of Bhagavan Sri Ramana Maharshi In His Own Words*, p. 50.

> Actually, the sun remains in its place. Similarly, it is not correct to say that the *ātman* is (actually) **in** the body — It remains as It is. Just as, when the face is reflected in the mirror, it is said that the face is '**in**' the mirror, in the same sense is the existence of the *ātman* 'in' the body. (Emphasis added) — XIII.1094-97

And finally, the *Gītā* declares:

> Just as the one sun illumines all the worlds, so does the (one) Subject animate all the fields, O scion of Bharata.
> — XIII.33

Now, what could be clearer than this?

The Bhāgavat, too, repeats the same view:

> Just as the Moon, though one, appears as many when reflected in many vessels of water, so does the one *ātman*, reflected in many individuals, appear to be manifold. — *Śrīmad Bhāgavatam,* XI.18.32

(Refer back to figure at the end of chapter 1.)

Some verses in the *Bhagavad Gītā* (like those which speak of the individual *ātman* travelling to various regions after death), are probably later insertions, for they do not fit in with the general tenor of the poem as described above, nor are they in agreement with its main philosophy.

To summarise, it is the Universal Consciousness which appears as individual life-forms (with, in the case of man, an **illusion** of separate consciousness). So in a manner of speaking we could say that the **Universal Consciousness** 'reincarnates' from one life-form to another.

There is no rebirth for the entity, for in actual fact there **is** no entity. However, if we insist on talking about reincarnation for the entity, then the process of 'rebirth' could also be understood in another way — it could be understood figuratively, **as occurring**

from moment to moment, as Alan Watts has explained.[19] The average man insists on carrying 'baggage' in the form of attachment to the past, into the next moment — and the next. One is thus being constantly 'reborn' so long as one identifies oneself with a continuing ego, which reincarnates itself from moment to moment. This mental 'carry-over' is totally absent in the case of the Liberated One, who lives from moment to moment, living each moment to the full and finishing with it, starting the next moment afresh. The average man carries the 'hangover' of each moment into the next. The *siddha* dies to every moment as it passes.

J. Krishnamurti has explained that the sage lives a life in which everything is constantly ending. He is dying to it, each day, each minute. And in such a life, then, there is that state of a "timeless dimension in which the movement we know as time is not".[20]

In other words, as long as psychological time remains, so long does the 'person' 'reincarnate' from moment to moment. The Liberated One has lost the sense of psychological time and is thus free of such 'rebirth'.

In the words of Coomaraswamy, not 'sudden death' at the end of one's life, but 'instant death' all through it.

Jīvanmukti and Videhamukti

The term *jīvanmukta* means 'Liberated during life' or 'Liberated while living'. It is generally wrongly understood to indicate the state of the Liberated One while alive, as against his state after the death of his body, which is called *videhamukti* (Liberation without the body). But what the term 'Liberated during life' actually implies is that this person has lost the illusion of the self (and hence the consequent conditioning and its related

19. Watts, Alan W., *The Way of Zen*.

20. Krishnamurti, J., *The Wholeness of Life*, p. 155.

psychological suffering), when alive, as contrasted with the average person who retains the illusion till death. After death, of course, the illusion is no more even in the case of the average person, as explained at the beginning of this chapter.

Śrī Ramaṇa Maharṣi:

> There is no difference (between *jīvanmukti* and *videhamukti* for the Liberated 'One'). For those who ask it is said that a Realised man with a body is a *jīvanmukta* and that he attains *videhamukti* when he sheds the body, but this difference exists only for the onlooker, not for him. . . . There are no degrees of Liberation. So there cannot be one stage of Liberation with the body and another when the body has been shed.[21]

Actually, in a sense, there **can** be degrees of Liberation, because the **process** of Liberation is a gradual process of de-conditioning. However, this does not really contradict the Maharṣi's statement above. What the Maharṣi obviously means here is that there are no degrees of the state of **final** Liberation, one with the body and another without it (as people wrongly understand by the terms *jīvanmukti* and *videhamukti*).

In the normal course, all will attain 'Liberation' (ending of the 'I'-illusion) at death. (That is why the Masters also assert that **all** will eventually attain Liberation.)

However, the *jīvanmukta* is the one in a million who has lost this illusion (and is hence 'Liberated') during life itself. In fact, if one were to consider any other explanation, the term *jīvanmukta* would lose relevance. By referring to a Liberated One as 'One who is Liberated while alive', the obvious implication is that others are Liberated upon death. Thus (and this should be a comforting thought to many), *videhamukti* is the prerogative of all!

---

21. Osborne, Arthur, *The Teachings of Bhagavan Sri Ramana Maharshi In His Own Words*, p. 236.

8

What Should 'I' Do?

IT is possible that the reader may still be left with the question, "What should I do (for Enlightenment to occur)?"

In the light of what has been stated in the preceding chapters, it should be clear that this question (as explained earlier in pp. 38-9, 57) is a flawed question at the outset. This is because there is really no 'I' to 'do' anything, and the realisation of this very fact is what Enlightenment is all about.

However, it would not be fair to ignore this question altogether, because most 'seekers' do start off from this point.

What answer could be offered to such a person in view of all that has been said so far? In other words, what should a seeker 'do'?

Enlightenment is an event which is spontaneous, unpredictable, and causeless. Causeless because it cannot be the effect of any specific cause. If it were, then it could have been predictably achieved by invoking that cause. The **intuitive** understanding which constitutes Enlightenment cannot be learnt or 'had' from another person, however great or illumined (chapters 3 and 6). Nor can it be brought about or induced by any particular effort, method or technique (as we saw in chapter 3, and as we shall be explaining presently). Therefore the only thing to be 'done' is to try and understand the situation **intellectually.**

> *nusta samazhūn ghyāyace āhe* (Understanding is all)
> — Nisargadatta Mahārāj

And then allow the understanding to sink in. **The rest will happen by itself. The intellectual understanding of the situation creates conditions favourable for the spontaneous occurrence of the intuitive understanding.** (Exactly how it does so will be described a little later). A comprehensive intellectual understanding is a prelude to Enlightenment.

> How can the 'I' eliminate itself? All that you need to do is to find out its origin and stay there. Your effort can extend only so far. Then the Beyond will take care of itself. You are helpless there. No effort can reach it. (Śrī Ramaṇa Maharṣi)[1]

Of course, even this 'doing' is not really volitional, but that will not be appreciated by the seeker at this stage. After Enlightenment all activity is non-volitional and is seen to be so; before Enlightenment also all activity is non-volitional but is **thought** to be volitional.

The Active Methods

We said that there can be no methods or techniques to 'achieve' Enlightenment, and the only thing to be 'done' is to understand the situation intellectually. But then how is this intellectual understanding to be reached?

(The word 'how' again implies methods, but since we are now talking about the intellectual understanding, which is a temporal understanding, like the understanding of any other worldly knowledge, we can legitimately talk of 'methods' to reach this understanding).

Understanding the situation implies the following very important points:

---

1. Osborne, Arthur, *The Teachings of Bhagavan Sri Ramana Maharshi In His Own Words*, p. 139.

1. Start with a clean slate, that is, discard (or at least temporarily set aside) all beliefs, preconceived ideas and notions about 'God', 'soul', Liberation, and so on. This is really the renunciation that is required — renunciation of your cherished beliefs and convictions. And indeed, it is the most difficult renunciation of all.

2. **Think for yourself**. Conduct research into spirituality in a spirit of scientific enquiry. Be ready to experiment, to find out for yourself. Reflect upon (*manana*) the conceptual knowledge gained from *guru*, scriptures or from the teachings of sages (*śravaṇa*), and ponder and deliberate upon it on your own (*nididhyāsana*). Replace your 'wrong' concepts with 'right' concepts, and be prepared to abandon even these finally. Clear your conceptual cobwebs by the light of your own clear logic, discrimination and understanding (*viveka*). This constitutes the theoretical aspect of the search for intellectual understanding.

3. The practical aspect is represented by actually **experimenting psychologically upon yourself**. Try to actually see, in your own particular case, how that which you have always considered to be 'yourself' (that is, your self-image), is nothing but a 'bag of edited memories' as Ken Wilber puts it. And it is this 'bag of memories' with which you have always been identifying yourself.

   Trying to see this for oneself in one's own particular case constitutes the practical aspect of the search for intellectual understanding, and it is this which is described as the method of 'Self-enquiry' by Śrī Ramaṇa Maharṣi, "inquiring after the inquirer himself" as Ku-yin put it.[2]

   Self-enquiry or asking oneself the question "Who am I"? obviously does not mean getting the answer "I am John

---

2. Wilber, Ken, *The Spectrum of Consciousness*, p. 325.

Smith". That much is usually understood. But what is often not understood is that it also does not mean getting the answer "I am *Brahman*", which, even if true, will still be a concept. This is obvious from the Maharṣi's own comment: "He who asks 'Who am I'? although existing as the Self, is like a drunken man who asks his own identity and whereabouts."[3]

The question 'Who am I'? actually consists in bringing ourselves face to face with the fact that **there is really no 'I'** (as a separate, independent, autonomous entity, apart from the Universal Self). It is rather meant to confront us with the truth that whatever doubts, questions, desires or ideas we may have, since there is in fact no 'I' for whom these questions would have been relevant, **that** is the point we should rather pay attention to and appreciate (rather than try to address each individual question, doubt, etc.).

The prescription "Enquire who am I" given to the average questioner must thus be understood to mean "(Enquire, find out, and) Understand who am I", or "Understand that there is no I".

In Self-enquiry ". . . the basis is not for the 'me' to ask the question and expect to get an answer, but to feel the absence of any entity. . . ."[4] (Also see Glossary)

4. You will know that you have finally reached the intellectual understanding when you begin to see clearly the utter futility (indeed the counter-productivity) of all 'me'-based spiritual effort (whether it is meditation or any other *sādhanā*).

The way in which the intellectual understanding creates

3. Sri Ramana Maharshi quoted in *Sunbeam*, April 1981, p. 22.
4. Balsekar, Ramesh (Conversations by air-mail), *Consciousness Writes*, p. 10.

conditions favourable for Enlightenment is by convincing the seeker of the futility of me-based efforts.

This part of the 'journey', starting with conceptual knowledge, and ending with the intellectual understanding, is what is termed *jñāna-yoga*.

Conceptual knowledge only serves as a starting point for the investigation, and is helpful but not absolutely essential. In a rare case, in a person so inclined, the practical Self-enquiry can start on its own, without the theoretical background of conceptual knowledge. This is known to have happened in the case of Śrī Ramaṇa Maharṣi. In such cases, therefore, there is generally no previous record of a *guru* or of a study of scriptures, which, as we explained in chapter 6, mainly confer conceptual knowledge.

However, such cases are rare. In the case of the average person, a theoretical background is important. If a person who has a strong existing (me-based) world-view follows the 'Enquiry' as a 'method' **without** first having a theoretical understanding of the situation, he is most likely to move around in circles, because he will not understand what is meant by the question in the first place.

The reason why Śrī Ramaṇa Maharṣi did not stress a prior theoretical understanding, (in fact, at times even discouraged it) was perhaps because, firstly, like most sages, he taught mainly the 'path', or rather the sequence of events which occurred in his particular case. And secondly, an excessive obsession with theoretical speculation alone, without an attempt at its practical application in one's own actual case (which is the method of Self-enquiry), will not work, and can even lead to the trap of 'false' knowledge (chapter 3).

After the Intellectual Understanding — The Shedding of Spiritual Effort

A deep intellectual understanding enables the person to see the futility of me-based effort, and as this understanding sinks in, the grip of the insistent demand for spiritual effort gradually loosens its hold. The common refrain of the average seeker is, "Give me *something* to do!" But as the understanding matures, the 'seeker' begins to think less of whether to do this or that technique, and begins to think of **who** it is that is to do the technique.

Once, the fact, that there **is no I** is deeply understood, the very realisation that there is nothing to be actively **done** or **achieved**, itself gives a tremendous sense of relief and peace, and results in the spontaneous dropping away of all conventional me-based (purposeful) spiritual efforts. Thus, the shedding of me-based efforts occurs before Enlightenment, upon the intellectual understanding. Indeed, it is this which creates a suitable environment for Enlightenment to occur, and it is an essential prerequisite, indeed a *sine qua non*, for the occurrence of Enlightenment.

This is because it is the me-based effort itself (and the idea behind it that one is a separate entity) which creates the obstacle to Enlightenment. It is somewhat like a person actively trying to fall asleep. The more he tries, the less likely he is to succeed. It is only when he gives up trying and lets go, that he will actually fall asleep.

In the jungles of Latin America, it is said, the natives trapped monkeys by keeping a tidbit inside an open jar. The jar's mouth was just broad enough to admit the monkey's open hand, but not broad enough for it to be removed once it closed its fist over the morsel. Though the monkey could let go of the food and free himself at any time, it would never do so, and be captured, screeching and screaming to high heaven.

Our 'bondage' is a little like that. It is of our own making. We refuse to 'let go' of our sense of being a separate 'self' and trap ourselves into bondage, and then yell for help. Rather than 'let go' of the idea that 'one' is 'doing' the spiritual effort, the general tendency is to intensify the effort.

(Of course, even this 'letting go' cannot be 'done'. It has to **happen**. And this is possible only when there is a clear understanding of the situation).

Thus, in a person with a suitable temperament who is potential material for the occurrence of Enlightenment, paradoxically enough, his very seeking of it[5] proves to be the final obstacle that prevents Enlightenment!

And an effective *guru* is one who is able to point this out to him. That is the meaning of the seemingly cryptic remark of the sage Aṣṭāvakra to his disciple Janaka "Your only bondage is that you practise meditation."[6]

The subtle point is that once the intellectual understanding has occurred, it is time to leave it alone, to allow it time to sink in. Trying to remember it constantly, or trying to 'keep it in mind', will again constitute me-based effort at Enlightenment and will be counter-productive.

> The one thing that remains thereafter, i.e., after the understanding is not any 'practising' as a deliberate effort, but merely to let our true understanding deeply impregnate our very being, passively and patiently, so that all illusions and obstructions gradually fall off by themselves.[7]

Any effort to remember this understanding is an

5. This applies to all me-based spiritual efforts except the search for intellectual understanding and its practical aspect—Self-enquiry. This is explained later.
6. Swami Nityaswarupananda, *Aṣṭāvakra Saṁhitā*, I.15.
7. Balsekar, Ramesh S., *Pointers from Nisargadatta Maharaj*, p. 211.

obstruction! Just leave it alone and the understanding **will work.**[8]

The intellectual understanding still comprises concepts. They are right concepts, but they are concepts nevertheless, and a time comes when even these have to be abandoned. Intellectual understanding will fail to result in Enlightenment if the person, after having had it, rather than leaving it alone to act on its own, continues to indulge in speculating and conceptualising on it as a continued intellectual exercise. The understanding needs time, without intellectual interference, to 'sink from the head to the heart'.

Most spiritual teachings have to be first understood, then practised. This is the one teaching which has to be understood, and if the understanding is true, will issue forth spontaneously in practice. In other words, all that is required is understanding — the practice will happen of its own. As Śrī Nisargadatta said, "Understanding is all".

The state of 'Spiritual Vacuum'

This is a state in which there is a complete absence of me-based spiritual effort, and an absence or near-absence of concepts regarding spiritual matters. It is a period of intellectual quiescence and spiritual 'non-action' (neither action nor inaction — see *sādhanā* later). The person drifts, floating in a spiritual vacuum. *And it is in this state that the phenomenon of Enlightenment occurs spontaneously.*

The Spontaneous Processes

A lot has been written (and said) about the various 'techniques' prescribed by the acclaimed sages, like for example the 'choiceless awareness' of J. Krishnamurti — (choiceless, non-judgemental

8. Balsekar, Ramesh (Conversations by air-mail), *Consciousness Writes*, p. 90.

observation, mere observation of the thought processes without desire or attempt to change them), and also various types of meditative techniques like for example *vipassanā* techniques said to be taught by the Buddha (the active practice of 'mindfulness'). But we must understand that there is an inherent contradiction in talking about 'methods' and 'techniques' in relation to Enlightenment, because 'method' implies something that is done to **achieve** a certain result desired **for** (and by) the 'me', and as explained earlier, any me-based effort is bound to be counter-productive in the context of Enlightenment (see chapter 3, 'The Paradox of Spiritual Effort'). As Śrī Ramaṇa Maharṣi said, it is like a 'thief turning policeman to catch himself'.

But how do we reconcile the fact that the sages did give these descriptions? The fact is that these are not methods or techniques in the strict sense of the term. They are rather spontaneous processes which occur or happen when there is an intuitive understanding of the entire situation, that is, after Enlightenment. In other words, these are not really techniques being prescribed, but processes being described by the sages, and they are spontaneous, effortless, post-Enlightenment processes.

The Buddha tried literally every single method known to him, and failed. It was in this state of total spiritual exhaustion that the light of understanding dawned on him. (When every known technique has been tried and has failed, the utter futility of me-based effort is self-evident. For discussion — see later). The spontaneous **process** which followed was described by him, and is known as *vipassanā*.

A person following these as techniques to achieve Enlightenment, falls into the trap of 'me'-based effort.

> Can you 'practise' awareness? If you are 'practising' awareness, then you are all the time being inattentive.
>
> — J. Krishnamurti

To repeat therefore, what we are now about to describe are **not** prescriptions to be followed by a 'me' seeking Enlightenment. They are processes which occur **after** the intuitive understanding. That is, these are post-Enlightenment phenomena. They are non-me-based, spontaneous occurrences — 'effortless' efforts, which cannot occur in a person in whom the fiction of the separate ego-entity or 'self-in-the-body' is maintained. This succeeding discussion is therefore purely academic, and the reader not interested in technical details may skip the next few pages and resume from the section entitled '*Sādhanā* or Spiritual Effort'.

(A very brief description of these processes was given in chapter 4, 'What actually happens to the thought processes after Enlightenment?').

The first change or process that occurs after Enlightenment is a **spontaneous silent observation** of the thought processes. 'Silent' in the sense that this is not *thinking* about thinking, but rather a non-verbal attention directed to one's own thought processes. This is a spontaneous 'inward turning' of the mind. It is Ken Wiber's Factor 1 (with some differences — see later).[9]

The earlier or formative portion of the thought processes do not ordinarily attract our attention, which is usually focused on the outside world; that is, this portion of the thought processes occurs unconsciously or subconsciously. (This is called 'inattention' by J. Krishnamurti). Our attention is drawn only at a later stage when the thoughts become more emotive and stronger, thus demanding our attention. After Enlightenment these subconscious processes become conscious and transparent. One can actually watch and see one's own thoughts form and grow into a chain of thoughts, one leading to another in quick succession — click-click-click. "Going into the machinery that builds images" as J. Krishnamurti has called it.[10]

---

9. Wilber, Ken, *The Spectrum of Consciousness*, p. 314.
10. *Ibid*., p. 318.

The important point to be noted is that the attitude of the person here is that of a neutral onlooker. **There is no desire to change**. That is the difference between this observation and analysis. Observation happens spontaneously out of an attitude of sheer interest. It is not done volitionally, with any motive. Analysis is done with a motive to change, to 'improve'. In observation there is no verbalising, no labelling, no judging as good or bad, desirable or undesirable. In analysis, there is always labelling. Labelling is required for analysis to proceed. Label, classify, change. That is the crux of the process of analysis. Classifying involves judgement — good/bad, desired/undesirable, etc.

Since this is occurring after Enlightenment, there is no more the 'I'-sense, and so while it may be seen (non-verbally) for example, that 'There is anger', there is no separate 'I' who is angry, therefore no question of 'I must not be angry'. That is, there is no **conflict** between the observer and the thing observed. In analysis, the observer is perceived as separate from the thing observed, which is then attempted to be modified, either increased or decreased. As this is not a real but an illusory separation, this unwittingly breeds conflict.

This is the same process that J. Krishnamurti calls "choiceless awareness". It is the spontaneous 'mindfulness' of Buddhism (as distinct from its active practice), and the *wu-wei* of the Taoists (spontaneous or non-volitional action or 'non-action').

This is the attitude of curiosity-based interest, the only activating force being the deep interest simply to know how one's thoughts form, how the processes work, simply to know 'what makes me tick'. It is the curiosity of the child who dismantles his watch just to see how it works. It is the detached interest of the scientist simply out to know how things work.

Unlike our description, Ken Wilber has not differentiated between the active methods and the spontaneous processes and includes Self-enquiry in his Factor 1. However, even if some descriptions may seem to so suggest, this is **not** an active volitional technique, but rather a spontaneous **happening**, resulting from the intuitive understanding.

This process leads inexorably to the next one — **the disappearance of unnecessary thinking**. When it is understood, not as a thought, but seen directly, non-verbally, actually, as it occurs or takes place, how the unnecessary thoughts habitually arise as a result of the (though now extinct) me-illusion,[11] there is an abrupt realisation of the absurdity of the whole situation, (the anomaly is seen for what it is). This leads to the breaking or halting of the thought-chain at some point, and this point occurs earlier and earlier as the understanding matures and settles, as the attention becomes more and more (spontaneously) vigilant. Till finally a stage is reached when the thought chain is never able to take off, that is, unnecessary thoughts fail to arise, being cut off at their very source.

This is the Factor 2 of Ken Wilber, which he calls 'Stopping'. Wilber has also shown that it has been called "suspension or stopping of image formation" by J. Krishnamurti, "subsidence of the mind" by Śrī Ramaṇa Maharṣi; in Zen, it is described as "a state of no-image, or no-thought" (*wu-nien*), and the Taoists have called it "mindfasting".[12]

Once the stage of no-thought is reached, the same attention described in Silent Observation continues to operate, now in its pure, naked form which we could call **Pure Awareness**, what Ken Wilber calls 'Passive Awareness' or 'Factor 3'. Since there are no more any unnecessary thoughts, the whole show is viewed or seen directly (without the intervention of unnecessary thinking).

---

11. Although the me-illusion diappears after Enlightenment, the me-based thought-patterns caused by years of conditioning do not disappear overnight, as explained in chapter 4. This residual effect of past (me-based) conditioning is known as *prārabdha* in Hindu spiritual literature.

12. Wilber, Ken, *The Spectrum of Consciousness*, pp. 314-31.

Śrī Ramaṇa Maharṣi has described this as "Reality manifests itself spontaneously as 'I-I'." In Buddhism this is called *prajñā*.

This is the final state of Liberation or *sahaja sthiti* which is incompatible with nothing. It encompasses everything. The occurrence of (necessary) thoughts, whenever present, do not interrupt the flow of *prajñā* — in other words, the first mode of knowing, when it operates (as when there is a requirement pertaining to everyday reality), is seen to be no different from the second mode of knowing.

The word 'witnessing' is sometimes used to describe this state, but this word suggests that there is a witness who is doing the witnessing in a detached manner, and is not a happy choice of word to describe the state of Pure Awareness. This word should rather be reserved for the state in which there is a sense of detachment, but the witness is nevertheless perceived as separate from the thing witnessed. Ken Wilber calls this the 'supra-individual Witness' or 'lesser mysticism' as against 'true mysticism'.[13] We could call this **detached, but dualistic viewing**. Such a state may occur in people who are practising Silent Observation or 'mindfulness' as an active technique.

The use of the word 'witnessing' may perhaps also give an impression of a person watching himself over his own shoulder like a peeping Tom. But this is exactly the position of the average man, which could be described as **involved, dualistic viewing.**

The state of Pure Awareness is a state where the perceived event is not seen as separate from the perceiver, whether it is an 'external' event, or an 'internal' one like (necessary) thought. Indeed, here the very distinction of external *vs.* internal ceases to exist. This is **non-dual perception**, with no **question** of detachment or choicelessness. In other words, here **viewing** is the same as **being**. This is experience-**ing** without an experience-**er**, the apparently fragmented triad of seer, seen and seeing

13. Wilber, Ken, *The Spectrum of Consciousness*, pp. 273-4.

being resolved to its original unity.

One of the most beautiful descriptions of this state has been given by J. Krishnamurti:

> There was an intense awareness of the country, of the occasional passing car, of the road signals, of the clear blue sky, of the body sitting in the car; but the mind was very still . . . a stillness that was very alert . . . there was no observer of this tranquillity; the experiencer was wholly absent. Though there was desultory conversation [indicating the presence of necessary thought], there was no ripple in this silence. . . The mind had no recollection of previous stillnesses, of those silences it had known; it did not say, "This is tranquillity". There was no verbalisation . . . for the word 'stillness' is not stillness. The movement of the mind was totally absent.
>
> . . . The barking of the dog, the unpacking of the car and the general disturbance in no way affected this extraordinary silence . . . here there was no time. . . .
>
> . . . The content of this silence is not to be measured in words.

* * * * *

To summarise, *prajñā* or Pure Awareness is ever-present.

In the average man, Pure Awareness is apparently eclipsed or obscured by unnecessary thoughts which also perpetuate the illusion that there is a 'me' (pseudo-subject) who is the 'thinker' of those thoughts.

After Enlightenment, Pure Awareness is intensely (and choicelessly) aware of unnecessary thinking, which is seen for the anomaly that it is, now that the illusion of the 'me'-the-'thinker' has disappeared. (Any choice is for the sake of the 'me'. Therefore, no 'me', no choice.) This is Spontaneous Silent Observation.

As a result, the unnecessary thoughts stop, or cease to be generated. This is the Disappearance of Unnecessary Thinking or the No-thought state.

What remains is Pure Awareness, which, however, as we just saw, was already ever-present.

And just what do we understand by the term Pure Awareness? Whatever we understand by it, it is not that — it is that within us **which is doing the understanding**.

We can summarise the entire process as follows:

> Intellectual understanding → Spontaneous shedding ('evaporation') of me-based spiritual effort → Spiritual Vacuum → Real or intuitive understanding (Enlightenment) → Spontaneous Silent Observation or motiveless attention (Factor 1 of K.W.) → Disappearance of Unnecessary Thinking ('No-thought' state or Factor 2 of K.W.) → Pure Awareness or *prajñā* (Factor 3 of K.W.), same as Liberation or *sahaja sthiti*.

As we have already clarified at several places, the word 'thought' in the term 'no-thought' state and its descriptions actually refers only to unnecessary thinking. It does **not** refer to necessary thoughts, which do **not** disappear, and which are not really counted as 'thought' in this context.

Most people take the description of the Silent Observation as a prescription of an active technique. The 'no-thought' state (the disappearance of unnecessary thinking) is then confused with *nirvikalpa samādhi*, in which **all** thoughts are suspended. But in *nirvikalpa samādhi*, the person is sitting in a trance and cannot function in everyday life as long as he remains in such *samādhi*, whereas *sahaja sthiti* (which is what we are dealing with here), is completely compatible with necessary thinking and with worldly activity, and a person in this state performs his worldly functions most efficiently — in fact, even more so than the average person. As mentioned earlier, *sahaja sthiti* is not a trance-like state — in fact, it is the most normal, natural state of the human being, and that is why it is called *sahaja sthiti*, which means 'natural state'. *Nirvikalpa samādhi* is a temporary state, dependent upon an active technique. But here we are talking not of any active technique or method but of a spontaneous process, leading to a state which is permanent, and **independent of any extraneous circumstance**.

In fact, if the process of Silent Observation is mimicked actively, that is, if a process similar to Silent Observation is carried out actively as a technique, (the active practice of 'mindfulness' for example), it may indeed lead to the temporary state of *nirvikalpa samādhi*. But it is only when Silent Observation occurs spontaneously that it leads to the enduring state of *sahaja sthiti*. The reason for this difference is that, in the former case, the process is not arising from the conviction or understanding that there is no separate 'I'. The person indulging in *nirvikalpa samādhi* still believes in the separate 'I', and he returns to that illusion as soon as he is out of the temporary *samādhi*. In fact, he is very likely to demand, and attempt to repeat the experience for the sake of that very 'I'. Śrī Ramaṇa Maharṣi has compared this state to a bucket of water submerged in a well, with the rope still attached, and which can be drawn out again by pulling on the rope.[14]

In practice, this is exactly what often happens. A sage describes the *processes* that occurred during his spiritual evolution, and his followers think he is describing methods to 'achieve' Liberation. They follow them actively, and some of them achieve states like *nirvikalpa samādhi*, and start believing that they have 'arrived'. Actually what they have got is no more than a faint whiff of the Reality.

---

14. Osborne, Arthur, *The Teachings of Bhagavan Sri Ramana Maharshi In His Own Words*, p. 225.

Sādhanā or Spiritual Effort

Traditionally, spiritual effort (*sādhanā*) aimed at achieving Enlightenment falls into two categories: 1. Self-improvement, and 2. Meditative (and other) mental and physical techniques.

Self-improvement: We have already shown in chapter 5 that cultivating virtue, while by itself a good thing, may not be of much relevance in the context of Enlightenment. (See chapter 5: 'True Virtue'.)

Meditative (and other) Techniques: We have also shown in chapter 3 and now in this chapter how me-based effort (in the form of meditative or other techniques) can in fact become a definite obstacle to Enlightenment.

This is not to say that such meditation should not be done. It merely means that **any** action done with the idea that a 'me' is doing it to 'achieve' something, will be counter-productive in the context of Enlightenment.

Should I meditate or not?
Do neither!

As long as there is the feeling that the 'me' is doing the action, whether it is meditating, or whether it is the avoiding of meditation, the result will be the same.

What is being described is not not-meditating as an action, but rather the shedding of the idea (through an intellectual comprehension of the real situation) that there is a 'me' doing the action, either meditating, or not meditating.

People often think that the sages have prescribed meditation, but the Masters often use the word 'meditation' not as a prescribed technique (as it is usually understood) but rather as a description of the *sahaja* state itself, and this is clear from the following examples:

> Meditation is your true nature . . . that is, . . . free from thoughts . . . Keeping away of other thoughts is now

called 'meditation'. But when (it becomes natural and continuous), . . . your real nature shows itself as true meditation. — Śrī Ramaṇa Maharṣi[15]

Why should one attempt meditation? Being the Self, one remains always realised. Śrī Ramaṇa Maharṣi[16]

When the mind becomes of its own totally silent, not made silent . . . then in that silence, truth, which has no path to it, exists. **That** is (true) meditation. (Emphasis added) — J. Krishnamurti

Krishnamurti's biographer, Mary Lutyens, too has noted that he used the word meditation differently (*The Open Door*, p. 63).

Thus, it will be seen that traditional *sādhanā* has really very little role to play in the occurrence of Enlightenment. Now this may startle the traditionalist. Yet, it is not anything new or original. This is the highest teaching in many philosophies. According to this teaching, telling the seeker to 'do' (or 'not do') certain things (*sādhanā*) only succeeds in perpetuating the illusion of the 'me'. Therefore, this teaching stresses only the understanding of the situation.[17] For example, the highest *Advaitic* teaching and especially that of the *Nāth* sect (as exemplified by Śrī Jñāneśvar and Śrī Nisargadatta Mahārāj) is the same. Ādi Śaṅkara too taught that it is only understanding (*bodha*) and not any other form of *sādhanā* that will lead to Liberation (*Ātmabodha*, 2,3).[18]

---

15. Osborne, Arthur, *The Teachings of Bhagavan Sri Ramana Maharshi In His Own Words*, p. 166.
16. Talks with Sri Ramana Maharshi, p. 436, quoted in *The Mountain Path*, Dec. '95, p. 76.
17. Balsekar, Ramesh (Conversations by air-mail), *Consciousness Writes*, p. 126.
18. (Tr.) Swāmi Nikhilānanda, *Self-Knowledge of Śrī Śaṅkarācārya*, p. 125-7.

> As long as enlightenment is sought under the compulsion of the 'me'-concept, how could it possibly be realised?
>
> . . . Attempting to become enlightened . . . no matter how sincere or genuine the effort, or apparently favourable the results, is activity having the same egoic basis . . . that one is trying to shed. . . . Consequently, *sādhanā*, or the common form of spiritual practice, is not prescribed in *Advaita*.[19]

Śrī Ramaṇa Maharṣi once told a devotee (who complained about being given no *sādhanā* to perform) that association with a sage was *sādhanā* enough. If that is obtained, then "to what purpose are the various methods of self-discipline?"[20]

> It is a sheer waste of energy to collect sticks to kill an (illusory) serpent. The only remedy to heal a wound caused in a dream is to awaken.
>
> — *Jñāneśvarī*, XV: 251, 254

Thus, according to the highest *Advaita*, no *sādhanā* is required (apart from understanding the situation), and in fact active *sādhanā* (spiritual effort) can be counter-productive.

Advaita has thus been called a

> most benign teaching, in the sense that it makes absolutely no demands on the seeker. Indeed, it releases the seeker from all demands placed on him by others as well as by himself.[21]

---

19. Balsekar, Ramesh (Conversation by air-mail), *Consciousness Writes*, pp. 17-18, 88.
20. Osborne, Arthur, *Ramana Maharshi and the Path of Self-Knowledge*, pp. 146-7.
21. Balsekar, Ramesh, *Consciousness Writes*, p. 126.

Ken Wilber[22] has shown how in the other spiritual traditions also, the same point has been made. He writes that in the original Ch'an (Zen) Buddhism there is no emphasis on any spiritual means or exercises, such as concentration or meditation (p. 322). He quotes Hui Neng, the Sixth Patriarch of Ch'an as saying that it is a mistake to think that sitting quietly in meditation is essential to deliverance. The truth of Ch'an, says Hui Neng, opens itself from within and it has nothing to do with the practice of *dhyāna* (sitting meditation).

And Wilber quotes Chang as saying that some people achieve a lucid thought-free state by suppressing all thoughts. This, however, is not Zen. (*Practice of Zen*, p. 101)[23]

And in Taoism, a systematic, forced, and ritual meditation practice was considered most un-Taoistic by the early Taoists, because trying to forget or get rid of the 'self' was considered no better than following its egotistical dictates. He quotes Chuang Tzu who asked, "Is not the desire to get rid of the self a positive manifestation of self?"[24]

It should be quite obvious and self-evident to the reader by now that, to a person who has really understood the fact that there is no separate 'me', that what-he-is is itself the Reality, and that there is nothing to be achieved, — to such a person then, there cannot be any **question** of spiritual effort. Effort for whom, by whom, and to what purpose? To such a person, the very idea of 'doing' spiritual effort to 'achieve' realisation would be absurd. On the other hand, in the case of a person who has not understood this basic fact, who still believes in his separate 'me', any effort is bound to be me-based.

Many seekers may not be ready for such a direct approach, and for them, the other, more conventional teachings are

22. Wilber, Ken, *The Spectrum of Consciousness*.

23. *Ibid.*, p. 324.

24. *Ibid.*, pp. 329-30.

available, which address relatively different levels of the reality. The conventional teachings begin by admitting (for the time being at least), the existence of a separate 'me', and, addressing this illusory 'me', give it a list of do's and don'ts to be followed.[25] However, beyond a certain point, the assumption of the existence of this 'me' itself becomes an insurmountable obstacle to spiritual understanding.

This is not to suggest that one teaching is superior to another. Rather, for a given individual, one teaching will be more appropriate than another, depending upon his mental make-up and spiritual maturity.

Thus it is the **intellectual understanding** which is the primary event, which leads to Enlightenment which in turn leads to the sequence of events culminating in eventual Liberation. So the only thing to be 'done' is to try to understand the situation intellectually. However, even this cannot be said to be a cause of Enlightenment. It only creates conditions favorable to its eventual spontaneous occurrence. It does this by removing the mental obstacles (like wrong ideas) which obstruct its occurrence.

> Self-enquiry leads directly to Self-realisation by removing the obstacles which make you think that the Self is not realised. (Śrī Ramaṇa Maharṣi)[26]

Natural Tendency to Enlightenment

We could say that there always exists in every individual a natural tendency towards the occurrence of Enlightenment, but this is obstructed by our present modes of thinking. Enlightenment does not **need** a cause. It will happen on its own,

---

25. Osborne, Arthur, *The Teachings of Bhagavan Sri Ramana Maharshi In His Own Words*, pp. 169, 199, 209.

26. *Ibid.*, p. 131.

provided we stop obstructing it by our fixed ideas and beliefs. This is because we always have a tendency to return to that which is our **natural state** (and Enlightenment is an event in that return journey).

Our volitional spiritual 'effort' can only reach as far as trying to understand the situation intellectually. (And even this is later seen to have been not really volitional at all.) Any other (apparently) volitional activity on our part aimed at the achievement of Enlightenment, being me-based, is bound to strengthen the me-illusion, making us go round in circles, like a dog chasing its tail, or like a man trying to kick himself in the rear. But intellectual understanding, even though initially occurring as a result of me-based effort, makes us aware of this very fact, and when this fact is clearly seen the effort (even further effort at intellectual understanding), eventually ceases to be me-based.

> The mind-intellect must be necessarily used in the early stages to try to understand the What-Is. Then the intellect comes to realise its own limitations, and with this surrender, intellect eventually becomes merged in the intuition.[27]

Thus attempts at intellectual understanding, though initially me-based, can be said to have a **boot-strap effect**, and boot back our consciousness into its original natural dimension. (In science, the 'boot-strap effect' is so-called because it is like a person lifting himself up by his own boot-straps.)

Apart from this, there is no particular regime of activity, or technique, or type of meditation, which will result in Enlightenment. What most of the commonly prescribed methods (like particular techniques of meditations) achieve are at the most a form of *nirvikalpa samādhi*, which is different from

27. Balsekar, Ramesh (Conversation by air-mail), *Consciousness Writes*, p. 124.

Enlightenment as we have explained earlier, but which many people confuse with Enlightenment. As Ramaṇa Maharṣi said,

> . . . there is no other means more effective than Self-enquiry. Even though the mind subsides by other means, that is only apparently so; it will rise again.[28]

To summarise finally, the main point being made in this chapter is that, in the final 'stages' (speaking phenomenally) of a sincere seeker's quest, **it is the seeking itself which prevents Enlightenment** because the seeking is based upon the false premise of the existence of a 'seeker' as a separate entity. As long as there is any seeking, this basic implied separation remains, and Enlightenment cannot occur. It is (intellectual) understanding of the situation which eventually makes the seeking cease, and it is in this state of 'vacuum' that the intuitive understanding (that is, Enlightenment) occurs. The role of the *guru* is limited to conveying conceptual knowledge in such a way that the seeker understands the true situation (intellectually), *with the result that his seeking stops.*

However, exceptionally, in a rare case like that of the Buddha, the state of Spiritual Vacuum is reached after actually attempting all the known techniques and seeing for oneself that they lead nowhere, until a state of spiritual exhaustion occurs. That is, the futility of me-based spiritual effort is seen not *a priori* through understanding, but by actually going through the entire gamut of the exercises and demonstrating or revealing their ineffectiveness to oneself. That is:

> Attempting unsuccessfully all techniques → spiritual exhaustion (futility of me-based spiritual effort seen by actual demonstration) → spontaneous shedding of me-based spiritual effort → Spiritual Vacuum → Enlightenment → Liberation.

---

28. Osborne, Arthur, *The Teachings of Bhagavan Sri Ramana Maharshi In His Own Words*, pp. 130-31.

As Krishnamurti declared at the historic meeting where he freed himself from the 'Order of the Star' and all other organisations

> "**Truth is a pathless land** and you cannot approach it by any path whatsoever."

Indeed, Truth can have no path to it, because :

> The spiritual quest is a journey without distance. You travel from where you are right now to where you have always been. From ignorance to recognition, for all you do is see for the first time what you have always been looking at.
>
> Whoever heard of a path that brings you to yourself or a method that makes you what you have always been?
>
> Spirituality, after all, is only a matter of being what you really are.
>
> — Anthony de Mello, S.J.

> To what shore would you cross, O my heart?
>
> there is no traveller before you, there is no road. . . .
>
> There is no water, no boatman, no boat. . . .
>
> Kabīr says: Put all imagination away and **stand fast in that which you are**! (Emphasis added)[29]

As Śrī Ramaṇa Maharṣi said:

> One goes through all sorts of austerities to become what one already is.[30]

That, then, is the paradox of the seeker seeking Enlightenment, for, though he does not know it, the seeker is indeed the sought — there is nothing really to seek.

---

29. (Tr.) Tagore, Rabindranath, *One Hundred Poems of Kabir*, XX.
30. Talks with Sri Ramana Maharshi, p. 63, quoted in *The Mountain Path*, Dec '95, p. 77.

9

Karma-, Bhakti- and Jñānā-Mārga

ALTHOUGH it was shown in the last chapter that there can be no real **path** to Enlightenment, it has been traditionally taught that Enlightenment can be brought about through three possible paths —*jñāna, karma,* or *bhakti*. These are usually presumed to mean three *alternative* paths, and the *mumukṣu* (spiritually minded person or seeker) is expected to choose the one most suited to his own particular temperament. What are these three, and why is there so much difference of opinion and confusion about the relative superiority of one over the other?

It seems to be generally conceded that *jñāna-mārga* (which includes Self-enquiry) is the penultimate step to Enlightenment. Śrī Ramaṇa Maharṣi said about Self-enquiry:

> . . . there is no other means more effective and adequate than Self-enquiry. Even though by other means the mind subsides, that is only apparently so, it will rise again.[1]

> "Enquiry. . . is the most important step." and "Self-enquiry is the ultimate route."[2]

The 'Sage who never speaks' said (to Paul Brunton):

---

1. Osborne, Arthur, *The Teachings of Bhagavan Sri Ramana Maharshi In His Own Words*, p. 175.

2. *Ibid.*, pp. 209, 65.

> . . . This backward turning of thought is the highest *yoga*.[3]

The Upaniṣads say,

> There is no other path except Knowledge for obtaining Release. (Sve. 3.8)[4]

But answering a direct question in the *Bhagavad Gītā* (V.2), Lord Kṛṣṇa says *karmayogo viśiṣyate* (*karma-yoga* is to be specially preferred). Yet, elsewhere in the *Bhagavad Gītā*, *jñāna* (knowledge) and renunciation are extolled, and Lord Kṛṣṇa says:

> . . . there exists here (in this world) nothing that is as purifying as Knowledge. That (Knowledge), one who has attained perfection in (*karma*) *yoga*, finds, in course of time, spontaneously within himself. — IV.38

> One imbued with faith wins that Knowledge . . . if he is intently after it. Having obtained the Knowledge, he in no time attains the Peace Supreme. — IV.39

Also see X.10 and XVIII.55 quoted later in this chapter.

The obvious implication in these verses is that **karma and bhakti lead to jñāna, which then** results in Enlightenment.

Ādi Śaṅkara (in his *Gītā-bhāṣya*) and Tilak (in the *Gītā Rahasya*) gave divergent interpretations of the *Gītā*'s meaning, Śaṅkara interpreting the *Bhagavad Gītā* as giving pre-eminent position to *jñāna*, whereas Tilak wrote the voluminous *Gītā-Rahasya* which is entirely devoted to refuting this opinion. He felt that the *Gītā* considers *karma-yoga* to be superior. Svāmī Ānandāṣram of Chitrapur agreed with Śaṅkara's interpretation.[5]

---

3. Brunton, Paul, *A Search in Secret India*, p. 113.
4. (Eng. Tr.) Sukthankar, Bhalchandra Sitaram, *Srimad Bhagavad Gita-Rahasya* by Bal Gangadhar Tilak, 6th edn., 1986, p. 432.
5. *Sunbeam*, p. 1-3, Feb 1979, April 1978, pp. 1-3.

On the other hand, saint-poets of the *bhakti-pantha* of medieval Maharashtra have sung of *bhakti-mārga* as the easy way to God (*bhakti-mārga sopā* — Tukārām), and this path has been upheld by Rāmānuja, Mādhvācārya and Vallabhācārya as well, in the past.[6]

(All talk of 'paths', 'levels', 'stages', 'progress', and 'reaching' or 'achieving' Enlightenment is of course from the point of view of the aspirant).

A lot of the apparent difference of opinion may be because the same or similar terms have been used to mean different things by different writers or speakers. At the outset, it must be seen that there are two different issues which are both in turn being discussed here, using similar terms, and thus causing confusion:

1. The **external path**, that is, the *outer mode of life* of the individual, and
2. The **inner (mental) path**.

In the *Bhagavad Gītā*, it will be seen that Arjuna's questions mainly relate to the external path, whereas Lord Kṛṣṇa is attempting to point out that the inner path is of more concern. Thus, the same or similar terms have been used sometimes with reference to the one, and sometimes to the other path. Arjuna admits his confusion arising from the terminology used saying:

> Thou art confusing my understanding with a riddle-like utterance. — III.2

In fact, at many places they can be seen to be virtually talking at cross-purposes.

The words *karma* and *yoga* themselves have several meanings, adding to the confusion:

6. (Eng. Tr.) Sukthankar, Bhalchandra Sitaram, *Srimad Bhagavad Gita-Rahasya* by Bal Gangadhar Tilak, 6th edn., 1986, pp. 22-5.

Karma can mean:

1. Vedic rites, rituals and *yajñas*.
2. Any action in general.
3. Actions pertaining to one's station in life.
4. The *karma* theory of action and its effects, the 'inexorable chain of causation'. (See Appendix).

The word *yoga* is also used in several different senses:[7]

1. Patañjali's *aṣṭāṅga-yoga* (see Glossary: *Yoga*).
2. *Samādhi* or superconscious experience.
3. Yoking or joining the individual self with God, integration.
4. In the sense of *yukti*, a trick or skilful device.
5. To indicate *karma-yoga*.

The External Path

Although a discussion about the external path would not seem very relevant today, when few people would seriously think of taking up *saṁnyāsa*, it is important to deal with it for two reasons:

1. Most of the ancient debate was on this point.
2. The similarity of the terms used may otherwise cause confusion.

A brief history of the evolution of Hindu religious and philosophical thought has been included to show how the idea of a monastic path (*saṁnyāsa mārga*) initially evolved, and thence, as a viable alternative to it, the path of the householder (*karma mārga*).

7. Harshananda, Swami, *A Dictionary of Advaita*, Ramakrishna Math.

HISTORY

The earlier portions of the Vedas contain descriptions of a lot of rites, rituals and *yajñas* (*karmas*) to be performed for different purposes (e.g., obtaining off-spring, rain, etc.). This part of the Vedas is therefore called the *karma-kāṇḍa*. According to the philosophy contained therein, (the Mīmāṁsā school), performance of such Vedic *karmas* would lead to worldly pleasures, 'heaven' and even to ultimate Liberation (*mokṣa*).

As philosophical thought developed, more importance came to be given to Knowledge (*jñāna*), and the latter part of the Vedas including the Upaniṣads (the *jñāna-kāṇḍa*) look upon the performance of these Vedic *karmas* as inferior, and do not agree that it can lead to Liberation. They say that only Knowledge can result in Liberation, and that ultimately such *karmas* have to be given up.

The Upaniṣads finally advised renunciation of the householder's life and the taking up of *saṁnyāsa* — the monastic way of life.[8] This path then came to be known as the **Saṁnyāsa-Mārga**. Some systems of Vedānta go to the extent of declaring that *mokṣa* is possible only through *saṁnyāsa*.[9]

To reconcile these conflicting views, (and perhaps to prevent a lot of able-bodied young men taking to monasticism) the later Smṛtis prescribed the four-stage mode of life in which a householder takes to *saṁnyāsa* at an old-age after completing his worldly duties. However, a better reconciliation was later developed in the form of **Karma-Mārga** or the Path of Action — the Householder's path, also called *karma-yoga*.

The *Bhagavad Gītā* was probably the first work to clearly

8. (Eng. Tr.) Sukthankar, Bhalchandra Sitaram, *Srimad Bhagavad Gita-Rahasya* by Bal Gangadhar Tilak, 6th edn., 1986, pp. 400-6, 435-6, 468-72, 480.

9. Harshananda, Swami, *A Dictionary of Advaita*, Ramakrishna Math, p. 65.

and concisely enunciate this method by which a **householder** could follow the spiritual path and achieve results equal to the *saṁnyāsī*. The *Bhagvada Gītā* mentions only two paths (III.3; V.1, 2, 5) *jñāna-yoga* and *karma-yoga*. These (here) obviously refer to the external paths, for as far as the external mode of life is concerned, there are only these two possibilities:

SAṀNYĀSA MĀRGA (THE MONASTIC PATH)

Synonyms: *nivṛtti-mārga, karma-saṁnyāsa-mārga, sāṁkhya-mārga, jñāna-marga, jñāna-yoga*, Pure *jñāna-mārga, jñāna-niṣṭha, smārta-mārga.*[10]

This is the path in which the individual renounces his home, family, and occupation and adopts a monastic way of life — in other words, becomes a *saṁnyāsī*. The idea is to minimise one's duties and spend maximum time in the contemplation of God.

Although it may have been so believed earlier (and that is why the terms *jñāna-mārga* or *jñāna-yoga*), we now know that the word *jñāna* used in this terminology does not mean that *jñāna* is the monopoly or prerogative of this path, nor does it imply that *jñāna* occurs earlier or more easily by this path. It simply indicates that this is the path in which spiritual knowledge is given supreme importance, to the extent of renouncing one's station in life (*karma*). Neither does it imply that *jñāna* is not important to the *karma-mārgī*. *Jñāna* is an essential preliminary to Liberation and any path which leads to Liberation must lead to *jñāna* first. The use of the word *jñāna* thus gives an unintended ring of superiority to this path.

KARMA-MĀRGA (THE HOUSEHOLDER'S PATH)

Synonyms: *pravṛtti-mārga, karma-yoga* (Path of Integrated

---

10. (Eng. Tr.) Sukthankar, Bhalchandra Sitaram, *Srimad Bhagavad Gita-Rahasya* by Bal Gangadhar Tilak, 6th edn., 1986, pp. 420-2, 491-8.

Action), *yoga* (the Integrated Path), *karma-jñāna-samuccaya-mārga* (Path of Synthesis of Action and Knowledge), *Karma-niṣṭha-mārga, bhāgavata-mārga.*[11]

This is the Path of Action, or the 'Householder's Path'. In this path, the person **continues his life as a householder**. The word *karma* here refers to duties of one's station in life, which are basically two-fold: professional (relating to one's occupation), and as a householder. In this path both duties are continued, and are, in fact, used as an aid in the spiritual journey.

> It is by (such) action all along that Janaka and others achieved perfection. —*BG*,III.20

Śrī Ramaṇa Maharṣi said,

> Actions performed with no thought of the ego purify the mind and help to fix it in meditation.[12]

Thus, the everyday duties (*karma*) are not abandoned but are **integrated** (*yoga*) into the spiritual path.

COMPARISON

Very few would seriously think of the first path in modern times, and those who do, are not usually encouraged by the sages. The path of *saṁnyāsa* was evolved when it was believed that a householder's life was incompatible with the spiritual search. The *Bhagavad Gītā* finally put this theory to rest, by showing how a householder can do as well spiritually as (if not better than) a *saṁnyāsī*. Like the *saṁnyāsī* he too can be, not just a part-time, but a regular full-time spiritual aspirant. The trick (*yukti, yoga*) is to know how to use the very action which was considered an

11. Sukthankar, Bhalchandra Sitaram, *Srimad Bhagavad Gita-Rahasya* by Bal Gangadhar Tilak, 6th edn., 1986, pp. 420-2, 491-8.
12. Osborne, Arthur, *The Teachings of Bhagavan Sri Ramana Maharshi In His Own Words*, p. 208.

obstacle, as an aid to spiritual progress. Nor will this hamper the efficient discharge of his worldly duties.

When the *Bhagavad Gītā* says that *karma-yoga* is preferable (V.2), it is to the external path that it refers to. It further gives very clear reasons for saying so. (III.4-5, 8; V.4-6)

The problem with *saṁnyāsa-mārga* is that in it, external renunciation (actual, physical renunciation) is given too much importance. What most sages including Śrī Ramaṇa Maharṣi and the *Bhagavad Gītā* have pointed out time and again is that external renunciation is of no use without internal renunciation (inner, mental detachment). And if there is inner detachment, there is then perhaps no necessity for external renunciation.

Śrī Ramaṇa Maharṣi is known to have often dissuaded people from taking up *saṁnyāsa*. Arthur Osborne has written

> He did not encourage the formal adoption of the saffron garb (external *saṁnyāsa*).[13]

> What do you mean by 'taking *saṁnyāsa*'? Wherever you go, . . . will your mind not go with you?. . . Why should your occupation or duties in life interfere with your spiritual effort? — Śrī Ramaṇa Maharṣi[14]

The person who has true detachment need not actually forgo action:

> Unattached to the fruits of actions, he who does what needs to be done, he is the one who has truly renounced, and who is a true *yogī*, and not he who relinquishes all action. — *BG*, VI.1

For him, no purpose of any kind is to be served by action

---

13. Osborne, Arthur, *The Teachings of Bhagavan Sri Ramana Maharshi In His Own Words*, p. 193.

14. *Ibid.*, p. 91.

> done, nor is any purpose whatsoever served by action not done. . . —*BG*, III-18

What holds true for action holds true for sensory experience or enjoyments also. (See chapter 5, 'True Detachment').

In fact, this point is the subject of a beautiful debate which is said to have taken place between Jñāneśvar and his father and is narrated in the *Mahā Bhakta Vijayam* of Nābhājī, which Ramaṇa Maharṣi had once produced on request for Śrī Manu Subedār (author of the first English translation of *Jñāneśvarī*).[15]

The story is interesting: Viṭhalpant, the father, was of ascetic bent of mind, and often retired to the forest to meditate alone. On one such occasion, he had left declaring that he would never come back. His wife then sent Jñāneśvar to convince him to return. This 10- or 11-year-old boy went to the jungle, and, sitting on his father's lap, carried on a philosophical debate with him and succeeded in convincing him to return home.

Jñāneśvar has herein given some beautiful arguments in favour of *karma-mārga*:

> Knowing one's Self and being that Self alone is '*Brahma-niṣṭha*', and not living in forests . . .
>
> *Ajñāna* will not be destroyed, nor the sense of 'I' and 'mine' be got rid of by living alone in a forest . . .
>
> *Sahaja-niṣṭha* consists in being free both from desires and aversions [also see *Bhagavad Gītā*, V.3]. Can hating the town and loving the forest be such *niṣṭha*?
>
> If one, who has given up all desires to engage in any activity, engages in the practice of *samādhi*, is not that practice also an activity, and why should not he who has this occupation have also the activity of the family?

15. Subedar, Manu, *Gita, the Mother*, pp. 311-16.

> The best *samādhi* is not to be in mere blank but, like meeting blow with blow, to engage in the affairs of the world.

Thus there now seems to be a near unanimity that *karma-mārga*, the householder's path, is preferable to *saṁnyāsa*, **as a path to Liberation**. However, if some person feels that he has the temperament fit for the life of a renunciate, he could still take to that path, but he should not be under any illusion that it will make Enlightenment and Liberation quicker or easier for him.

As we have repeatedly said, there is really no path to Enlightenment or Liberation. The term 'path to Liberation' is used here in the sense of 'external mode of life to be followed by the spiritual aspirant'.

The Inner (Mental) Paths

We have already shown (chapter 3) that the disappearance of the illusion of the entity cannot be 'achieved' (because any achieving is done by the entity itself) — it can only **happen**. We have also seen (chapter 7) that there are no cut and dried methods or techniques to make it happen. Thus, in fact, there can be no real inner 'paths' to Enlightenment. What the three terms — *bhakti-*, *karma-* and *jñāna-yoga* — refer to are rather **mental attitudes** of the aspirant prior to Enlightenment.

All three are required by **all** persons, whether externally following the householder's path or the monastic path, although depending upon temperament one aspect may be more dominant than another in a particular individual. *They are not alternative methods or paths.*

Even *jñāna mārga* enthusiast Ādi Śaṅkara has shown (in the *Upadeśapañcakam*)[16] how it is only a combination of *karma*, *bhakti* and *jñāna* that will lead to Knowledge.

---

16. Ed. V.R. Bhat, *Ānandabodhāmṛt*, pp. 11-5

> And Śrī Ramaṇa Maharṣi said: The . . . *mārgas* . . . are not exclusive of one another. They are described separately in classical works only to convey an idea of the appropriate aspect of God to appeal readily to the aspirant according to his predisposition.[17]

The *Yoga-Vāsiṣṭha* says:

> Just as the bird is able to fly by virtue of its two wings, so too by (means of) both *jñāna* and *karma* is obtained the enduring (state of) *Brahman*.

JÑĀNA-YOGA (THE INTELLECTUAL ASPECT)

We saw in the last chapter that there can be no methods or techniques to 'achieve' Enlightenment, and the only thing to be 'done' is to understand the situation intellectually. And this intellectual understanding creates conditions conducive to the spontaneous occurrence of Enlightenment. We also saw that conceptual knowledge is the starting point for the seeker's own investigation.

The part of the 'journey', starting with conceptual knowledge, and ending with the intellectual understanding, is *jñāna-yoga*. It consists of a theoretical aspect (*śravaṇa, manana, nididhyāsana*) and a practical aspect (Self-enquiry).

This (as already discussed in chapter 8) is an investigation into the working of our own mind and thought processes, into the matter of how our conditioning affects the way we see things and the way we think. It is the enquiry into the way our minds distort the reality and present us with a false version of it. And when we can really see this for ourselves, when we can actually observe it happen in our own mind, without any effort to change it, without any desire to change it, then **this very seeing** paves the way for a very fundamental change.

17. Osborne, Arthur, *The Teachings of Bhagavan Sri Ramana Maharshi In His Own Words*, p. 224.

This investigation or enquiry constitutes *jñāna-yoga*. *Jñāna-yoga* thus denotes the **intellectual** aspect of the search.

BHAKTI-YOGA (THE DEVOTIONAL ASPECT)

Bhakti is the **emotional** attitude towards God in the interim period (until Enlightenment). It is the aspect which gives the immediate flavour, the immediate sweetness to the search. Without *bhakti*, there is no incentive to pursue *jñāna*.

It is 'the path of love and devotion, worship and surrender'.[18]

Love cannot be made to order, it has to develop. Therefore several means are used. Worship leads to devotion, which leads to love, which ends in surrender. The *nava-vidhā-bhakti* suggests nine techniques of *bhakti*, the last of which is *ātma-nivedanam* (self-surrender).[19] But truly total surrender is not possible for the unenlightened, for **total surrender is itself Enlightenment**.

> Complete surrender is another name for *jñāna* or Liberation. — Śrī Ramaṇa Maharṣi[20]

And surrender is really complete when the word 'surrender' itself loses all meaning (for who is to surrender what and to whom?):

> If . . you merge in the Self there will be no individuality left. You will become the Source itself. In that case what is surrender? Who is to surrender, and to whom?
>
> — Śrī Ramaṇa Maharṣi[21]

18. Osborne, Arthur, *The Teachings of Bhagavan Sri Ramana Maharshi In His Own Words*, p. 193.
19. (Eng Tr.) Sukthankar, Bhalchandra Sitaram, *Srimad Bhagavad Gita-Rahasya* by Bal Gangadhar Tilak, 6th edn., 1986, p. 573.
20. Osborne, Arthur, *The Teachings of Bhagavan Sri Ramana Maharshi In His Own Words*, p.198.
21. *Ibid.*, pp. 195-6.

merā mujhamen kucha nahīn, jo kuch hai so terā;
terā tujhako soumpate, kyā lāgai hai merā.

— Kabīr

There is nothing in me that is mine, all that exists is yours;
What (sacrifice) does it require of me to give you what is already yours?

In that state there remains no 'one' to surrender anything:

jab mai thā tab hari nahīn, ab hari hain main nāhīn.

— Kabīr

When 'I' was, the Lord was not; now He is, and I am not.

As J. Krishnamurti said, if you **know** Reality, you *cannot* surrender to it, because **you cease to exist**.

Thus, we see that total surrender is synonymous with Enlightenment, and therefore truly total surrender is not possible for the unenlightened. But partial surrender is possible:

> Complete surrender is impossible in the beginning but partial surrender is possible for all. In due course of time that will lead to complete surrender.
>
> — Śrī Ramaṇa Maharṣi[22]

BHAKTI AS AN ALTERNATIVE 'PATH'

Height of devotional fervour, for example in the case of an exceptional *bhakta* like Tukārām, may sometimes lead to experiences of Unity. The exceptional clarity of vision obtained during that state may enable the *bhakta* to apperceive the adual Reality directly, as may have perhaps happened in the case of Tukārām.

---

22. Osborne, Arthur, *The Teachings of Bhagavan Sri Ramana Maharshi In His Own Words*, p. 198.

> We have now come to know Thy real nature. There is neither saint nor God (Tukārām).[23]

> Through that devotion he perceives in reality the essential nature of My being; and so, knowing Me in My real essence, he subsequently enters therein.
>
> — *BG*, XVIII-55

How could such intense *bhakti* lead to Enlightenment? It could do so by inducing total (or near total) surrender. And as we just said above, total surrender is the same as Enlightenment, because total surrender implies the complete and irrevocable surrender of the 'me', which means Enlightenment.

Or, after such experiences, Self-enquiry may automatically and imperceptibly follow (What was that state? Where was I then? *Who am I*?). This would then be an example of *bhakti* leading to (and merging into) *jñāna-yoga*.

However, these are exceptional cases, and *bhakti* otherwise is not an alternative path, and should not be considered as such, though sages may sometimes prescribe this to a seeker who is temperamentally or otherwise not ready for the intellectual understanding.

> . . . if the aspirant is temperamentally unsuited for Self-enquiry, he must develop devotion.
>
> — Śrī Ramaṇa Maharṣi[24]

Total surrender is more easily said than done, and in any case, is unlikely to happen unless there is at least some intellectual understanding of the real situation (that the 'me' is an illusion). Even Tukārām almost certainly had the theoretical knowledge of the basic premise of *Advaita* from the beginning.

---

23. Balsekar, Ramesh, (Conversations by air-mail) *Consciousness Writes*, p. 209.
24. Osborne, Arthur, *The Teachings of Bhagavan Sri Ramana Maharshi In His Own Words*, pp. 208-10.

Bhakti without any attempt at intellectual understanding would, in most cases, lead to spiritual stagnation. At the same time, pursuing spiritual knowledge as a purely intellectual exercise without any element of *bhakti* would only make a person a spiritual scholar, and nothing more. What is required is an appropriate mix of both, the actual proportions depending on the person's inherent nature and temperament.

Thus, ultimately, the actual 'path' towards Enlightenment taken by any one 'seeker', or rather (to be more accurate), the course of events occurring in any one individual body-mind antecedent to the happening of Enlightenment in it, will depend upon its individual characteristics — whether it is more given to intellectualism, or has more of an emotional inclination, or perhaps a little of both. In that sense, therefore, one could say that there are as many paths as there are individuals, and every 'individual' must beat out for himself the 'path' that most suits his own temperament.

> *Bhakti* and *jñāna* are not really different. In the final stages, in the case of both, the identity with the individual entity does disappear. . .[25]

> . . . and it is clear that they are not separate paths for 'attaining' the Ultimate. There is really no question of 'selecting' one or the other. In the mystical experience the 'individual' is totally annihilated, whatever the circumstances — that is to say, whether the take-off stage was reached through devotion, or through knowledge, or by a combination of both.[26]

---

25. Balsekar, Ramesh (Conversations by air-mail), *Consciousness Writes*, p. 206.
26. *Ibid.*, p. 207.

KARMA-YOGA (THE PRACTICAL ASPECT)

Karma-yoga is the practical aspect, relating to the attitude to be adopted towards one's everyday duties and actions. It is the art of integrating everyday activities into the spiritual journey, and using them as an aid to spiritual maturity.

> *yogaḥ karmasu kauśalam*
>
> (*Karma*) *yoga* means the art of action.
>
> — *BG*, II.50
>
> (*kauśalam*: skill, craftsmanship, art).

This art is essential for the *saṁnyasī* as well as the householder, but it forms the main basis or plank of the householder's path.

The actual art (the key or the secret) of *karma-yoga* is to perform action without the idea that one is the 'do-er', that is, without the idea that 'I' am doing the action. Now if the person could actually fully perceive this fact, then he would be already Enlightened, and indeed in that case such action (without the idea of 'doership') would occur spontaneously. (*BG*, III.27-28) Since the unenlightened person does not actually see this fact for himself, he is told to perform action with the idea that God, and not he, is the doer — and he, the person is merely the instrument, the conduit, *nimitta-mātra*. (*BG*, III: 30-1; V.8; XI.33) And if he finds it difficult to do even this, then he is advised to perform action without worrying about the results — *karma-phala-tyāga*. (*BG*, II.47-8, XII.8-11) In fact, this latter is a sound management technique — concentrate on the work on hand, and do not be unduly bothered about the result. Management experts now teach that excessive concern about results interferes with the efficiency of the activity.

COMPARISON

As mentioned earlier, the three are not alternative techniques or paths. Nor are they clear-cut stages, one ending before the other. They all happen concurrently, representing the intellectual, emotional, and practical aspect of the search respectively.

The *Bhagavad Gītā* says:

> With mind fixed on Me, O Pārtha, practising *yoga*, [that is, *karma-yoga*] with Me as refuge (having surrendered to Me) [that is, *bhakti-yoga*,] hear how you may know Me in entirety and with certainty [that is, *jñāna-yoga*].
>
> — VII-1

However, in a sense, *karma-yoga* can be said to be the most preliminary, for a novice *sādhaka* can practice it right at the outset, even before *bhakti* has developed, or Enquiry has begun. But it is continued all throughout till Enlightenment (after which it becomes spontaneous).

Bhakti can be practised without Enquiry, and can therefore be said to be the next in order, (but a *sādhaka* at this stage would actually be practising both *bhakti-* and *karma-yoga*).

Jñāna-yoga or Self-enquiry is the final process which precedes Enlightenment. Here again, *bhakti-* and *karma-yoga* are not abandoned.

Thus, the three merge one into the other, and will all be occurring simultaneously towards the end. *Jñāna-yoga* can be said to be the final lap, when conceptual knowledge leads to intellectual understanding, which in turn paves the way for 'true' knowledge.

All Methods Lead to Jñāna-Yoga

Śrī Ramaṇa Maharṣi said "All other methods lead up to Self-Enquiry."[27]

---

27. Osborne, Arthur, *The Teachings of Bhagavan Sri Ramana Maharshi In His Own Words*, p. 170.

The *Bhagavad Gītā* also affirms that *karma-yoga* and *bhakti yoga* lead to *jñāna-yoga*:

> In such persons of constant application [*karma-yoga*] who adore Me full of love [*bhakti-yoga*], I cause to arise that mental-absorption [*jñāna-yoga*] by virtue of which they come to Me. — X.10

The practice of *karma-yoga*, it is expected, would lead to equanimity of mind (*sama-buddhittva*) and purity of intention (*citta-śuddhi*), which then, along with the practice of *bhakti*, could create a mental state conducive to pursue Enquiry (*jñāna-yoga*). It is obvious that a mind fluctuating with the vagaries of fortune, and lacking sincerity of purpose would hardly be inclined to pursue *jñāna-yoga*.

As already discussed, *bhakti* is not really an alternative to *jñāna*. But it may be prescribed as an alternative activity *till such time* as the aspirant is ready for *jñāna-yoga*. *Bhakti* if carried to its logical conclusion will inevitably lead to Self-enquiry. The ninth prescription of the *nava-vidhā-bhakti* is *ātma-nivedanam* (surrender). To surrender oneself, **one must first know who one is**, which is where Self-enquiry starts.

> Surrender is giving oneself up to the original cause of one's being. One's source is within oneself. That means that you should seek the source and merge in it. . . . This constitutes devotion, wisdom and Self-enquiry. Thus, you see, devotion is nothing more than knowing oneself.
>
> — Śrī Ramaṇa Maharṣi[28]

* * * * *

To avoid confusion, there should really be a standard terminology. Perhaps the following could be considered:

---

28. Osborne, Arthur, *The Teachings of Bhagavan Sri Ramana Maharshi In His Own Words*, pp. 195-6.

External 'Path' (Mode of Life)

1. *Saṁnyāsa-mārga* or *nivṛtti-mārga* for the path of monasticism.
2. *Karma-mārga* or *pravṛtti-mārga* for the path of the householder.

Inner 'Path' (Mental Attitude)

1. *Karma-yoga* for attitude towards work,
2. *Bhakti-yoga* for emotional attitude towards (personal or personified) God,
3. *Jñāna-yoga* for intellectual attitude, and Self-enquiry.

The True Gist of the Bhagavad Gītā

The *Bhagavad Gītā* advises us to stick to the external path of the householder (*karma-yogo viśiṣyate*, V.2) even in adversity. Abandoning this path to take *saṁnyāsa* only because conditions have become unfavourable is escapist, and is the way of the coward (II.33-6). At the same time, we are shown how we should bear ourselves internally (mentally):

Do action without regard to the results (II.47-8), without the idea that 'I' am the doer (V.8), with *inner* detachment which is true renunciation (V.13) — that is *karma-yoga*; with devotion to God (XII. 6-8) — *bhakti-yoga*; and with the diligent mind of the sincere enquirer into Truth (IV.33-5), that is *jñāna-yoga*, until the advent of Knowledge (VI.15, 28).

After Enlightenment — Advaita-Bhakti

The very term *advaita bhakti* would appear to be a contradiction in terms, for *bhakti* presupposes duality — the duality of the lover and the loved, God and the devotee, the *bhakta* and the object of his *bhakti*. In that sense then, *bhakti* should be incompatible with true *Advaita*, for the ultimate *Advaitic* truth expresses the absolute 'inseparateness' of 'oneself' (one's presumed separate self) and the Totality or God, and when this truth has been realised, *bhakti* in the ordinary sense would be an impossibility. And yet, we see that confirmed *advaitin*s like Ādi Śaṅkara and Jñāneśvar have to their credit verses virtually dripping with the emotion of *bhakti*. The *Bhaja Govindam* and *Hymns to the Goddess* are well-known examples of Śaṅkara's devotional poems. Jñāneśvar's devotional *abhaṅga*s too are well-known.

> I have woven my thoughts into a shawl,
> and offered it to the Lord Viṭṭhal, consort of Rukmiṇī.
> He, the dusky, lovely one, *pītāmbar*-clad,
> With beauty so alluring, Him have I beheld. . . .
> Viṭṭhal, the Lord of Bliss, consort of Rukmiṇī,
> My body, mind and speech, all has He drawn to Himself.

One could explain these verses by saying that they may have been composed in the pre-Enlightenment period of the sage's life. But these devotional compositions often contain unmistakable mystical references, thus proving that these were indeed composed after Enlightenment, in the full light of the Great Understanding. To give examples from Jñāneśvar's compositions:

> *darpaṇi pāhatā rūpa, na dise ho āpule,*
> *bāpa rakumādevī vare, maza aise kele.*

> On looking into the mirror, I see no more my form,
> Thus has the Lord, consort of Rukmiṇī, made me.

And again:

> Today is a golden day,
> The clouds are raining showers of nectar (*amṛta* = elixir of life),
> I have seen Hari, I have seen Hari,
> He permeates everything inside-out, the Divine Flutist.

What really happens is that after Enlightenment, the very **concept** of 'God' disappears. God becomes an actuality. As Tukārām sang, "Now whom shall I worship, God is inside as also outside."[29] There can indeed be no more *bhakti* as it is usually understood, for there is no more a '*bhakta*!'

Such a person cannot then indulge in *bhakti* in the traditional dualistic meaning of the word, for he no longer sees God as 'another', separate from 'himself.'

However, this is not to say that there can be no *bhakti* or Love after Enlightenment. What remains is the most supreme form of Love, without the slightest trace of duality or separateness. There is Love, but there is no 'one' who loves, and no separate 'one' being loved. Thus we come to what appears to be a paradox — that the mystic (*advaitin*) cannot even think of God or pray to Him in the usual dualistic sense, and yet he can and does manifest emotions of Love which are indistinguishable from *bhakti*. We could call this ***advaita-bhakti***.

Svāmī Ānandāṣram of Chitrapur also said that the *advaitin* does not have to forgo the bliss of *bhakti*.

Here *advaitin* must be taken to mean not simply a believer in the doctrine of *Advaita*, but a person who actually sees this truth for himself, in other words, an Enlightened or Liberated person.

Although I have not come across the term *advaita-bhakti* anywhere, such *bhakti* has been unmistakably referred to by most mystics and sages. It also appears in the *Bhagavad Gītā* in the last verse of the chapter on *dhyāna-yoga* (VI.47):

> And of all *yogīs*, he who, possessed of faith, adores (worships) Me, abiding in Me in his innermost self (*madgatena-antarātmanā*), such a one is deemed by Me

---

29. (Eng. Tr.) Sukthankar, Bhalchandra Sitaram, *Srimad Bhagavad Gita-Rahasya* by Bal Gangadhar Tilak, 6th edn., 1986, pp. 318, 598.

to be the best *yogī*, (or the most completely united with Me).

Jñaneśavar's commentary on this verse (*Jñāneśvarī*, VI. 482-5):

> He who may be called a (true) *yogī* — know ye that he is the (very) God of gods and My sole happiness — indeed My very life. In the totality of his experiencing, worshipper, worship and worshipped have all become My very Self. Then the love between him and Me cannot be described in words. If that unitary love has to be described by a metaphor, then it can only be this: that I am the body and he the soul.

And Jñaneśavar has also described it elsewhere:

> However small the wavelet, yet it is no different from the ocean, in the same way am 'I' no different from God: the joyous state of vision emanating from such consciousness of full identity, is what we call devotion [In other words, this is *real* devotion].
>
> — *Jñaneśavarī*, XIV.386-7

Kabīr has talked of it:

> *prema gali ati sānkari, yā mein do na samāhi*
>
> The lane of Love is too narrow, it cannot accommodate two.

This *advaita-bhakti* does not involve any actual act of worship by the *advaitin*. For him, there is no need for such. Whatever he may be doing at the time, is his worship. His very oneness with God, indeed his very being, is his act of worship. As Jñaneśavar describes in Lord Kṛṣṇa's words:

> Whatsoever he may speak, that is My praise,
> Whatsoever he looks at, that is My form,
> With his walking do I move, inseparably bound (to him)
> by non-duality.

Whatsoever he may be doing, that is itself My worship,
Whatever he thinks, that is My contemplation,
His very being itself, O Arjuna, is his absorption (meditation) in Me . . .
As the wave is to the water, the fragrance to the camphor, the lustre to the gem, so also is he inseparable from Me. — (*Jñāneṣvarī*, XVIII.1180-3)

Advaita-bhakti is thus the most sublime form of Love. It is Love without an object, and, even more important, without a subject. Subject and object both have dissolved, merged irrevocably without a trace, into one unitary reality of indescribable Love.

The *advaita-bhakti* which is described here is not an emotion or an experience in the ordinary sense. It is unitary or adualistic experiencing, that is, experience-**ing** without an experience-**er**. And yet, we are not referring to the unitary love and bliss experienced by the person who goes into *nirvikalpa-samādhi*. *Nirvikalpa-samādhi* is the result of a particular technique, whereas *advaita-bhakti* is the description of the waves of loving bliss which **spontaneously** engulf the mystic from time to time. The mystic does not volitionally indulge in such acts of Love, or attempt to induce them by any particular effort. They occur naturally, as manifestations emanating from his deep Understanding. The practitioner of *nirvikalpa-samādhi* retains his sense of separateness, though it is suppressed for the duration of the *samādhi*. With *advaita-bhakti* on the other hand, the blissful feeling of all-encompassing Love may come and go, but the basis of that love — which is the Understanding of Oneness — never leaves the mystic.

To conclude, *advaita-bhakti* is the most supreme, most sublime form of love possible. It is love without a cause, without a subject and without an object. If at all we must demonstrate a purpose for Creation, it could be this. We could say that the universe was created so that this, its most sublime expression, could be possible.

10

God

Does God really exist? And if he does, what is his true nature? If there is a God, and if he is all-merciful, then why is there so much suffering in the world? Anyone with even the slightest trace of curiosity must have certainly pondered over these questions sometime in his life.

But before we attempt to answer these, we must first be clear what we mean by the word 'God', because the term may mean different things to different people.

The Common Man's God

Most people who believe in God imagine him to be a wise, benevolent being with superhuman powers. He would be all-knowing and all-powerful, and the creator and master of the universe. He would be endowed with all the good qualities that we can conceive of and that we normally consider desirable in man, and will therefore be the epitome of love, compassion, beauty, generosity, kindness, and so on.

To most of us then, God is a benign superman. Thus we can define the common man's God (that is, the common man's perception of God), as an omnipresent, omniscient and omnipotent, benevolent Person. This is the anthropomorphic God (God with human form) conceptualised by the human mind. It is but natural that man should imagine God thus — as an exalted image of himself. As Svāmī Vivekānanda once said, if a cow were philosophical and had religion, she would imagine God to be a cow; and if cats became philosophers, they would imagine a cat ruling the universe.[1] Spinoza said that if a buffalo could think, he would think of God as a large, benevolent buffalo. Baron de Montesquieu said . . . if triangles invented a god, they would make him three-sided.

But this is not God. It is merely our **concept** of God.

How far is this concept of God based on (or related to) reality? In other words, is this God of our concepts for real? Or is this idea the result of fantasy and wishful thinking, related to man's subconscious craving for security in an insecure world?

Let us then briefly see how this idea of God originated and evolved to its present form. Historically, the idea of God was born when man began to **think**. Animals do not have a concept of God. In Man, the concept of God began with Fear. The early God was a God of Fear.

And he still remains so for many people. Even today we use the term 'God-fearing' to indicate a religious person.

Primitive man lived in a bewildering, frightening world with absolutely no control over his own life or future. His world was filled with many strange, inexplicable and often powerful and dangerous phenomena over which he had very little or no control. This bred insecurity and fear. He therefore attempted to devise ways and means to regain some control over these events. Even if that control was imaginary and illusory, it gave him some peace of mind. It gave him a feeling of psychological security, which though false, was effective in relieving his immediate stress. This control was achieved by deifying the very elements which scared him, and attempting to propitiate and appease them by worship and prayer.

---

1. *The Complete Works of Swami Vivekananda*, Vol. II, Mayavati Memorial edn., Advaita Ashram, Calcutta, p. 155.

Eventually almost anything and everything was deified. The elements — the earth, fire, water, air, the ocean, the sky, rain, lightning, forests (Pan), the stars, the sun and the moon. As man evolved, so did his God, and to the list of gods were added the deified versions of Love (Cupid, *Madana*), wealth (Mammon, *Lakṣmī*), war (Mars), ancestors, birds, animals, Time (*Kāla*), and Death (*Yama*). For convenience, the gods were symbolised by images of clay, stone, or wood. Intricate techniques and elaborate rituals were developed to keep these various gods happy. The multitude of gods formed a world of its own, with its own hierarchy, and its own politics and intrigue. Gods fought with other gods, gods destroyed gods.

Man created God in his own image (not the other way around) and filled him with his own petty ambitions and emotions.

God is your own projection of yourself. (J. Krishnamurti)[2]

Over the centuries, these various gods slowly evolved into the concept of a single supreme, universal God who was nevertheless a Person.

The average man's concept of God today is a somewhat vague mixture of the two pictures above.

It is important to realise that the God in our minds is ultimately a **concept**, which may or may not have any relation to the reality. It is an image of **thought** just as there is an image of clay or stone.

> We should not confuse the image of God as man conceives him with the reality of God.[3]

Even the 'Cosmic Form' revealed to Nārada (in the *Mahābhārata*) was a concept, as Lord Kṛṣṇa himself immediately clarified:

That My form which you see is an **illusion** (*māyā*)

---

2. Krishnamurti, J., *The Wholeness of Life*, p. 71.
3. Radhakrishnan, S., *Religion and Culture*, pp. 61-2.

created by Me. (Emphasis added)[4]

But to the average man, this concept is **more important than the reality**:

For years the *bhakta* had prayed for a vision of his deity, Lord Rāma. Finally, the Lord appeared before him, but in the form of Lord Kṛṣṇa.

"Who are you?" asked the devotee.

"I am God" answered Lord Kṛṣṇa. "I am He to whom you have been praying all these years. I am pleased with your devotion. You wished to see Me, so here I am!"

"Go away" said the devotee. "I do not recognise you. I prayed to Lord Rāma, and I want to see God in the form of Lord Rāma only."

(You see, his concept of God was more important to him than God Himself. That is how it is with most people).

To most people, God is not a reality, but a **belief**. Moreover, they are content with this belief, with their idea of God, and are not the least interested in knowing what he is really like (or whether he really exists at all). This is not to say that the atheist is any different. The atheist is also a believer, for he believes in the absence of God. He is not any different because he too does not really know and does not want to find out.

The mystic, on the other hand, knows but cannot say. For the reality of God is beyond expression : *avāṅgmanasagocaram*. He certainly does not believe in God, for, to him God is not a mere belief, he is a burning reality, an actuality. Just as a man does not believe that he exists — he knows it and feels it. But strangely, for this very reason, mystics have often been labelled as atheists.

4. Shantiparva 339-44, quoted in (Eng. Tr.) Sukthankar, Bhalchandra Sitaram, *Srimad Bhagavad Gita-Rahasya* by Bal Gangadhar Tilak, 6th edn., 1986, p. 280.

> To believe in God is not to find God. Neither the believer nor the non-believer will find God. (J. Krishnamurti)

> I do not believe in anything... I have no belief and it does not mean that I am an atheist, or that I am ungodly... It means that the mind is free from all the entanglements of belief.[5]

It is said that the Buddha was unwilling to speak about God. He considered such idle speculation as useless and distracting from the main issue, which was to find out about one's own self. Śrī Ramaṇa Maharṣi, too, when asked about God, replied "Why do you want to know what God is before you know what you are? First find out what you are."[6] Arthur Osborne writes that though the Maharṣhi often spoke of God, that was really a concession, for so long as the concept of the individual self as a real and separate being continues, the concept of God as the Creator of that being must also continue.

> Bhagavān (Ramaṇa Maharṣi) was willing to speak to each person in the idiom of that person's understanding, but to those who would open their hearts to his teaching he pronounced only the final truth: that there is no God and no you *apart from the Self*.[7]

Śrī Ramaṇa Maharṣi said explicitly,

> There is no God apart from the Self, for if there were he would be a Self-less God, which would be absurd[8]

Kabīr lamented:

> Alas! the true fountain of life is beside you,

---

5. Krishnamurti, J., *Questions and Answers*, p. 35
6. *Mountain Path*, Dec '95, p. 83.
7. *Ibid.*
8. *Ibid.*

and you have set up a stone to worship.[9]

Kabīr decried idol-worship, rites and rituals. He said:

Worshipping the stone idol will not destroy delusion,
Such will not obtain peace even in their dreams,
their delusion will increase day by day. [10]

They rush to the temples, to bow their heads,
But the Lord is seated within your heart,
Seek Him there within[11]

Japa (chanting) and austerities,
Pilgrimage and vows, futile are they all[12]

. . . my *Guru* showed me the Path,
I abandoned all rites, all rituals,
no more do I bathe in the holy waters,
nor ring the temple bell
no more do I set the idol on its throne
nor worship it with flowers — Kabīr

When at the temple of Jagannāth, Guru Nānak saw the image being worshipped with lamps waved before it and flowers and incense offered on gold salvers studded with pearls, he burst into song:

The sun and the moon, O Lord, are thy lamps;
the firmament, thy salver
and the. . . stars the pearls set therein.
The perfume of the sandal (tree) is thy incense;

---

9. (Eng. Tr.) Tagore, Rabindranath, *One Hundred Poems of Kabir*, XXI.
10. Singh, Dr. Jaidev and Singh, Dr.Vasudev, *Kabir Vani Piyush* (Hindi), part II, p. 100.
11. *Ibid.*, p. 102.
12. *Ibid.*, p. 101.

the wind is thy fan;
all the forests are thy flowers,
O Lord of light.[13]

We see therefore that what people believe in, think of and worship as God is really a concept in their minds. It has no relation to the reality of God. This is what the sages try to point out. And the sages usually discourage idol-worship and rituals not because these are bad in themselves, but because people invariably tend to become so involved in this symbolism, that they completely forget the Reality that the symbol stands for.

The Reality of God

THE GOD OF THE MYSTIC

So far we have seen what God is **not**. We have seen that what the common man calls God is merely a concept of God. We have also seen that the common man thinks of God as a Person. But God is not a person. Then what is God? And does he exist at all? And how can we be sure?

Like the Upaniṣadic *neti-neti*, it is indeed much easier to say what God is not than to say what he is. Indeed it is nothing short of an attempt to define the indefinable, to express the inexpressible, comprehend the incomprehensible. The description is bound to be grossly inadequate, but the attempt must be made.

What then does the mystic mean when he talks about God? The mystic may mean two things, and not necessarily in an exclusive manner. That is, one meaning may not necessarily exclude the other.

1. The actual or main meaning: 'God' is the Absolute or All-that-is. An indefinable, **impersonal** force which is the basic substratum (ground) and essence of all that exists,

---

13. Radhakrishnan, S., *Religion and Culture*, p. 144.

and yet is at the same time not different from it. It is itself the creation, its ground, its essence, its potentiality, and what remains after all this, that is, its transcendency. It is the Becoming, Being, and that which is 'More than Being'.[14] Yet, It is not an abstraction (as these descriptions may well appear in the mind of the reader). To the mystic, It is the one actuality.

It is the Absolute in its triple aspect, that is, the actual (the Creation itself), the immanent (its basic underlying principle or Essence) and the Transcendent (all that remains over and above and beyond the Creation). It is not merely infinite and eternal, It is beyond concepts of finitude (finiteness) and time — beyond the duality of finite and infinite, transient and eternal. For in timelessness there can be no eternity.

To put it simply, God is not only the Creator, but also the Creation and the Created, He is both the Cause and the Effect, both the thinker and the thought. In short, He is all there is.

2. The same Absolute, in its personal aspect, becomes the loving God, the beloved '*fakīr*' of Kabīr and of Sāi Bābā (of Śirḍī), the *parvardigār* of the Sūfi mystics, whom Jesus called 'my Father'. But (and this is most important), *at no time does even this aspect of God become a concept to the mystic*, as it inevitably does to the non-mystical hearer. To the mystic, God always remains the actuality, whether he describes him as the Absolute, or as the Divine Lover, or whether he does not describe him at all and remains silent, abiding in pure Being.

And what is our proof that such a thing exists? How do we know that the Universe is not just what it appears to be — matter and

14. (Eng. Tr.) Tagore, Rabindranath, *One Hundred Poems of Kabir*, p. 9.

energy, and nothing more esoteric than that? Indeed, this was the basic assertion of several philosophies like the Materialism of ancient Indian *Cārvāka*,[15] Hedonism, and the more recent Nihilism (Russia, nineteenth and twentieth centuries). Haeckel, a pure Materialist, was of the opinion that there is no Fundamental Element which is at the root of or beyond the visible world.[16]

The mystic, on the other hand, says that there is something, some active principle, which underlies all that exists, and which is itself beyond the duality of existence and non-existence. It is the potential plenum from which all things arise, and it is at the same time all those things. The mystic says that he knows and feels this principle, indeed he (and all else) **is** this principle.

Even the Buddha, who did not talk about God, did assert (like all other mystics) that there *is* some active principle which underlies all that exists. He said:

> There is an Unborn, Unoriginated, Uncreated, Unformed. If there were not this Unborn, this Unoriginated, this Uncreated, this Unformed, release from the world of the born, the originated, the created, the formed would not be possible.[17]

The *śūnyavāda* of Buddhism (Nāgārjuna, second century AD) was not the same as Nihilism. Whereas the Buddha had refused to theorise or speculate on these matters, considering it as a waste of time, and insisting on actual experience, Nāgārjuna merely said that the supreme essence or truth cannot be conceptualised or described in words. All that we can call it is *śūnya*, nothingness or void. Not because it does not exist, but

---

15. (Eng. Tr.) Sukthankar, Bhalchandra Sitaram, *Srimad Bhagavad Gita-Rahasya* by Bal Gangadhar Tilak, 6th edn., 1986, pp. 105-6.

16. *Ibid.*, p. 369.

17. Goswami, Amit, *The Self-Aware Universe*, pp. 51-2.

because it is devoid of describable qualities, and is even beyond the concepts of existence and non-existence. In the *Mādhyamaka-śāstra*, Nāgārjuna describes it as:

> **That** which cannot be known through (the experience of) another, where there is the subsidence of all concepts, which cannot be described in words, which cannot be conceived by the mind, in which there is no plurality.[18]

Thus this *śūnyavāda* is not different from the *neti-neti* description of the Vedas.

Now can we prove this assertion, and if so, how?

THE PROOF

It is generally assumed that the existence of God (meaning the Reality or *Brahman*), or the mystical awareness, has never been (and can never be) proved scientifically. The common error made in this assumption is that we look for what we could call External Proofs or Indirect Proofs or Conventional Proofs. An external proof is a proof that is separate from the thing proven. This is the type of proof that science is used to (though this type of proof may not apply in quantum mechanics). To explain it in a very simplified manner, in such a proof, Statement *A* is proved by Statement *B*. However, you have to either assume the correctness of Statement *B* without any basis, which is unscientific, or prove it by Statement *C*. But then Statement *C* has to be assumed or proved by Statement *D*, and so on. Now this can either go on *ad infinitum*, or must necessarily lead somewhere back to Statement *A*; that is, Statement *Z* is proved by Statement *A*, thus forming a complete circle. An external proof is an example of 'Circular Logic', or a 'closed' system of thought, as Ken Wilber calls it.[19]

---

18. Singh, Dr. Jaidev and Singh, Dr.Vasudev, *Kabir Vani Piyush* (Hindi), Part I, p. 33-4.

19. Wilber, Ken, *The Spectrum of Consciousness*, p. 33.

Godel's "Incompleteness Theorem" also states something similar — that every encompassing system of logic must have at least one premise that cannot be proven or verified without contradicting itself.[20]

This is not to say that such proofs have no value at all. These proofs are valid for all events 'within' the 'circle of logic' that they circumscribe. But they cannot hold true for events outside that circle. In other words, they have limitations. For example, Newton's Laws of Motion were based on observation of everyday reality, and they were considered authentic because everyday reality both supported them and could also be predicted by them. A classic example of *A* proving *B*, and *B* proving *A*. But what they could not predict or prove was quantum reality, which was not everyday reality.

Usually the circle of logic is quite large, and the implied reconnection merges back so imperceptibly that we fail to notice it. But we notice the absurd nature of such proofs when the circle is very small (that is, when most events fall outside it). An example: An inmate of a lunatic asylum told a visitor "I am God". (Statement *A*). Other inmates agreed with him. When the visitor asked another inmate why they believed him, he got the answer "Because God does not lie". (Statement *B*). A proves *B*, *B* proves *A* — Q.E.D.! Absurd? But most worldly proofs are only more sophisticated versions of this logic. In fact, this is an inferior type of proof as compared to what we may call Internal or Direct Proof. Such proofs are really themselves self-evident truths or inherent truths, which require no formal proof at all. In other words, **a self-evident truth is its own proof**.

The Reality has always been said to be Beyond-proof or Self-Proven, or Self-Known (*sva-samvedyā* as Jñāneśvar has called it: *Jñāneśvarī*, 1:1, *Amṛtānubhav*, 6:13, also see 2:29, 5:54). For example, when one asks about the existence of *Brahman*, the

---

20. Quoted by Wilber, Ken, *The Spectrum of Consciousness*, p. 36.

existence of the questioner is taken for granted. If asked to prove that formally, one would face difficulties. How can you prove, or who is to prove the existence of the verifier or the one who demands the proof? Is not the very demand for proof the proof of his (the questioner's) existence? In fact, the question seems absurd. And this is typical of the nature of self-evident truths. So too, the demand for proof of the existence of the Reality sounds absurd to the mystic, for the Reality is itself All-That-**Exists** (including the questioner); where is the question of proving its existence; and to whom? The fact that you exist is self-evident. This 'proof' does not depend upon anything else. And yet, (if someone were to question it), you would have a hard time proving it to him in a laboratory.

At the same time, we must understand that the mystic's vision is very different from a mere hallucination. A hallucination can only be seen by the one suffering from it. It cannot be seen by others. Whereas the mystic state has been attested to by innumerable sages by means of identical descriptions, and it can be experienced (though experienced may not be the exact word), by anyone (including you), who is interested. The mystic's situation is rather like a person seeing a beautiful landscape, which others cannot see only because they insist on keeping their eyes firmly shut. How can he prove it to them? He cannot, except by showing them how to open their eyes and making them see for themselves — this is the only proof.

In fact, there are many worldly things which cannot be externally proven but whose existence we accept unquestioningly, like our emotions (love, hate, anger), subjective qualities like beauty, colours, taste, and so on. We accept these not because they have been scientifically proven to exist, but because we can see or feel them too. So internal proofs are not so alien to us after all.

The existence of *Brahman* or the mystical awareness is a matter which cannot be proved by an external proof. Yet, for the sake of the sceptic, we do have two scientific ways of demonstrating the veracity of mystical awareness. The main criteria of a scientific proof are Consistency, Repeatability and Predictability.

The first proof we have is the extra-ordinary **consistency** in the assertions of the mystics, and the almost unbelievable concurrence of their sayings, which are in perfect agreement with each other, however far apart in time or distance or culture or education the speakers may have been. From the sparsely educated Kabīr of medieval India, to J. Krishnamurti of our times; from the Sūfī mystics of the Middle East, to Meister Eckhart of Europe; and so the list goes on. Without basing their observations on any theoretical considerations, without any reference to other sources, time and again these mystics have described what they saw and felt for themselves. And what they said has been in absolute accord with each other. That this is so should be evident from the various quotations given in this book alone. Indeed, their opinions have been so "impressively universal and unanimous", a "philosophical consensus of universal extent", that this universal philosophy has been given the name *philosophia perennis* or the "Perennial Philosophy". (Leibniz; Aldous Huxley.)[21]

This is surely significant corroborative evidence for those who will look at it.

> There is a reality which coming upon the mind transforms it . . . there is that state unquestionably. In saying this I am not speculating, nor am I saying it as an experience of yesterday. It is so. There is that state. (J. Krishnamurti)[22]

The other sort of scientific evidence is when we are able to **repeat** any experiment for ourselves with predictably similar results.

21. Wilber, Ken, *The Spectrum of Consciousness*, pp. 23 and 169; also (ed.) White, John, *What is Enlightenment*, p. 27.

22. Jayakar, Pupul, *Fire in the Mind*, Foreword, pp. xiv-xv.

Therefore, if we question further, the mystics say, "Do not take our word for it. Come, find out for yourself. That is the only certain way. Be yourself a mystic." And we cannot go any further than that.

> If you really experiment with what I am saying you will discover the truth of it for yourself.
>
> Experiment, . . . and you will find out for yourself. (J. Krishnamurti)[23]

As Ken Wilber has pointed out, Vedānta and Zen are not theories, philosophies, psychologies, or religions — rather, they are primarily **a set of experiments** in the strictly scientific sense of the term. They are not mere theoretical speculation, but are actually based upon an experimental insight into the Reality.[24]

And thus, as Wilber says,[25] we have only two options open to us in judging the reality of mystical awareness — either we can believe the sages who have experienced it, or we can attempt to experience it for ourselves. But if we cannot do either of these things, we should withhold judgement. The Reality or God or Consciousness **cannot be externally proven**, for the simple reason that there is no place one can go that is outside of it so as to be able to verify it. Indeed, that 'one' who is attempting to prove or verify it is himself part of that Consciousness. It can be proven experimentally by any individual who is willing to become a mystic himself, but this proof is not an external one.

Therefore, says Wilber, if a scientist denies the reality of Consciousness as so much mystical nonsense without himself performing the experiment, then he would be behaving in as

---

23. *Krishnamurti's Talks in America — 1954* (*Verbatim Report*), pp. 5 & 17.

24. Wilber, Ken, *The Spectrum of Consciousness*, pp. 23, 164.

25. *Ibid.*, p. 275.

unscientific a manner as if he had denounced the experimental data of one of his colleagues without himself repeating that experiment.[26]

As Ananda Coomaraswamy has said, it would be unscientific to say that such attainments are impossible, unless one has himself made experiment. The reality of Consciousness and of the mystical awareness cannot be demonstrated in the classroom.

> At the same time, it would be unscientific to deny a presupposition for which an experimental proof is possible.[27]

Ironically, when you do find the proof, you will have the same difficulty in proving it to others — because the existence of God (the real God), can **only be proved to oneself**, **for oneself**. It can never be satisfactorily proved to another.

Yet, as we have just seen, it can be proved and it has been proved, though not in the way we usually expect things to be proved.

One way to answer that eternal question "Does God exist?" is by saying "Yes and No! Yes he does, but not in the way you think". God as a personal, personified concept exists only in the mind of the worshipper, as a concept. But the mystic's definition of God is quite different. For the mystic, he himself has long ceased to exist. All that remains, is God. The whole point is that the original question is asked under the basic presumption that the questioner exists as a separate entity, which is a false presumption in the first place. Hence, the question is itself flawed. Therefore, another way to answer it could be:

> Does God exist?
> God alone exists. It is **you** who don't exist.
> (God is the only thing that exists).

---

26. Wilber, Ken, *The Spectrum of Consciousness*, p. 309.

27. A.K. Coomaraswamy, *Hinduism and Buddhism*, pp. 18, 69.

For asking if God exists is somewhat like the fictitious character in a story asking if the author exists.

God — The Reality

Synonyms: The Absolute, The Reality, **That**, That-Which-Is, (Universal) Consciousness, the Self, *nirguṇa Brahman*, the (Universal) *ātman*, *tattva* (Essence), *Tao*, the Knower, the Witness, Absolute Subjectivity, the Host (Ch'an Buddhism), the *Tathāgata-garbha*, the Godhead (Christianity), *Dharmadhātu* (Buddhism), Mind, Universal Mind, Self-nature, Buddha-nature, Noumenon.

Definition: The reality of God could be defined, rather inadequately, as **All-That-Is**.

Stephen Hawking, famous physicist and confirmed atheist, is reported to have said:

> The Universe is totally self-contained and it does not need the postulation of any outside agency to create it, like 'God'. The Universe is just **there**. It just **is**. (Emphasis added)

The mystic would be in complete agreement. The outside agency which Hawking refers to is the common man's God, which, as we have already explained, is a mere concept, not the reality. The God of the mystic *is not an outside agency*. As Hawking says, the Universe just **is**, *and that very '**Is**-ness' is the God of the mystic.*[28] Furthermore, the mystic sees this not as a mere description or a definition, but as a living, pulsating, throbbing Reality which he can feel but can find no adequate words to describe.

---

28. In fact, in Hindu spiritual literature the word *sat* meaning 'IS-ness' or 'existence' is used to describe the Reality (*sat-cit-ānanda*). The word '**Is**-ness' (German: *istigkeit*) has also been used to describe God or the Reality by Meister Eckhart, the thirteenth century European mystic.

When the stifling, suffocating sense of personal individuality is lost, the awareness which remains is one with (or rather, 'inseparate' from) what may be called the Universal Awareness or Consciousness, which is the sense of God. That is, the mystic has lost the sense of separateness which makes a man feel that his consciousness is distinct from that of any other living organism. The lack of this feeling of separateness is itself the feeling of oneness with everything that exists. The mystic does not identify with the rest of creation. Rather, he feels no separation between himself and the rest of creation. It is this Unicity which is called God by the mystic. This God is not different from himself or from anything else. It must be understood that ultimately this feeling of unitary awareness cannot be fully conveyed in words, it has to be felt for oneself. But it is not an abstraction, a theory or speculation. To the mystic, it is the reality, the actuality — indeed, it is the only reality.

In the language of mathematics, we can define God as the **Universal Set**, the Set which contains all possible sets, **and some more**.

But we have said that sometimes the mystic also refers to a personal aspect of God. How can we define the Reality in its personal aspect, the *fakīr* of Kabīr, the beloved *Viṭhu* of Jñāneśvar?

We have said that God or the Absolute is not a person. However, it is the definite experience of the mystics that the Absolute can, on occasion, behave **as if** it were a person. This is the personal aspect of the God of the mystic. Mathematically, we can define the personal aspect of God as **that function of the Absolute, by which it sometimes acts as if it were a person**.

It is because God is not a person that there is so much apparent contradiction in the world-view of the common theist. (Why does an all-merciful God allow so much sorrow and injustice in his world?) But it is because (the real) God acts sometimes as if it were a person, that we see the expression of so much Love (but without duality) from the mystics (what we have earlier called *advaita bhakti*).

The Avatāra

The Hindu concept of the *avatāra*, the incarnation of God, or the 'descent' of God in human form, is based upon the idea of a God who is a person. But, as we have just shown, there is, in fact, no personal, anthropomorphic, all-seeing, benign God (as commonly believed) except as a concept. There is only an indefinable force which is variously referred to as *Brahman*, *tattva*, or merely as **That**, which can, however, on occasion, act **as if** it were a person. Therefore, there could not be such a phenomenon as an *avatāra* as is traditionally understood.

Kabīr wrote:

dasaratha kula avatari nahin āyā, nahin lankā ke rāv
satāyā,
nahīn devakī ke garbhahi āyā, nahīn jasodai goda
khelāyā, . . .
hoya barāha dharani nahin dhariyā, . . .
nahin gobaradhana kara gahi dhariyā, nahīn gwālan
sang ban-ban phiriyā, . . .
jehi rākhehu anumān kai, so thūl nahīn asthūl.[29]

He did not incarnate in the household of Daśaratha, nor
did he harass the Lord of Laṅkā,
He did not arise in Devakī's womb, nor did he sport on
Yaśodā's lap, . . .
Neither did he support the earth in the form of the
Varāha-avatāra, . . .
He did not hold Govardhan (hill) aloft, nor did he roam
the forests with the milk-maids.
He whom I have fathomed, is not gross but subtle.

29. Singh, Dr. Jaidev and Singh, Dr.Vasudev, *Kabir Vani Piyush* (Hindi), Part I, p. 31. (See Glossary: *Avatāra*)

But from time to time a mystic is born, who sees the Reality for himself — he is the *tathāgata*, the one who has 'been there', the messiah, who brings the message of Reality to the rest of humanity. His ordinary followers seize upon his teaching, study its words, dissect its verbal nuances, and eventually distort it to suit their own feeble understanding. In course of time the message is so corrupted that there has to be another messiah to set the record straight. This is the real meaning of the verse in the *Bhagavad Gītā* (IV.7):

> *yadā yadā hi dharmasya...*
>
> Whenever there is the decline of *dharma*, then do I incarnate Myself . . .
>
> When Krishnamurti dies, which is inevitable, . . . you will build a temple, . . . have ceremonies, . . and create philosophies. . . . you will be caught . . . in that temple and you will have to have another Teacher come and extricate you from that temple. But the human mind is such that you will build another temple round him, and so it will go on. (J. Krishnamurti)[30]

In a way then, the mystic is the messiah, and is the nearest thing to an *avatāra* that one can get. Kabīr said:

> *sādhū pratași deva hai*
>
> The sage is God incarnate.[31]

But the sage is not the all-knowing all-powerful being that the common man believes an *avatāra* to be (see chapter 5).

In fact, rites, ritualistic religion, *avatāra*s, and such are of

30. Krishnamurti, J., *The Last Talks*, p. xii.
31. Singh, Dr. Jaidev and Singh, Dr.Vasudev, *Kabir Vani Piyush* (Hindi), Part II, p. 100.

interest only to those who fail to understand the reality of God as All-that-exists.

Mirzā Ghālib has made the most beautiful, yet the most concise statement on God. He wrote:

> *jabki tuzha bin nahīn aur koi moujūd,*
> *phir yah haṅgāma ai khudā kyā hai?*

> When there exists nothing apart from you, O God,
> then what is all this racket about?

. . . .which really says everything in just two lines.

Why

C.H.L Lewellyn Smith, nuclear scientist, said:

> To paraphrase St. Augustine, the deepest question that mankind can ask is why is there something rather than nothing.[32]

In other words, why does the universe exist?

The answer to that question may lie in a second question: Given that the universe exists, why has it become aware of itself (through the countless different points of awareness which constitute the living beings of the universe)?

Obviously, it is through these various individual points of awareness that the universe is able to perceive, comprehend, experience, appreciate and wonder at its own immensity and diversity, beauty and grandeur.

If there were not this awareness, the universe may have existed, but who was to know of it? Like a beautiful work of art lying forgotten in the attic, its beauty and grandeur would have remained unseen, unheard, unknown and unappreciated. Thus

32. Report in *Times of India*, 6.4.1996.

we could say that the universe developed awareness in order to experience its own spectacle.

And so it is that Eckhart describes God's activity as play "played eternally before all creatures". Yet, he makes it clear, "play and audience are the same".[33] Omar Khayyām calls it the Drama which "for the pastime of Eternity, He doth Himself contrive, enact, behold".

Hindu philosophy, too, has traditionally answered it by calling it the sport (*līlā*) of God — a spectacle for His own enjoyment and wonder, but where actor and spectator are not different.

> As the spider weaves its thread out of its own mouth, plays with it, and then withdraws it again into itself, so also the Supreme Lord evolves the whole universe out of himself, plays with it, and again withdraws it into himself. (*Śrīmad Bhāgavatam*, XI.9.21)

Thus, as G. Spencer Brown has said,[34]

> we cannot escape the fact that the world we know is constructed in order to see itself.

The corollary which follows from this is that **the purpose of life is the living of it, the experiencing**.

Kamā Bābā of Bombay (a disciple of Sāi Bābā of Śirḍī) was often heard chanting this verse:

> *Rāma kī duniyā, Rāma kā khel,*
> *khāo ciḍiyā bhara bhara peṭ.*

> It is the Lord's world, it is the Lord's sport,
> Eat your fill, O bird, eat your fill!

---

33. Quoted by Wilber, Ken, *The Spectrum of Consciousness*, p. 155.

34. *Ibid.*, p. 14, quoting from *Laws of Form*.

In fact, this was the only philosophical statement this writer heard him make in his over decade-long association with him. A cryptic saying, but in fact, it says it all. It says what it is, it says why it is; and after disposing off this theoretical aspect, it gives the very practical advice as to what a person is to do — to simply live and experience life to the fullest. (The bird is the typical example of living in the moment). That is really all there is to it — look, listen, feel, experience, Live. . .

When Fa-ch'ang was dying, a squirrel screeched on the roof. "It's just this," he said, "and nothing else".[35]

Through the Eyes of the Mystics

Finally, let us see how the mystics have described God. Let us have it in their own words.

The mystics have made it clear at the outset that the Absolute is without qualities and attributes which allow description. It is *agr̥hya* (beyond comprehension) and *avarṇanīya* (beyond description) (*Br̥hadāraṇyakopaniṣad*, IV.5.15).[36]

> That which is not visible to the eyes, and which cannot be described by speech.
>
> — *Muṇḍakopaniṣad*, 3.1.8

> It does not possess the five qualities of sound, touch, colour, taste and smell . . . and is without beginning, without end and imperishable.[37]

A similar description is given in the *Vedānta Sūtra*, 3.2.22-30.

> *yato vāco nivartante aprāpya manasā saha*[38]
>
> — *Taittirīya Upaniṣad*, 2.9

---

35. Watts, Alan W., *The Way of Zen*.

36. (Eng. Tr.) Sukthankar, Bhalchandra Sitaram, *Srimad Bhagavad Gita-Rahasya* by Bal Gangadhar Tilak, 6th edn., 1986, p. 285.

37. *Ibid.*

that is, it is beyond comprehension by the mind or description by speech: *avāṅgamanasagocaram*.

Since that which has no qualities cannot be described in ordinary language, it is sometimes described by mutually contradictive adjectives, like:

> the *Brahman* is neither *sat* (existent) nor *asat* (non-existent) —*Ṛgveda*, X.129
>
> It is smaller than an atom and larger than the largest —*Kaṭhopaniṣad*, II.20
>
> It does not move and yet it moves, it is far away and yet It is near —*Iśāvāsyopaniṣad*, V; *Muṇḍakopaniṣad*, III.1.7

Ultimately, the Upaniṣads say '*neti-neti*' (It is not this, It is not this) (*Bṛhadāraṇyakopaniṣad*, II.3.6, IV.2.4, etc.).

In a remarkably similar statement, Ruysbroeck described it as 'Neither This nor That'.

Śrī Ramaṇa Maharṣi said:

> *Brahman* is not to be seen or known. It is beyond the three-fold relationship of seer, sight and seen, or knower, knowledge and known. The Reality . . . is neither light nor darkness but beyond both.[39]

Thinking About God

It is often believed that the mystic is in 'constant contemplation of God', that is, he is continuously thinking of God. This is a fallacy.

We have already seen that the mystic does not, nay cannot, believe in God. But can the mystic **think** about God?

38. *Srimad Bhagavad Gita-Rahasya*, p. 287.
39. Osborne, Arthur, *The Teachings of Bhagavan Sri Ramana Maharshi In His Own Words*, p. 47.

For the mystic, who lives in the very **actuality** of God, to think of God would be to reduce that actuality to a base concept, a 'thought-idol no better than a stone-idol'. To the mystic, this would be tantamount to sacrilege! To him, who is forever (or rather timelessly) one with God, it would be to introduce separation where there is none, to imply distance where none exists. The mystic does not think about God, he **is** God. (In fact, we are all God, but the mystic alone is fully aware and conscious of this truth, not as an intellectual fact, but as an undeniable living, throbbing awareness or 'knowledge of being'). To think about God as (if He is) separate from himself would be a denial of that **Is**-ness, that oneness (or rather lack of separateness). The mystic does not worship God by thinking about Him, he worships God by **being** God.

> God or truth cannot be thought about. If you think about it, it is not truth. (J. Krishnamurti)[40]

> The highest Reality is the eternally unthinkable. (*Lankāvatāra sūtra*)[41]

Ken Wilber writes that if we form any positive mental conception of God, that conception must be a myth. He quotes St. Augustine,

> If any one in seeing God conceives something in his mind, this is not God.

Wilber writes that you cannot think about God because **it is He who is doing the thinking**.[42]

This is not to say that man must not think about God. It only means that if he does so, he must be careful not to confuse the myth with the reality.

We had mentioned that the mystic is often misunderstood by

---

40. Quoted by Wilber, Ken, *The Spectrum of Consciousness*, p. 316.
41. *Ibid.*, p. 67.
42. *Ibid.*, p. 113.

people, and called an atheist, but in a way, we have seen here how it is the common man who 'believes' in God and who 'thinks' about God who is the real atheist.

> Anyone content with what can be expressed in words is aptly styled an unbeliever. (Ken Wilber)[43]

The *Bṛhadāraṇyaka Upaniṣad* says (II.4, 12-14):

> It is only in duality that one can see another, speak of another, think of another, know another. Where everything has become the Self itself, whom and by what should one think? By what can we know the Universal Knower?

Oneness

Like many other words used in talking about the Absolute, the word 'Oneness' is used for want of a better word. In actual fact, there is not even oneness, for the idea of oneness can have meaning only when there is the possibility of the many. And in the Reality or Absolute there is no question of 'many'. That is why the word *'a-dvaita'* or 'non-duality' is used in Sanskrit (rather than 'oneness' or 'unity').

> The Eternal One is so infinitely real that we dare not even give it the name of 'One', since oneness is an idea derived from worldly experience (*vyavahāra*).
>
> *ek kahau to hai nahīn, doya kahau to gār,*
> *hai jaisā vaisā rahai, kahain kabīr bicār*
>
> If you call it One, it is not so; but calling it two is a falsehood as well; it is what it is, this is how Kabīr would express what he feels.[44]

---

43. *The Spectrum of Consciousness*, p. 65.
44. Singh, Dr. Jaidev and Singh, Dr.Vasudev, *Kabir Vani Piyush* (Hindi), Part I, p. 29.

To summarise, in the words of Dr. S. Radhakrishnan:[45]

> God is not an abstraction but an actuality. He is Truth, formless, *nirguṇa*, absolute, eternal, infinite, beyond human comprehension. . . . The ideas we form of him are intellectualisations of that presence. . . . Silence is the only adequate expression of that which envelopes and embraces us. No word however noble, no symbol however significant, can communicate the ineffable experience of being absorbed in the dazzling light of the Divine.

And yet, in spite of all this, the mystics have not refrained from describing God. Let us look at two such examples.

Kabīr

Kabir was the archetypical mystic. Living in fifteenth-century Benāres in Northern India, by profession a weaver, he was a simple and unlettered man. Yet, poet *par excellence*, his spontaneous outpourings form an excellent example of the typical mystical expression. Persecuted by the religious orthodoxy, he was finally banished from Benāres in the interests of peace by the ruler Sikandar Lodhī. Then almost sixty, he lived the rest of his life in exile and died in Maghar near Gorakhpur.

Seeing people search for God in vain, Kabīr sang out:

> Where do you seek Me, O friend?
>   I am right here beside you;
> Neither in temple nor in mosque am I,
>   nor in Kābā nor Kailās,
> Nor am I in rites and rituals,
>   nor in *yoga* or renunciation;

Asked to describe God he exclaimed:

> The brilliance of the *Para-Brahman*

45. Radhakrishnan, S., *Religion and Culture*, p. 143.

is beyond imagination,
It does not bear description,
it can only be understood
When one sees for oneself

But surely, (he said),

That (idol) which can be enclosed in a box,
that cannot be the Lord,
He pervades the entire Universe,
that is the reality of God

* * *

He is apart from the Universe,
yet the Universe is in Him,
Sayeth Kabīr: such a Lord do I serve,
there is none apart from Him

* * *

. . . Neither with form nor without,
Subtler than the perfume of a flower,
such is his Incomparable Essence

Describing the adual state of the mystic union, Kabīr says:

Water it is that exists as ice,
water it is when the ice melts,
I have become That which I was always

* * *

When the wave rises, it is water;
and when it subsides, it is still water
Where, pray tell me, is the difference?

He now sees God everywhere — the 'me' is no more:

I came into this world to see the various forms,
Sayeth Kabīr: O Sādhus, but I saw
the Incomparable in every form.

In calling out to You, I was transformed into You,
There is no more any 'me' left in me now,
I have surrendered to your Love,
Now Wherever I look, I see none but You

* * *

My mind has merged with the Lord,
and He has merged with me
just as salt dissolves in the water,
and the water pervades the salt

The seeker is the sought but knows it not:

The musk is in the deer,
but it seeks it not within itself,
it wanders in search of grass

And an unmistakable reference to Self-enquiry:

I inverted my mind,
and found the fountain (of bliss),

Surrender your 'I', says Kabīr:

Love is not grown in the fields,
Nor is it sold in the market,
Be he King or commoner,
He alone obtains it
who gives his head ('I'-sense) for it

Kabīr as the *bhakta* longing for his beloved:

For so long have I waited for you, O Rāma,
My heart yearns for you,
my mind knows no peace

* * *

My body and my mind grieve for You,
    O my Beloved! come to my home.
As water is to the thirsty,
    so is the lover to the bride.
O Who will carry my message to my Beloved?

The fever of his yearning is beyond endurance:

I will make a lamp of my body,
    and for wick use my soul,
my blood will be the oil,
    O when will I see my Beloved?

And when he finds Him — the bliss of *advaita-bhakti*:

    Love has lighted up my whole body,
The eternal flame (of Love) has erupted (within),
    All doubts are resolved,
now there is only bliss,
    I have found my Beloved[46]

Jñānadeva (Jñāneśvar)

If Kabīr presents to us the picture of the elderly, impatient *Sūfi* saint — unorthodox, simple, unlettered, and using the earthy metaphors which were familiar to him, Jñāneśvar, in contrast, is the learned, orthodox Hindu, boy-saint-poet who lived a century and a half earlier. Yet what they both said was essentially the same. It had to be, for they were describing the same thing. . . .

Jñānadeva, also called Jñāneśvar, was born at Alandi near Poona, in AD 1275 (Śaka 1197). He was initiated into spirituality

---

46. Singh, Dr. Jaidev and Singh, Dr.Vasudev, *Kabir Vani Piyush* (Hindi), Part I, pp. 38, 42, 51; Part II, pp. 16, 23, 39, 40, 47, 49, 102, 108, 109 see also (Tr.) Tagore, Rabindranath, *One Hundred Poems of Kabir*, XIV, VI.

by his elder bother Nivṛtti, himself said to have been initiated into the *Nāth Panth* when he was only 7 years of age by *guru* Gahininātha. Orphaned at an early age (when Jñānadeva was 12), the children continued their spiritual pursuits, and Jñānadeva composed his famous commentary on the *Bhagavad Gītā*, the *Bhāvārtha-Dīpikā*, (better known as the *Jñāneśvarī*), when he was only 15 years of age.

Subsequently, he composed the *Amṛtānubhav* (Experience of Immortality), a poetic tribute to the highest philosophy. He also wrote the brief *Cāngdev Pāsaṣṭī*, a concentrated capsule of wisdom addressed to Cāngdev, a well known *yogi* of the time.

This is what Jñānadeva wrote:

The basic premise:

> There is in this world an all-pervading and hidden spiritual essence which the wise recognise to be the Reality. — *Jñāneśvarī*, II.126

> That one indestructible essence which exists everywhere, and pervades all bodies, know That to be the Universal *ātman*. Everything that happens, happens spontaneously because of Its (the Universal *ātman*'s) inherent nature. — *Jn.*, II.177-8

The description:

> **That**, from which the entire universe has emanated, has neither any name nor form, nor colour, nor any characteristic. It is timeless, all-pervasive, without birth or death, indestructible.
>
> — *Jn.*, II.134-5

> He is without origin, eternal, self-illuminated, perfectly pure, without any limitations, . . . beyond reason, beyond contemplation, beyond thought. — *Jn.*, II.145-9

That which is not the illumined but the Light itself... It can only be compared to Its own self.

— *Jn.*, XV.546-56

The Creation, the Universe, and His relationship to it:

Blending with forms, He sports as the forms Himself. Yet does His formlessness remain unaffected.

— *Jn.*, V.81

I am that beginningless, spontaneous (*sahaja*) seed of the Universe, which expands to the ends of the sky during creation, and which appears as the Universe as long as the Universe exists, and, after the dissolution of the Universe, relapses into its original nothingness (pure potentiality). — *Jn.*, VII.40-2, abridged

I support the Universe as the string does the beads in a necklace. Furthermore, just as if beads made of gold were to be woven onto a golden thread (thus making the entire ornament gold), even so do I uphold the Universe, pervading it inside-out. — *Jn.*, VII.31-2

That pervades the universe just as the sky pervades all of space, the thread pervades cloth in the form of its fabric, wetness pervades water, brightness pervades the lamp in the form of its light, the fragrance pervades camphor in the form of its essence, in short, just as gold pervades every particle of gold, in the same way does **That** pervade everything and every body.

— *Jn.*, XIII.892-5, abridged

Even when gold is made into an ornament, it still remains gold — it is only conceptually an ornament. In the same way, when one perceives the Creation and the various created beings upon My pure (unmanifest) Being, these are actually all appearances in one's imagination (that is, conceptualisation). When this conceptualising power ends, the illusion of creation is demolished at the outset, and My Pure Being alone remains.

When seen without this deluding conceptualisation, then it is clearly seen that all this talk of My being in created beings, or they being in Me, cannot be even imagined in a dream. Now saying that I am the sole sustainer of all beings or that I dwell in them, is like the delirious ravings of an unsound mind. I am the cause of the (illusion of) created beings, *but yet am not different from them*, just as the sun and its light are one and the same. Is there scope for any distinction here?

Hence, never consider created beings as different from Me, nor Me as separate from them.

— *Jn.*, IX.77-88, abridged

(In short, it is not so that 'they are **in** Me' or that 'I am **in** them'; the truth is that they **are** Me and I **am** them).

Sweetness and jaggery (sugar), camphor and its fragrance, cannot be separated.

— *Amṛtānubhav*, I.23

Just as, whichever way you look at it, the wave is nothing but water, similarly there is nothing apart from Me in this universe. — *Jn.*, X.114

What is called the *paramātman*, know that He is thus: like the sun which, though reflected in the water, is not wetted by it. Moreover, the sun existed even before the water was, and will exist even after. It is only in between (these two states) that it is seen reflected in the water.

— *Jn.*, XIII.1094-95

I (*Brahman*) am the Father, 'Gross-*Brahman*' (that is *māyā* — the root cause of the illusion) is the Mother, and

> the entire universe the off-spring. (And yet all three are the same as Me). Just as the diverse waves become the 'progeny' of the sea, in the same way is the relationship between the universe and Me, or as the fire and flames are both simply fire, so am I related to everything.
>
> (Furthermore, the appearance of the universe does not diminish Me or affect Me in any way). Can a ruby be diminished by its own lustre? Does gold become any less the gold by being made into an ornament? Or when the lotus blooms, does it cease being a lotus?
>
> — *Jn.*, XIV.116-24, abridged

Mahad-Brahman ('Gross' *Brahman*), *māyā*, *mūla-māyā* or *śakti* are the names given to the **energy** which results in the appearance of the universe, upon the ground substance of *Brahman*. If *Brahman* is potential energy, *māyā* or *śakti* is kinetic energy, and the result is the universe. If Naṭarāja, the divine dancer, symbolises *Brahman*, the motion of the dancer is *śakti* and the dance itself represents the cosmos or creation. The dancer, his movement, and the dance cannot be separated, for they are only conceptually, and not really separate. The same holds true for *Brahman, śākti*, and the Universe.

Brahman and *śakti*, the two different aspects of the one same Reality, are sometimes poetically referred to as lovers:

> The Lover, to satisfy His urge for love, has Himself become His own consort.
>
> They are not one (conceptually), yet they are not two (in reality); how is one to describe the relationship between the Reality and its appearance?
>
> Behold this wonder: to experience the bliss of the Self, the One has become the two, and yet not lost its Unicity.
>
> —*Amṛt.,* I.2, 4, 5

> So it is that in its own womb it shows itself this scene (sport). It lays out the triad of seer-seen-and-seeing.
>
> — *Cāng. Pās.*,18

Impersonal nature of God versus the common man's perception:

> To one whose taste is lost due to fever, even milk tastes bitter. In the same way though I am impersonal, I am mistaken to be a person. Such a superficial way of seeing Me is not right perception; one can never attain immortality through the elixir tasted in a dream.
>
> Ordinarily people know Me through such superficial knowledge, but it is precisely such ideas that keep them from the real knowledge. Those people who go through life thinking that I am a person, know that they have, instead of the moon, grasped at its reflection in the water. Can one obtain grain by pounding mere chaff? Can one be said to have drunk water merely by tasting froth?
>
> Thus, blinded by such delusion, men attribute to Me earthly fortunes like birth and death. I, who am nameless, they endow with name, they impute form to Me who am formless, and Me who am all-pervading, they confine to a specific location. Into an idol am I, the self-risen (*svayambhū*), installed and invoked. Whatever idol they see before them, they worship it as God.
>
> Thus in various different ways do they reveal that they consider Me to be a person, and these their erroneous beliefs keep out of their reach the real knowledge of My true Being. —*Jn.*, IX.142-71, abridged

Where is He?:

> It is not that the sweetness of the sea of milk is greater in the middle and less near the banks, in the same way

is **That** equally perfect (completely present) everywhere.
—*Jn.*, XIII.916

Knowing Him:

It (the Supreme *Brahman*) is the sound that cannot be heard, the nectar whose fragrance cannot be perceived (for who is there apart from It to hear or perceive It?)—and yet, though invisible, it can be seen without a seer! It is Knowledge without a knower or the known (object of knowledge). It is neither the effect nor the cause, it is neither qualified by dualism nor by adualism, it is that which is known only by Its Own Self (*āpaṇayā je zāṇ āpaṇaci*) (for there is no other to know it).
—*Jn.*, XV. 74-8

For one's own sentience ('knowingness') to know itself would be like the eye seeing the eye. Can the dagger stab itself? —*Amṛt.*, VI. 88, 90

Upon the occurrence of Self-knowledge, devoid of the sense of 'I' or 'me', one sees one's own true form (reality), which cannot be described as 'this' or 'that'. But ignorant people look into a mirror and conceive of two faces where there is only one: do not be so (and conceive of duality where there is none).

Like the tongue tasting itself, or the eye seeing itself, or like light merging into light, or the sky rolling on itself, or water filled into a bag made of water, such is this adual viewing of oneself. —*Jn.*, XV. 267-74

Proof of its existence:

Where silence is speech (That which can only be expressed in silence), where not knowing is itself knowledge (absence of temporal knowledge and conceptualisation); where even the idea 'I am That' does not remain, where

> the narrator becomes the very act of narrating (the *raconteur* becomes the recounting), where the seer and the seen both disappear, but then — (just because there is neither seer nor seen) — it is not right to say that It does not exist.
>
> Thus when the seer and the seen have both disappeared, *then* what is experienced is Its true form (then what remains is the true experiencing: experience-**ing** without the experience-**er**) — *Jn.*, XV.541-5, abr.

When everything is the *ātman*, who is to prove Its existence, to whom, and by what?:

> Can one ever marry oneself? Or can the sun eclipse itself? Can the sky (space) emerge out of itself? Can the ocean dive into itself? Or can the hand grasp itself? Does the sun set with respect to itself? Does fruit bear fruit? Or can fragrance smell its own perfume?
>
> — *Amṛt.*, VI.76-8

Conclusion:

> O Dhanañjaya (Arjuna), He the Self-illuminated One — what more can I say about Him? There exists nothing apart from Him (He is All-there-is).
>
> I am that attributeless One, beyond the mortal and the immortal, and hence the Vedas call Me the Puruṣottama (the Supreme Being). (*Jn.*, XV. 557-8)

* * * * *

Besides these works, Jñānadeva also composed many *abhaṅga*s (short poems) in which the personal aspect of God is addressed.

> I have woven my thoughts into a shawl,
> and offered it to the Lord Viṭṭhal (Viṣṇu), consort of Rukmiṇī.

He, the dusky, lovely one, *pītāmbar*-clad,[47]
He with a beauty so alluring, Him have I beheld . . .
Viṭṭhal, the Lord of Bliss, consort of Rukmiṇī,
My body, mind and speech, all has He drawn to Himself.

In a devotional mood, he expresses his poignant longing and ardour for the Lord:

Behold the two crows cawing up yonder, be they an omen perhaps?
Fly away, O crow, I will paint your feet with gold,
I will feed you balls of rice and curd, and bowls full of milk,
Tell me the truth: will the Lord of Pandharpur be a guest in my house today?

* * * * *

The clouds are thundering, the wind blows, . . .
I do not feel happy without my Lord, son of Devakī,
Rub my body with sandalwood paste, (but it will not soothe me),
Will the Lord of the forest (*vanmāḷī*) come speedily?

But even Jñānadeva's devotional compositions contain unmistakable mystical references:

darpaṇi pāhatā rūpa, na dise ho āpule,
bāpa rakumādevī vare, maza aise kele.
On looking into the mirror, I see no more my form,
Thus has the Lord, consort of Rukmiṇī, made me.

āji soniyācā dinu . . .
Today is a golden day,
The clouds are raining showers of nectar (*amṛta,* elixir of life),

47. The *pītāmbar* is an Indian silken lower garment.

I have seen Hari, I have seen Hari,
He permeates everything inside-out, the Divine Flutist.

* * * * *

O Jñānā, thou hast become Pure! Thou hast understood thyself!
Thou art thine own God, thou art thine own faith (support).
All doubts about other (external) principles are now eliminated.
After inverting the mind, did arise the understanding . . .
The light is within the lamp itself, the (other) flames have faded,
The wicks have sputtered into emptiness.
Worldly existence (*vr̥tti*) has itself become the renunciation (*nivr̥tti*);
Everything, everywhere, has become Paradise.

Appendix

Advaita

We started with a scientific approach to spirituality, but the thesis that we have finally outlined is identical with the doctrine of *Advaita*. Let us therefore have a brief look at what this original doctrine is about. (Also see Glossary).

Advaita is the Hindu or Vedāntic name for the doctrine of monism. *Advaita*, which can be literally translated as 'adualism' or 'non-dualism', but is generally referred to as 'monism', is not the same as monotheism. (Monotheism is the belief that there is only one God, as contrasted with polytheism which believes in many gods.) *Advaita* is not even the same as pan-theism ("all things are God"). The basic principle of *Advaita* is that there are no 'things' — there is only God. In other words, all that exists, is God — 'things' are mere appearances.

The basic tenets of *Advaita* could be stated as follows:

1. There is One basic underlying Reality or Source of the entire manifestation, which is variously called *Brahman*, *Nirguṇa*[1] *Brahman*, Consciousness, etc., or just '**That**'.

   Unlike the common perception of God, in reality God is not a person — 'God' in *Advaita* refers to this same impersonal, indefinable force.

   This force cannot be accurately described in words, and so any description must be accepted with that caveat.

1. '*Nirguṇa*' means without attributes or qualities.

2. The *Nirguṇa Brahman* has not **created** the manifestation (phenomenal universe), it has **become** the manifestation, and that too, **only in appearance**. In this becoming, the essential nature of *Brahman* remains unchanged (indeed *Brahman* is, by its very nature, changeless). In other words, this becoming is only an **apparent** becoming. The example given is that of a screen (*Brahman*) and the pictures projected on it (the manifestation).

3. 'We', as the separate individual entities that we unquestioningly take ourselves to be, are also not different from *Brahman* or the Source. Our sense of being separate psychological entities each with our own separate individual consciousness, **is an illusion** caused by our distorted or defective way of thinking.

   We are not even a 'part' of *Brahman* in the sense of being a 'small part of a bigger whole'. We **are** *Brahman* by another name.

4. Thus it follows that the 'we' and the rest of the manifestation are also not separate, since both are the same as *Brahman*, different only in appearance (like the screen and the different pictures projected on it).

5. Subjectivity, which is that in us 'by which we are doing the thinking (or knowing)', is the most important function of *Brahman* in this manifestation. It is by this function that 'we' (as apparently separate subjects) know (are aware of) the manifestation. And in relation to the manifestation, 'we' can only conceive of *Brahman* as 'Absolute Subjectivity', that is, that power that 'sees' or 'knows' the manifestation (including 'ourselves') **through** 'us'. Thus sentience or subjectivity, that by which we perceive or know anything, is really a function of the Absolute Subjectivity that is *Brahman*.

6. From all the above it could be inferred that the

manifestation (including ourselves), the awareness that perceives it, and the Source that is *Brahman*, are really **one and the same thing**.

7. Thus, in effect, the ultimate *Advaitic* truth expresses the absolute 'inseparateness' of 'oneself' (one's presumed separate self) and the Totality or God or *Brahman*.
8. The actual (not merely intellectual) perception or 'apperception' of this truth is called Enlightenment.

The important point is that the seeking of Enlightenment or of 'union with *Brahman*' is an unsustainable paradox, a contradiction in terms, for the seeker **is** the sought. There is no question of 'union' with *Brahman*, for all there is, is *Brahman*. In other words, the seeker is already *Brahman*, for *Brahman* is all that exists.

The Law of Karma and the Effect of 'Past lives'

The so-called Law of *karma* refers to the law of cause and effect, or what may be called the inexorable chain of causation. This simply means that any action or event will necessarily have its natural effects, which are inevitable. These unavoidable consequences are inherent in the action (or event) itself. For example, one cannot drop a fragile glass bowl and expect it not to fall, and perhaps break.

Conversely, all that happens today is the sum total of the effects of past events and actions. The actions are not necessarily of the same person, they may be of different people. For example, we suffer (or enjoy) the consequences of the acts of our ancestors, and our descendants will have to endure the fruits of our actions. The entire nation may have to bear the effects of the leaders' actions.

Admittedly, this sounds too obvious a truism to be honoured by calling it a 'Law'. But if we observe the way people behave, it will be clear that most of them do indeed act as if they will not have to bear the consequences of their actions.

However, the law of *karma* is generally misinterpreted to mean that the present events in a person's life are the results of 'his' **own** actions in a 'past life', and further, that his current actions will affect 'his' 'subsequent lives'.

Now this is simply not true, for, as explained earlier, there is no 'one', no entity, to have such 'past' and 'future' lives. This queer interpretation is merely a convenient argument to explain the otherwise unexplainable events in the world, where 'evil' often triumphs over 'good', and decent people often have a hard time of it.

But then sages have been sometimes known to refer to 'past lives'. For example, Śrī Ramaṇa Maharṣi said (*Mtn.Path*, Dec. '95, p. 134):

> Countless *vāsanā*s or tendencies caused by past *karma* reside in the mind. These have accumulated from time immemorial, through untold past lives.

When a sage makes such a remark, it should be understood that he is not referring to the 'past lives' of the same 'soul' or *jīva*, for he has usually already declared that there is no such thing as a separate soul or a *jīva*. What is being referred to, is past lives in general, that is, evolution and inherited traits. In other words, it refers to tendencies evolved over several lives, but not of the 'same' 'individual'. Indeed, the crux of the sage's message is that there is **no separate individual**. (Or the 'past lives' referred to, could be understood to be of the one Universal *ātman*.)

> When the half-wit heard that a man is hit by an automobile somewhere in the world once every 8 seconds, he said "O, the poor man".

> The same sort of misunderstanding also led a man to name his third child 'Lin Yoo Ping' because he had heard that every third child born in the world is Chinese.

The true meaning of the law of *karma* is that the consequences of one's actions cannot be avoided and will have to be suffered (or enjoyed), but not necessarily by the same person. This is specifically clarified in the *Mahābhārata*, where Bhīṣma says to Yudhiṣṭhira (Śāntiparva, 129.21):

> O King, although a particular man may not be seen to suffer the results of his evil actions, yet his sons, grandsons and great-grandsons have to suffer them.

The idea of an 'account' carried over to 'future lives' of the same 'individual', as commonly understood, is nothing but pure fantasy. Indeed, this life is all there is — so make the best of it! As Kabīr said:

> O *sādhu*! Finish your buying and selling; have done with your good and your bad, for there are no markets and no shops in the land to which you go.

For, 'your' account will be closed when 'you' die.

Paranormal Phenomena

It was mentioned at the outset (chapter 1) that in this book we are concerned only with the core of the spiritual message, in the form of the central teaching of the sages, and not with the peripheral events in their lives like 'miracles', etc. Also, the subject of this book has really nothing much to do with the so-called paranormal, occult, or psychic phenomena like ESP, for example.

However, people generally connect spirituality with mystery, miracles and magic. Hindu philosophy mentions the *siddhis*, miraculous or occult powers. More important, those who believe in occult phenomena often consider their occurrence to be the ultimate proof of the existence of a 'soul' and 'rebirth'.

For the above reasons, these topics are dealt with, albeit briefly.

There are several questions involved here. The first is whether such phenomena really do occur.

From those that are reported, after excluding those which are plain fiction, or undue exaggeration, we are left with those events which may have certainly occurred, but whose explanation is to be determined. Many of these may be explained by the known laws of science. Those which finally remain are the possibly genuine 'paranormal' phenomena. The question which really concerns us here is, whether these indicate proof of the existence of an individual 'soul' or *jīva*?

If there is no such thing as an individual 'soul', then these phenomena should have other explanations. Again, it is not our intention here to go into the exact *mechanism* of each such phenomenon. That is a matter for researchers into those particular subjects. Our present purpose will be served if we can only show that other explanations are at least possible. And that is what we propose to do here. And if those explanations also fit in with the general scheme of things outlined in this book, that will be an additional corroborative bonus.

Paranormal phenomena can in general be classified into the sensory type, called extra-sensory perception (ESP), and other phenomena like psycho-kinesis, etc.

ESP is the acquiring and possession of knowledge or information which would not have been available through normal channels (or channels considered normal as of today).

When the information is about a current or past event, it is termed (a) **telepathy** when that information exists with some other human individual, and (b) **clairvoyance** when it cannot exist with any human individual. When it is the knowledge of an event which is to occur in the future, it is called (c) **precognition** (fore-knowledge).

Telepathy is the transfer of information from one brain to another, or the simultaneous occurrence of similar thoughts in two different minds.

But if in reality Consciousness is universal, then the wonder is not that such phenomena occur, but that they do not occur more often. If there is, in fact, no separation between one person's consciousness and another's, the question should be, not how they can sometimes read each other's thoughts, but why they normally cannot?

The answer to this could be that entitification causes an (apparent) fragmentation of consciousness, and this blocks the free flow of information from one brain to another. One would therefore expect such phenomena as ESP to occur most easily in the case of a Liberated person, and they probably do (see later: 'miracles').

Actually, in the mystic sense, there is really no question of 'transfer' of information, for Consciousness is one. In that sense therefore, telepathy is no more remarkable than a person knowing his own thoughts.

If we could only lower the barriers created by our constricting sense of individuality, our 'I'-based thinking, perhaps these phenomena would occur more frequently.

Ken Wilber, authority on transpersonal psychology, writes that extra sensory perception and other such occurrences occur

> in the bands of the spectrum of consciousness where the boundary between self and other has not been completely crystallised.[2]

The feature that such occurrences have in common, he says, is a suspension of the distinction between the self and not-self (which he calls the Primary Dualism),

---

2. Wilber, Ken, *The Spectrum of Consciousness*, p. 120.

> so that although the self is still experienced as being more or less separate from the world, it nevertheless has greatly extended some portion of its boundary.[3]

Rebirth

There are reported cases where a person, usually very young, 'recalls' events from his 'past life' which are then found to closely correlate with the life of a deceased person. People often jump to the conclusion that this is evidence of 'transmigration' of 'soul'.

Actually all that has happened here is that a person possesses information about another person, which should not normally be available to him. That is, this is at best evidence of 'information transfer'. In other words, it is no different from telepathy, only the other person (the thought or information 'donor') is not alive. If both persons were alive, we would call it telepathy and would not invoke explanations involving 'souls'. This is then telepathy 'out of sync' in time. If information can flow across the 'barrier' of space, there is no reason why it cannot flow across time. After all, we do recollect our own past experiences 'across time'. Very young persons would be expected to naturally have a better developed sense of ESP as their sense of individuality is not yet fully developed. In most such reported cases, the recollections pass off as the person grows into an adult.

Ghosts

Reported instances of 'ghosts' are actually instances of apparitions or appearances of what are thought to be ghosts. They are really no more than that — **visions.** In such cases, a common theme is that the viewer cannot interact with the 'ghost', a point in favour of its being a mere vision. A vision of a past (or occasionally future) event is again an instance of ESP. It does not imply the existence of a 'soul', any more than a hologram does.

---

3. Wilber, Ken, *The Spectrum of Consciousness*, p. 275.

Instances of '**after-death**' **experiences** are actually no more than *near*-death experiences. The sensations described may perhaps be explained medically by, among other things, inadequate oxygen supply to the brain. The great sensation of peace which is often a part of such experiences may be attributable to the loss of the distorting sense of individuality and of 'I'-based thinking in the sinking brain, as the failing brain regresses into the pre-personal stage.

Since death is, by definition, irreversible, there can be no genuine 'after-death' experience.

Miracles

The lives of saints often abound in miracles. Many of these reported events are hearsay, matters of faith, lucky coincidences, and generous exaggerations. The stories grow as they are handed down from generation to generation. Max-Müller has called this the 'Dialogic Process'. But a few of these events may be genuine 'paranormal' phenomena. The saint may have a heightened sense of ESP because of which he may be liable to have flashes of telepathy, clairvoyance, precognition, and the like. The heightened ESP may be explained by his 'oneness' with the Universal Consciousness and by the fact that in his case the blocking effect of individualistic thinking is absent. But this is not proof of his 'all-knowing' nature. Such occurrences may happen to the sage, but they are unpredictable and a matter of wonder, even to himself.

Faith healing or 'psychic healing': This is dealt with at some length because it forms a very important part of the aura of miracles surrounding a saint.

Most non-medical persons fail to appreciate the extreme complexity of the human body, and the multiplicity of factors involved in the resolution of any disease process. As a result, people very often give credit where it is not due, whether it is to a system of what is called 'alternative' medicine, or to a saint's intervention. Many unexplained cures may be explained by one of the following:

1. Self-limiting nature of the illness.
2. Natural exacerbations and remissions (important in conditions like rheumatoid arthritis).
3. Inappropriate diagnosis and imprecise documentation. Many people who claim to have been cured may not really have been ill at all in the first place. They only *thought* they were ill.
4. Psychosomatic effect (very important in conditions like asthma for example).
5. Placebo effect.
6. Simultaneous effect of conventional therapy which is usually taken for granted.

Instances of genuine 'faith healing' are mostly examples of accelerated healing or improved immune response. Better names for these phenomena could be 'Psyche Mediated Accelerated Healing' (PAH) and 'Psyche Mediated Immuno-Augmentation' (PIA).

Depression and other similar psycho-affective states are known to lower the immune response of the body. It is therefore known that the mind can affect the healing and immune processes. It is also known that healing is faster and better in children than in adults, and even more so in animals than in humans, and both healing and immunity are superior in wild animals as compared to domesticated species. In other words, as one goes down on the 'thinking' scale, the body seems to work better.

It could be postulated that it is the blocking effect of our individualistic thinking which interferes with the wholesome working of the mind-body complex, and retards these natural processes, and that this effect is present not only in obvious states like depression, but even in average people, who, we can now see by our understanding of Enlightenment and Liberation, are not really 'normal' or fully natural. The process of Liberation would remove the psycho-somatic blocks which retard healing. One would therefore expect both healing and immunity to be better in a Liberated person, than in an otherwise physically comparable but unenlightened person.

We could even postulate further and say that a similar effect could be temporarily induced in an unenlightened person if his blocking way of thinking is at least temporarily suspended or set aside. This could perhaps be due to a state of 'surrender' caused by intense faith. The mere physical proximity to a sage is also known to passively induce a state of great peace of mind, a "peace that passeth all understanding". Paul Brunton, describing his first meeting with Śrī Ramaṇa Maharṣi, talks of a sensation as if there was a a 'river of peace' flowing by his side.

Interestingly, a new form of therapy called 'Dolphin Assisted Therapy' (or DAT) is recently being investigated. Improvement is said to have been induced in patients suffering from various disorders ranging from cancer to AIDS, simply by sessions of being in the water with dolphins. Such improvements are believed to be due to improved immune response and are reportedly associated with an increase in the T-cell count. These changes are thought to be mediated through the CNS because measurement of brain wave patterns have shown that in 75 per cent of such persons, the chaotic 'normal' brain wave patterns are replaced, after being in the water with the dolphins, with remarkably different, stable, theta patterns, with synchronised activity seen between the left and right sides of the brain. The actual sensations felt by the person has been described as 'soothing' and a sensation of being 'at peace with the world.' (Discovery TV channel, November 17, 1996, 11. 00 a.m. IST)

We on our part can easily understand how this happens. This is the effect of the person's participating in (or rather losing the feeling of separation with) the Universal Consciousness. The actual physical interaction with the dolphins, and the physical act of being in the water with them, perhaps provides the trigger to the process. In short, the physical participation facilitates the mental reunification (or rather 'un-separation') with Nature. The dolphin is merely a catalyst.

But why dolphins? The dolphin has perhaps the highest level of nervous development next to humans in nature, stopping just short of formed symbolic thought. This state of a high level of neurological development without symbolic thought is most conducive to the spirit of 'inseparateness' with the rest of Nature. This in fact was the condition of Man (the state of beatitude) before his 'fall from grace' which occurred with (misuse of) symbolic thought. The physical proximity to the dolphin may act in a way somewhat similar to physical proximity to a Liberated person. (See chapter 5: 'The Liberated One, the Animal and the Child'.)

What is happening in such cases is not some magical process, but rather a relaxation or reversal of the psycho-neurogenic blocks, an undoing or dismantling of the kinks which interrupt the otherwise natural processes of immunity and healing.

These topics have been dealt with only to satisfy curiosity and to ensure completeness, to round off the topic. They are not really relevant to our study of Enlightenment and Liberation. Miracles are not important in the understanding of the Reality. They are merely side-issues. We could rather say that the Liberated person is himself a living miracle.

And to the Enlightened person, the whole of the manifest, phenomenal universe, and everything in it, is a wondrous miracle.

Śrī Ramaṇa Maharṣi said about **clairvoyance**:

Can one see or hear without the Self? What difference

> does it make if you see or hear anyone close up or at a great distance? . . . Why then should there be any glamour about clairvoyance or clairaudience?[4]

Nirvikalpa Samādhi and Sahaja Sthiti

Most people, it appears, fail to distinguish adequately between *nirvikalpa samādhi* and the *sahaja sthiti*—between trance-like states occurring as a result of effortful meditative practices, and the natural way of life of the sage. Even those who do distinguish between them, are usually convinced that *nirvikalpa samādhi* is a preliminary exercise to realising the *sahaja sthiti*.

But actually the two are quite different and unrelated, as we have already pointed out several times in this book. *Nirvikalpa samādhi* is not *sahaja sthiti*, nor is it a precursor or preliminary stage of *sahaja sthiti*. It neither leads to nor results in *sahaja sthiti*. *Nirvikalpa samādhi* is basically an artificial state of trance brought upon as a result of certain techniques. It is a temporary, artificial experience of the Unity of the original state. But the basic misconcept of the 'I' as a separate entity (who is 'doing' the practice and who is 'achieving' the superconscious states) **still exists**. It is, as Śrī Ramaṇa Maharṣi explained, like a bucket of water lying submerged in the well with the rope still attached. When the person comes out of the trance of *nirvikalpa samādhi*, he will find that his ego is as strong as ever, and in all likelihood. even stronger because of his recent achievement. Indeed, to attempt to attain *nirvikalpa samādhi* is "to wear out your brain trying to make things into One without realising that they are already One. . . ." (Chuang Tzu)

Sahaja sthiti, on the other hand, is our natural, original state. It is really nothing but ordinary everyday living, devoid of the sense of being a separate entity. Now, in the words of Zen,

---

4. Osborne, Arthur, *The Teachings of Bhagavan Sri Ramana Maharshi In His Own Words*, p. 223.

'the bottom of the bucket has broken'!

The feeling of being a separate self, and the resultant 'me'-based thinking (or 'separatist' thoughts) lead to the (apparent) fall from that state in the case of the average man. It is only in the complete absence of all me-based thinking that this original state can be experienced. Since the average man has such me-based thoughts at all times, in the sense that the idea of being a separate entity is the very basis of almost all his thinking, that is why for him, the absence of me-based thinking would only be possible when there is **absence of all thought**. That is, for an average man to get even a brief, temporary glimpse of his original state, the only immediate way for him would be to eliminate all thought, which is what is sought to be done in *nirvikalpa samādhi* and other trance-like states. The sage, on the other hand, is at all times free of me-based thinking, and hence he is always in that original state, whatever he may be doing or thinking. There is clearly no need for him to exclude all thought. Nor is there any need for him to go into a trance. The sage sees very clearly that there is, in fact, no separate 'self' with a separate consciousness — no 'me'. So, me-based thinking is spontaneously cut off at its very source. In contrast, what the exponent of *nirvikalpa samādhi* does is to avoid me-based thinking by simply banishing **all** thoughts, which is rather like cutting off the head to cure a headache.

The experience of *nirvikalpa samādhi*, when described, may sometimes **sound** like the mystic's description of the *sahaja sthiti*.

For example,

> There is . . . no meditator, and no meditation, nor is there any awareness of an absence of these.[5]

Yet, *nirvikalpa samādhi* is a state of trance, whereas *sahaja*

---

5. Hixon, Len, *Coming Home*, quoted in Wilber, Ken, *The Atman Project*, p. 73.

sthiti is very definitely not so. But to compound the confusion, the term *sahaja samādhi* is often used for *sahaja sthiti*, thus making people think of it as a trance-like state.

Although descriptions of *nirvikalpa samādhi* may sometimes sound convincingly like the *sahaja sthiti*, *nirvikalpa samādhi* finally remains a *temporary experience* brought on by means of some particular practice (as a result of it). *Sahaja sthiti* is a *way of life*, the natural, original way, indeed, the only way. It is not an **experience**, and is not **dependent** on any practice. (See *Vivekacūḍāmaṇi*, 529). It is not something to be **achieved**, rather, it is something to be **realised**. *Nirvikalpa samādhi* leaves the experiencer with a sense of achievement. In *sahaja sthithi* **there is no experience-er**, and therefore no question of a sense of achievement. Rather, there is a sense of freedom, of relief, a floating sense of non-volitional living, and of wonder.

Although in *nirvikalpa samādhi*, the experiencer (the ego) may be apparently absent for the duration of the *samādhi*, he is very much alive and well in the background. He may be said to be merely dormant for the moment as in deep sleep, and reappears at once upon the termination of the *samādhi* — when 'the bucket is pulled up from the water'.

The Enlightened or Liberated person is therefore not to be confused with a practitioner of *nirvikalpa samādhi*. You can distinguish the two without too much difficulty. The sage in *sahaja sthiti* will always emphasise the **ordinariness** of the state, its **naturalness**, how **easy** it is to realise it. (Indeed, it is too easy, so much so that most people miss it precisely because they expect it to be difficult, to be something esoteric. They refuse to believe that it can be something commonplace, spontaneous, effortless). He will always stress that it already exists,[6] and it is within the capability of every man to realise it. The adept at *nirvikalpa samādhi*, on the other hand, will usually talk of it as

6. In a sense, (from the viewpoint of the sage), it could be said that everything is *sahaja sthiti*, including ordinary everyday life. (See →

a feat, and a very difficult one, requiring extensive practice in the art of meditation, intense concentration, and years of effort. Nor is he wrong. All that is true of *nirvikalpa samādhi* — but not of *sahaja sthiti*.

Sahaja sthiti is nothing spectacular, it is not super-consciousness. It is simple everyday living but without the feeling that one is a separate entity with a separate consciousness. The feeling of separateness (of being a separate entity, or of 'having' a separate consciousness or 'soul') is an artificiality which has been foisted on us very early in life. It is now so ingrained that it has become 'second nature' with us.

The essence of the spiritual understanding is thus to unlearn this feeling of separateness, to lose it, and **not** to gain or learn or achieve a feeling of 'oneness,' which would be adding another artificiality, compounding the confusion.

- Original (Unity of) Consciousness + feeling of separateness = Average Man
- Original (Unity of) Consciousness + feeling of separateness + feeling of 'oneness' = most so-called 'spiritual' experiences, including *nirvikalpa samādhi*
- Original (Unity of) Consciousness (unmodified) = The sage

Thus what is required is not to learn or achieve something new, but rather the dismantling of the structures built by thought.

To learn something new requires **effort**, but to dismantle something already learnt (but which is untrue) requires **understanding** or **insight**.

→ pp. 105-9). But though everything is indeed *sahaja sthiti*, the average man in his delusion does not see it as such. So we can say that *sahaja sthiti*, (as the term is used in this discussion, and for all practical purposes), is the condition of the person who **knows** or **realises** that everything is *sahaja sthiti*.

Many people believe that *sahaja sthiti* cannot be realised without going through active meditative techniques. However, this is patently wrong. *Sahaja sthiti* can be realised directly. In fact, it is to be realised directly. Active techniques can prove to be a real diversion and distraction, and deepen or strengthen the illusion that one is a separate ego-entity. The only active technique that could be useful is Self-enquiry because this directly attacks (or questions) the root illusion. All other techniques proceed on the assumption that this illusion is reality.

This is not to say that *nirvikalpa samādhi* should not be practised. Only, it should be clearly understood that it is of no value in the search for Enlightenment, except perhaps to give a person a brief glimpse of a state devoid of me-based thinking, and to convince him that such other possibilities (other than his average, daily me-centred living) do at least exist.

This is also not to say that meditative techniques are of no value at all. Some of them may have their uses as preliminary techniques to quieten an agitated mind which would otherwise not be conducive to receiving the real teaching (that is, more in a therapeutic capacity). They may also be prescribed as interim techniques for the spiritual seeker who insists on being given something to 'do' (see 'Meditative Techniques' next).

Meditative Techniques

We had seen in chapter 8 that the Masters sometimes use the word 'meditation' to refer to the *sahaja sthiti* itself, and sometimes to describe the mental processes which occur spontaneously *after* Enlightenment. But to the average spiritual seeker, 'meditation' invariably means **effortful** meditative techniques, or 'sitting meditation', and it is these which are usually given pride of place in the search for Enlightenment, whether in the East or in the West. It is because of this misplaced importance given to such effortful techniques of meditation that it was thought necessary to include a short discussion on this topic.

The reader may point out that it has already been shown in this book that in reality, everything is spontaneous, so where is the question of labelling certain practices as 'effortful'? However, the average person does not see everything as spontaneous, so by 'effortful techniques' we mean those practices performed under the **illusion** that the seeker is doing them wilfully, and to 'achieve' a certain goal, usually Enlightenment.

A large number of methods and techniques of meditation have been described (and are practised), but they all fall into one of two basic types or categories, which are very different from each other:

(1) *The 'Discursive' type*,[7] also called the 'Concentrative-absorptive' type:[8] In this type of meditation, directed thinking in words (sacred verbal formulae or *mantrās* like 'I am *Brahman*') or images (of a deity for example) is used to produce the desired mental changes in the meditator, a process somewhat similar to 'auto-suggestion'. In its higher forms, it involves severe mental concentration and strenuous and prolonged control of thought. The immediate aim is a mind occupied with one idea to the exclusion of all other thoughts (these being seen as irrelevant or undesirable). This is called 'one-pointedness'. Most Hindu systems of meditation are of this type.

(2) *The 'Receptive-defocal' type*: In this type, thoughts are simply observed or watched neutrally, not forced one way or the other (though this is much easier said than done — for an unenlightened person, that is). The

---

7. Kretschmer, W., "Meditative Techniques in Psychotherapy", in *Altered States of Consciousness*, ed. by C.T. Tart.

8. Wilber, Ken, *The Atman Project*, pp. 93-9.

emphasis is on lack of selection or direction. For example, the active practice of 'mindfulness' in Buddhism (as distinct from its spontaneous occurrence after Enlightenment).

It will be seen that these two are complete opposites. The first involves extreme mental concentration, while the second is more a method of mental relaxation. They are as different from each other as heavy physical exercise is from complete physical relaxation.

Concentrative-absorptive techniques are more likely to culminate in *savikalpa samādhi* (absorption in the object of thought because of intense mental concentration upon that object) which may then perhaps lead to *nirvikalpa samādhi*, whereas defocal techniques may lead to *nirvikalpa samādhi* without the intervention of *savikalpa samādhi*.

The concentrative-absorptive types of meditation may be useful in improving concentration as required in learning mental or physical skills for example in studies or in sports. However, they can also have adverse effects on the personality (like increased irritability), and can also lead to a fixation, or addiction to their effects.

As regards their practice for spiritual purposes, if the meditator's goal is a type of *samādhi* in the sense of a trance-like state, they could achieve that limited purpose, but as we have shown in this book, *sahaja samādhi* (*sahaja sthiti*) is something quite different.

Defocal techniques may have their uses in the domain of psychiatry. They may, for example, help a person gain an insight into his own neuroses (like obsessions). They may also be used as a type of relaxation exercise.

In the spiritual context, the defocal type of meditation may be prescribed as an interim 'technique' to be performed by the aspirant or seeker who insists on being given **something to 'do'**.

Practically speaking then, should a 'seeker' practise meditative techniques, or should he avoid them (or, if he is practising them already, give them up) since they, by themselves, cannot lead to Enlightenment? The answer is simple — if he **feels the necessity** to perform effortful meditative techniques, then he should by all means do so. When the time comes, he will not have to 'give up' the practices. Rather, he will **no longer see the need to do them** (as techniques for Enlightenment) and they will fall away of their own. (Even if he continues to do them, there will no longer be the idea that they are being performed as a 'means' to Enlightenment.)

The return to the *sahaja sthiti* involves a process of dis-identification through **understanding** (not effortful meditation). Meditation may at the most take one to a take-off stage, but beyond that it is understanding or perception (insight) which is required. It is a change of view or focus, in the absence of which the meditator will stagnate spiritually. To take the snake-rope example, however much one may concentrate one's vision to see the 'snake' clearly, finally it is the recognition that it was never a snake that ends the fearful illusion.

After Enlightenment, the Enlightened person does whatever comes to him naturally. Thus, he may show no change whatsoever in his external life, or, at times, on the other hand, (as described in the life of Śrī Ramaṇa Maharṣi) he may sit by himself, absorbed in Unity. In the case of the latter, this is not a 'practice' of meditation to attain some end. This is a spontaneous, purposeless happening.

Turīya

As discussed in chapter 5 ('States of Consciousness'), in Hindu spiritual literature the word *turīya*, technically speaking, refers to the waking state of the Liberated One, which is different from the three states known to the average man, and is therefore called *turīya* (the fourth). However, in a broader sense, the word *turīya* is used more often to denote the state of the Liberated One in general, that is, *sahaja stithi* (and by implication, Awareness or *prajñā* itself). The discussion about *turīya* which follows refers to the word when used in this latter, broader sense.

The average person is aware that he passes through the three states of waking, sleep and dreaming. He is aware of these because there is a basic underlying awareness (which Jñāneśvar has called *jāṇaṇe*), which enables him to know this fact. He thinks he is some 'one' who is aware (or has awareness) of these three states.

But the truth is that he is not some-'one' or some-'thing' who 'is aware' or 'has awareness'. He is in reality the very Awareness itself which underlies all the three states, and which is unable to see (or be aware of) itself, because of its very nature (of being aware-**ness**) — just as the eye cannot see itself, and the tongue cannot taste itself. The average person, in the words of Śrī Ramesh Balsekar, has (as the pseudo-entity) 'usurped the subjectivity' of *Brahman* (which is Absolute Subjectivity), thus creating an illusory pseudo-subject, which he calls his 'self'.

Once, this fact is realised (actually, intuitively), then Enlightenment is said to have taken place, and then there is no more the identification with a pseudo-subject who 'is aware'. In other words, the sage is not (as often erroneously described) 'one who is aware of all the three states' — that is in fact a description of the average person (who thinks he is so). The sage is one in whom the false identification with this 'one' who 'is aware' is lost, and who has realised his true nature as the very aware-**ness** itself which underlies all the three states. And *this* is the condition of *turīya*. It is not therefore a state by itself, nor is it a level of consciousness. It is simply a word used to indicate the realisation of one's true identity as the unknowable Awareness which underlies all the states of consciousness.[9]

Turīya is called as such (*turīya* or the 'fourth') only in relation to the three states of consciousness. But as we have just seen, *turīya* (when the word is used in its broader meaning) is not a state of consciousness. Therefore, the term 'fourth' is not very appropriate in that sense. Hence, sometimes, it is also referred to as *turīyātīta*, that is, 'that which is beyond the fourth'. Thus, *turīya* is itself *turīyātīta*.

> Since in *turīya* those three states
> Are seen as false appearances,
> The Fourth is also that beyond
> The Fourth, *turīyātīta*.
>
> The Garland of Guru's Sayings, by Muruganar.
>
> — *Mountain Path*, June '97, p.71

Perhaps technically it would be better if the word *turīya* was reserved to describe the waking state of the Liberated One, and the word *turīyātīta* was used to denote the Liberated state in general (or Awareness or *prajñā*). For the Liberated state is independent of (and the Liberated One does not identify with) any of these states of consciousness, hence *turīyātīta*, meaning 'beyond (even) the fourth (state)'.

9. (Tr.) Swāmi Nikhilānanda, *Self-Knowledge of Śrī Śaṅkarācārya*, pp. 66-8, 270. Also, *Śrī Vāsiṣṭha Saṅgraha*, XXXI, 14-18.

Questions and Answers

WHENEVER there is a discussion on spirituality and on the Enlightened or Liberated state, there are some questions which seem to constantly recur. Some of these are tackled below.

Q. How can one identify a Liberated person from outward appearance? In other words, how does a sage look?

A. People often imagine a sage to be some sort of other-worldly person with a saintly air and a halo around his head. If they do, they are in for a disappointment. In fact, the Liberated One may be outwardly unremarkable and may not differ from the average man in any obvious way. He would neither be susceptible to sudden trances, nor will he necessarily have a ring of followers surrounding him. Like any ordinary person, he may be busy earning his livelihood and looking after his family, and you may never hear him talk about his Liberation.

The general impression seems to be that upon Enlightenment, a person will retire from his trade or profession, and become a hermit, or lead a rather inactive life, doing nothing much apart from teaching his followers. In reality, there is absolutely no reason why he should do so. As explained in chapter 4, after Enlightenment a person may simply continue in his trade or profession (and his role as a householder) without any obvious change in his external life. The fact of Enlightenment is not, as people seem to think, a bar to working in the material world. In fact it is a boon, as a person works much more efficiently when not burdened with unnecessary thoughts which interfere with efficiency.

The Enlightened One may therefore be very active in worldly life, and may be materially successful too for that matter (like the legendary Janaka and Kṛṣṇa). After Enlightenment, a person becomes an adept at the art of living, and there is no disinclination to work. Rather, there is a zest for living, and a freshness and vigour to one's work. To retire from active life after this would be like training for a difficult skill, and then retiring just when one has acquired that skill to perfection. As Jñāneśvar said to his father:

> The best *samādhi* is not to be in mere blank but, like meeting blow with blow, **to engage in the affairs of the world**. (Emphasis added)[1]

However, some Enlightened persons may live a retired life and have the time and inclination to guide people, and it is usually these who become well known as sages. This leads to a stereotyping of that particular image of a sage in the popular mind.

On the other hand, the Liberated person who is a householder and professional would live his life like any other average person except that the me-based element will be absent in his thinking. Thus he will (for example) make plans, execute them, try to expand his business, arrange his finances and, in short, go through the routine of everyday life just like anyone else. Only, there will be no undue worrying about the results, and no pointless regrets or recriminations in case of failure. It is not that his life would be completely smooth and without turmoil or problems of any kind. But the Liberated person possesses the quality of great mental resilience. In the face of adversity, he recovers or bounces back quickly and does not lose his emotional stability and mental poise. He has thus been compared to a *Daruma* doll (spherical Japanese rocking doll which if tipped over, quickly regains its balance and cannot be toppled). As there is no me-based mental conflict, the mental disturbance, if

1. Subedar, Manu, *Gita, the Mother*, pp. 311-16.

at all it appears, is superficial and short-lived. Sāi Bābā of Śirḍī once appeared greatly agitated when one of his followers was dying, but after a time, all of a sudden he seemed to reconcile himself to the inevitable.

Thus the sage is a person who is completely practical, down-to-earth, objective, mature, tolerant and exceedingly compassionate, but otherwise, quite ordinary—for, in the words of Zen, Awakening is *wu-shih*, nothing special!

Q. The world is said to be unreal and an illusion. But it appears very real.

A. This (that the world is an illusion) is one of the most misunderstood statements from Hindu or Vedāntic spiritual literature. Most people take it to mean that this world does not really exist, and, as a corollary, that it is to be entirely disregarded.

Actually the world is said to be an illusion in the sense that this material world **is not all there is**. As Jñānadeva says in the *Jñāneśvarī*, there is a hidden, all-pervasive Reality underlying this physical, material universe. But what we ordinarily perceive with our senses is only this material universe, which is merely one aspect or **appearance** of the underlying Reality. Calling the world an illusion therefore means that what we are seeing is only an appearance, not the final Reality. It does **not** mean that the appearance does not exist. It means that it is not the **only** thing that exists, and that **the unseen Reality which is not seen is more important than the appearance which we see**. The sage does not deny the world. He merely asserts that it is not the ultimate level of reality, which is also what the modern physicist says. Sir James Jeans (physicist) says:

> As the new physics has shown, all earlier systems of physics, from the Newtonian mechanics down to the old quantum theory, fell into the error of identifying appearance with reality; they confined their attention to the walls of the cave, without even being conscious of a

deeper reality beyond.[2]

The mention of the cave is a reference to Plato's famous example. Plato picturised man's condition as that of a person engrossed in watching the shadows on the walls of a cave, while ignoring the Reality which is the light behind him that is creating the shadows on the wall.

The sage does not deny the world — he gives it just the importance it rightly deserves, no more, no less. This is the meaning of the statement by Jesus:

> Render unto Caesar the things which are Caesar's and unto God the things which are God's.

The idea that the world is *māyā* or illusion is often attributed to Ādi Śaṅkarācārya, the eighth-century *Advaitic* sage. But Ādi Śaṅkara did not simply state that the world is an illusion, as is commonly believed. He, too, accepted three *degrees* of reality:

> *prātibhāsika satya*: apparent truth, corresponding to our thought-world, our opinionated, subjective view of the world, (it is this which is referred to as an illusion created by *māyā*);
>
> *vyāvahārika satya*: day-to-day practical, objective reality, or the actual physical reality; and
>
> *pāramārthika satya*: the highest Truth or the ultimate Reality, which is *Nirguṇa Brahman.*[3]

On similar lines, let us now define the three degrees of reality.

1. The **subjective** or **common man's reality** — that is 'reality' as perceived by an average man who takes his ego-entity to be very real, and who perceives every

---

2. Commins and Linscott, *Man and the Universe*, p. 384.
3. Harshananda, Swami, *A Dictionary of Advaita*, Ramakrishna Math, pp. 5-6.

event, every issue coloured by this belief. This could be called 'Level 1 Reality'. (The *prātibhāsika satya* of Ādi Śaṅkara). The average man's life is largely centred around this 'reality'.

2. The **objective everyday reality**. This is the objective world, seen in its pure 'suchness' or *tathatā* only by the sage, and to which the sage reacts and responds in his everyday phenomenal living. This is 'Level 2 Reality'. (The *vyāvahārika satya* of Ādi Śaṅkara).

3. The highest or **Ultimate Reality**. This can be called 'Level 3 Reality'. (The *pāramārthika satya* of Ādi Śaṅkara). This is Absolute Subjectivity or the Absolute (or God in the real sense) described in chapter 10. This is neither anything that is perceived nor anything which apparently perceives, it is the perceiver-perceiving-perceived triad resolved to its original, timeless, spaceless unity.

The average man lives in two worlds. A physical world common to all (Level 2 Reality), and a private mental world different for each one of us (Level 1 Reality). This mental world is the prism through which we see this physical universe and all that is in it. That is why it appears different to different people.

Thus while in our dreams, we live in a thought-world (Level 1 Reality), in our waking state too we live in a thought-world (also Level 1 Reality) but which is superimposed upon the actual physical world (Level 2 Reality). And most of us live more in our 'thought-worlds' than in the actual physical world, that is, our presence is much stronger in our emotional and mental world than in the physical world, to which we are often oblivious. That is why this life is often compared to a dream.

It is this thought-world (Level 1 Reality) which is said to be an 'illusion' and which is said to disappear after Enlightenment. The physical world (Level 2 Reality) does not disappear after Enlightenment, but is, in fact, seen as it actually is for the first time! The Liberated One is the only person who has no emotional thoughts (no unnecessary thoughts, only necessary or technical thoughts), and hence he alone will be able to see the physical world as it really is.

> If you really heard a bird sing, if you really saw a tree . . .
> you would know.[4]

Thus 'delusion' or 'illusion' simply refers to our subjective way of seeing things.

To summarise, the sages tell us that what they call the Absolute is the highest level of reality there is, **compared to which**, both our subjective as well as our objective reality are **relatively** unreal. It is a misconception to think that when the sages say the world is an illusion they mean it does not exist **at all**. The sage himself may take the events of this world very seriously and act upon them, but he is always aware that he is like a sincere and dedicated actor living his part on stage. And he lives it up to the hilt, because even though these are events in a drama, the drama does exist.

At a mystical level of consciousness, however, the sage may remark, like Śrī Ramaṇa Maharṣi, that 'there has been no creation', or 'nothing has happened' or, like Hui-Neng (seventh century AD), that 'not one thing exists'. This is because with reference to the Ultimate Reality, all 'happenings' in Space-Time are relatively unreal. The description 'nothing exists' is not nihilism but is simply an inadequate verbal description of that which the sage sees and which cannot be described in words.

Q. If there is no free will, then why should I do (or decide to do) anything at all? Also, I should not be held responsible for any of my actions.

A. This is a common problem which a religious person faces when he hears that there is no free will. The fallacy in the question is

4. Mello, Anthony de, *The Song of the Bird*, p. 17.

that the absence of free will is not a fact to be heard, believed, and acted upon by the 'one' who hears it. It is rather an inevitable conclusion which follows from the discovery that **there is no 'one' to have any free will**. The idea of free will in religion is fundamentally based upon the belief in the existence of a separate, autonomous entity. But we have already shown that such an entity does not exist. However, what usually happens is that the average hearer misses the main implication of the statement, namely that there *is* no entity to have free will, and takes the statement to mean that *the entity* has no free will. Actually, belief in the separate entity (the 'self') and belief in free will go together (and they disappear together). You can have both or neither, but you cannot have one without the other. The average man believes in both, while the Enlightened One sees both to be illusions. So long as the belief in a separate self remains, the person will perforce believe in free will. It should be understood that telling such a person about the absence of free will is merely for his intellectual understanding, and not a prescription to be followed.

What then does this statement imply, apart from simply explaining the way the brain functions? It also implies the very important fact that there is no moral responsibility (no personal blame or credit) for any action, which takes us to the second part of the question, and another very common misconception. Again the situation is that there can be no moral responsibility because there is no 'one' to have any such responsibility. And again this follows automatically when (and only when) it is seen very clearly that there is really no 'one', no entity, who exists. It does not mean that the person keeps believing in the presence of the entity, and then believes that *the entity* has no moral responsibility. This would again be a double fallacy, which would only make the situation worse. And that is why this knowledge is said to be not such that can be shouted from the rooftops to all and sundry.

The fact that in reality there can be no moral responsibility however, does not mean, for example, that a person should not be punished for his actions. For although there is no entity who can have any moral responsibility, the body-mind unit does continue to have a legal and social responsibility, and will **have** to answer for its (the body-mind's) actions in life. The individual person, meaning a biological unit constituted by one body-mind complex, will have to bear the consequences of his actions, just as a company or a nation, for example has to. Thus one could say that there is no moral blame, but there is legal responsibility.

Entitification is in fact the 'original sin', the cause of all the misery. For a body-mind which still suffers from it, the facts about free will and moral responsibility are merely for satisfaction of curiosity, or for intellectual understanding, and not recipes to be acted upon. It is only when entitification has disappeared that these facts will be seen for oneself, and will automatically become a reality in daily life.

A person who continues to believe that he is a separate entity cannot justifiably say that 'he' is not responsible for his actions. His saying so will only be a clever way of using words. It is only when entitification has actually disappeared in a particular case that it can be legitimately said so. To such a person this is then a living fact, not a theory.

Theorising apart, the practical implication of all this for a particular individual is that, in actual life he must behave **as if** there **is** free will — till such time as he actually **sees** for himself that there is no entity to have free will — and then everything becomes spontaneous, or rather everything is seen to have been spontaneous all along.

Q. What is meant by the cryptic reference to the 'inverted *aśvattha* tree of Life' in the *Bhagavad Gītā* (chapter 15)?

A. The *Bhagavad Gītā* speaks of an inverted, imperishable *aśvattha* tree, which is to be cut down by the sword of detachment (resulting from Knowledge). It is also said in the *Gītā* that he who understands what this tree is about, truly understands. It is believed that this cryptic reference contains a message which is the key to the mystery of Life.

Seekers after Enlightenment attempt all sorts of spiritual exercises (*sādhanā*), both physical and mental, to achieve the state of Awakening. But all these efforts turn out to be fruitless, because, as we have explained, any me-based effort is bound to be counter-productive in the context of Enlightenment. It is also traditionally believed that the seeker should exercise 'mind-control' and suppress all desires. But neither any spiritual *sādhanā* nor simply leading a virtuous life will by itself lead to Enlightenment. This is because all these exercises do not tackle the root of the problem (which is entitification). They all operate on the same illusory level of reality as the problem itself (Level 1 Reality)—that is, they are all done with the assumption of the existence of the 'me' as a separate real entity. The only way out of the impasse is by *understanding the situation*, that is by intellectual understanding, which alone can lead to the intuitive understanding that is Enlightenment.

No amount of effort on the part of the illusory 'me' can lead to its own demise. It is only when it is **seen** very clearly that **there is no separate 'me'** that the root or source of me-based desire is destroyed, and the entire make-believe world wholly based on the fiction of the illusory 'me' comes crashing down.

(See chapter 3 'The Paradox of Spiritual Effort', chapter 5 'True Virtue', and chapter 8 '*Sādhanā*').

The tree symbolises the tree of *saṁsāra* (worldly life). The picture of an inverted tree suggests the reflection of a tree in a lake, implying thereby that it (the tree of *saṁsāra*) is an illusion. The tree of *saṁsāra* is a reflected appearance of the Reality of *Brahman*.

The inverted tree of *saṁsāra* or manifestation

Nirguṇa Brahman (Void, 'Noumenon')

↓

Manifestation, sentience in living beings, conscious awareness

↓

(through 'Ignorance', delusion or *māyā*)
Identification, 'Entitification', the illusory entity 'me'

↓

Me-based desires

The *Jñāneśvarī* explains (XV.72-260, abbreviated):

> The formless adual Supreme *Brahman* is the upwending root of this tree. Indeed the *nirguṇa Brahman* is beyond existence and non-existence, and beyond attributes like above and below. It is only said to 'exist as the topmost level of the tree' in a relative sense with reference to this illusory tree.
>
> *Māyā*, acting upon this *Brahman*, causes the deep ignorance of its own nature, and there sprout below innumerable and diverse forms, into which sprouts egotism.
>
> This tree is called *aśvattha*,[5] but this perennial tree only *appears* to be everlasting. It is actually appearing from moment to moment, (giving an illusion of continuity), like the spinning wheel of the chariot or a whirling top appears immobile, or a firebrand whirled around looks like an unbroken circle of fire. Thus is the tree of life rooted in delusion and is unreal and momentary.
>
> How can such an (apparently) vast and strong tree be felled down?
>
> Indeed, is it ever necessary to (actually, physically) drive

5. *Aśvattha*: *Pīpal*, a long-lasting tree (*Jñāneśvari*, XV. 115).

> away a goblin conjured up to frighten children? What (physical) effort is required to pluck the (illusory) horns of a hare? In the same way, know that this tree of worldly life is an unreality. Its detailed study and description is like filling the house with the children of a barren woman. Can crops be grown on the water of a mirage? (What is required is not actual physical efforts, but merely seeing the unreal as unreal).
>
> So long as the illusion is not removed by right thinking (*viveka*), there would be no end to the tree of *saṁsāra*.
>
> The unreal tree keeps growing on account of Nescience (Ignorance). Therefore, O Arjuna, cleave it with the weapon in the form of Knowledge of the Supreme Self. The greater use you make of other remedies (considering the unreal affairs of this world to be real), the more entangled you will get in the meshes of this tree, and then there will be no limit to your wanderings up and down the branches of this tree. It is a sheer waste of energy to collect sticks to kill an illusory serpent.

In other words, all efforts, whether physical renunciation and asceticism, or whether spiritual *sādhanā* ostensibly aimed at removing desires, will invariably be fruitless, for they do not address the root of the problem. They are equivalent to merely beating around the bush (or travelling up and down the branches of the tree). Only when the core or heart of the problem — the illusory 'me' — is tackled, will true detachment set in and desires fall off by themselves. As Jñāneśvar has said, **the only remedy to heal a wound caused in a dream is to awaken.**

In Zen, too, the method of Self-enquiry has been likened to an indestructible sword,[6] and ignorance to a tree. Suzuki states that as one goes on inquiring after the inquirer himself, a time will eventually come when the tree together with the entwining

6. Wilber, Ken, *The Spectrum of Consciousness*, p. 324.

wistaria breaks down, that is, when the distinction of subject and object is utterly obliterated, when the inquiring and the inquired are fused into one perfect identity.[7]

*****

When the Fifth Zen Patriarch wished to select his successor, he told his monks to express their wisdom in a poem. The head monk, who was the most learned, was full of expectation. After much deliberation, he wrote:

The body is the *Bodhi*-tree,
The mind is a bright mirror standing,
Take care to wipe it all the time,
And allow no dust to cling.

On reading this, the Fifth Patriarch knew that the head monk had not yet found his original nature.

Hui Neng, on the other hand, was a disciple who couldn't even write. So someone had to write down his poem for him. But when the Fifth Patriarch saw it, he immediately gave him the insignia of his office. This is what the poem read:

There is no *Bodhi*-tree,
Nor any bright mirror standing;
Fundamentally, not one thing exists,
So where is the dust to cling?

---

7. *Zen Buddhism, Second series*, p. 131 quoted in Wilber, Ken, *The Spectrum of Consciousness*, p. 325.

Who's Who

Ānandāṣram, Svāmī (1902-66); sage and highly revered religious leader of the small community of Chitrapur Sārasvat brāhmaṇas in India. Ordained at the tender age of 13 years, he lost his ailing *guru* within days of that event. His thirst for knowledge was fulfilled later through his subsequent preceptor Svāmī Kṛṣṇācārya Sarasvatī of Rishikesh in northern India.

Aṣṭāvakra; legendary Indian sage, *guru* of King Janaka. Said to have been physically deformed since birth ('Aṣṭāvakra' means 'deformed in eight places'). His advice to Janaka is recorded in the form of the *Aṣṭāvakra Gītā* (*Aṣṭāvakra Saṁhitā*).

Asimov, Isaac (1920-92); Russian-born American author. He wrote about science and technology, both fiction and non-fiction.

Aspect, Alain; experimental physicist at the University of Paris-Sud acclaimed for the 1982 experiment named after him that established quantum non-locality.

Augustine, Saint (354-430); Christian mystic, philosopher and theologian.

Balsekar, Ramesh (*b.*1917); sage, disciple of Nisargadatta Mahārāj. A graduate of London University, he was a banker by profession till his retirement in 1977. He often acted as interpreter during Mahārāj's talks. Now author of several books, he holds regular talks at his residence in Mumbai (Bombay).

Brunton, Paul; an Englishman who toured India in the first half of the twentieth century. It was his book *A Search in Secret India* which introduced Ramaṇa Maharṣi to the Western world.

Cārvāka; ancient Indian philosopher who proposed the doctrine of materialism.

Chuang Tzu (*circa* 360 BC); co-founder of Taoism along with Lao Tzu (*circa* 500 BC). According to tradition, he followed Lao Tzu, but some people believe him to be the original Taoist.

Coomaraswamy, Ananda Kentish (1877-1947); born in Ceylon (now Sri Lanka), later settled in Boston; scholar, art historian, author of several books on art and religion.

Dakṣiṇamūrti; legendary Indian sage who is said to have taught in silence.

De Mello, Father Anthony (1931-87); Jesuit priest of Lonavla in western India, teacher, preacher, mystic, author. Wrote in a simple but distinctive style combining the philosophy of all religions.

Eckhart, Johannes (1260?-1328?); German theologian and mystic. He is usually called Meister (Master) Eckhart.

Eknāth (sixteenth-seventeenth century); saint-poet of western India, known for his commentary on the main (eleventh) section of the *Śrīmad Bhāgavatam*. He rewrote the *Jñāneśvarī* in 1584 as it had been distorted over the years. His *guru* was Janārdan Svāmī, a soldier.

Feynman, Richard Phillips (1918-88); American physicist; developed an improved theory of quantum electrodynamics in the late 1940s. Shared the 1965 Nobel Prize for physics.

Freud, Sigmund (1856-1938); of Austria. Founder of psychoanalysis based on the theory of 'unconscious motivation.'

Ghālib (Mirzā Ghālib) (1797-1869); famous Indian poet, author of some of the most beautiful compositions in the Urdu language. Said to have had a liking for wine and women, but some of his poems reveal a rare mystic insight.

Godel, Kurt; Austrian mathematician who, in the early 1930s, demonstrated that for any logical system, there are always theorems that cannot be proven either true or false by the axioms within that system.

Guru Nānak (1469-1539) founder of Sikhism and the first *guru* of the Sikhs.

Haeckel, Ernst; materialist, author of *Riddle of the Universe* (1899).

Haldane, J. B. S. (1892-1964); British scientist who made many contributions in the fields of mathematics, physiology, biochemistry, and biology.

Hawking, Stephen William (*b*.1942); British theoretical physicist, author of the best seller *A Brief History of Time* (1988). Generally regarded as having made the most important discoveries about gravity since Albert Einstein.

Hui Neng (638-713); the sixth patriarch of Ch'an (Zen), the most famous Ch'an master in Chinese history. Before Hui Neng, Ch'an was still influenced by Indian Buddhism, which emphasised the importance of meditation, study and metaphysical debates. Hui Neng taught sudden, direct awakening through introspection and understanding, and gave little importance to practices of meditation (sitting meditation). He stressed that it is the attitude of mind that is important, and not the physical posture, because truth can be found standing, walking, or lying down.

Huxley, Aldous (1894-1963); famous writer, author of *The Perennial Philosophy* (1944) besides other books.

Jalāluddīn Rūmi (1207-73); Sūfī saint and poet from (what is now) Turkey. Authorship was unimportant to him, and he called his collection of poems (the *Divani Shamsi Tabriz*) the work of his preceptor, Shams, the wandering minstrel of Tabriz. He also wrote the didactic *Mathnawi*.

James, William (1842-1910), famous American psychologist and philosopher, brother of novelist Henry James.

Janaka; legendary Indian King, father of Sītā (the bride of Rāma). Said to have been Enlightened, yet continued to function as a most effective and excellent king, and is therefore often quoted as the ideal example of the *karma yogī*.

Jeans, Sir James Hopwood (1877-1946); British scientist, contributed to the understanding of the behaviour of molecules, especially to the kinetic theory of gases. He also suggested a theory of the creation of the universe.

John the Baptist, Saint (6 BC?-AD 28); a prophet, considered the forerunner of Jesus Christ.

Kamā Bābā (-1978); of Mumbai, sage, disciple of Sāi Bābā of Śirḍī.

Krishnamurti, J. (1895-1986); famous Indian philosopher. Adopted as a child by Mrs. Annie Besant (president of the Theosophical Society) and educated in England. In 1929 he cut himself off from all organisations, and from that time until his death, he travelled round the world speaking as a private person.

Leibniz, Gottfried Wilhelm (1646-1716); German philosopher, mathematician, and scholar. He was the first to use the term *philosophia perennis.*

Mādhvācārya (1119-98); philosopher and religious teacher of south India. Taught that *ātman* and *Brahman* are eternally separate, that is, the doctrine of *Dvaita* (dualism). See Glossary: *Vedanta*.

Mansur al-Hallaj (tenth century); Sūfi mystic. He was put to death for declaring "I am the Truth".

Max Müller, Prof. Friedrich; German-born British scholar, renowned Orientalist of the late 1800s.

Muruganar; disciple of Ramaṇa Maharṣi.

Nāgārjuna (second century AD); a Buddhist philosopher. Founder of the Mādhyamika school of Buddhism, which represents the negative way of demonstrating the Reality, called *sūnyavāda*.

Nāmdev; saint-poet of mediaeval India, believed to have been a contemporary of Jñāneśvar.

Nārada; legendary sage referred to in several ancient Hindu texts.

Nisargadatta Mahārāj (1897-1981); sage from Mumbai. He was a householder, and, by profession, a cigarette stall owner. He became known to the West after the book *I Am That* by Maurice Frydman, a Polish Jew, became a best seller. His *guru* was Siddharāmeśvar Mahārāj of the *Nāth* sect.

Omar Khayyām (twelfth century); Persian mathematician, astronomer and Sūfi poet. His *Rubaiyāt* is an immortal classic.

Osborne, Arthur; Englishman, later settled in India. Biographer of Ramaṇa Maharṣi. Also wrote *The Incredible Sai Baba*, a brief biography of Sāi Bābā of Śirḍī.

Patañjali (second century BC); founder of the system of *Yoga* (better termed *Pātañjala Yoga*, to avoid confusion with *Karma Yoga*, etc). *Pātañjala Yoga* consists of systematic efforts to attain perfection. See Glossary: *Yoga*.

Plato (427?-347? BC); Greek philosopher; one of the most important thinkers and writers in the history of Western culture.

Radhakrishnan, Sarvepalli (1888-1975); Indian philosopher and statesman and India's president from 1962 to 1967.

Ramaṇa Maharṣi (1879-1950); renowned sage of Tiruvannamalai, in south-east India. He did not have a regular *guru*.

Rāmānuja (1017?-1137?); philosopher and religious teacher of south India. Mainly taught the path of *bhakti* (devotion). Expounded the doctrine of *Viśiṣṭa Advaita* (qualified adualism). See Glossary: *Vedānta*.

Ruysbroeck, Jan van (1293-1381); Dutch mystic.

Sage Who Never Speaks; a sage in Madras (now Chennai) described by Paul Brunton in his book *A Search in Secret India.*

Sāi Bābā of Śirḍī (?-1918); sage and mystic of unknown antecedents who settled in Śirḍī, a village in western India, which is now a famous place of pilgrimage. He kept his early life a secret, and like Kabīr, attempted to bring Muslims and Hindus together.

Schroedinger, Erwin (1887-1961); Austrian theoretical physicist, founder of quantum mechanics.

Śaṅkarācārya (AD 788-820); also known as Ādi Śaṅkarācārya or Śaṅkara; great sage and philosopher. Born in Kerala, south India. Most important exponent of the doctrine of *Advaita* (monism or adualism).

Spinoza, Baruch (or Benedict), (1632-77); Dutch philosopher; strong supporter of religious and political liberalism. In his masterpiece, *The Ethics*, he stated that "God or Nature" is the only substance, and all finite things (such as human minds and bodies) are only modes or states of the attributes of God. Spinoza did not view God as some superhuman being who created the universe. He identified God with the universe.

Tiḷak, Bāḷ Gaṅgādhar (1856-1920); from western India. Journalist, Sanskrit scholar, philosopher, and early leader in the Indian freedom struggle. He wrote the *Gītā Rahasya*, a commentary on the *Bhagavad Gītā*.

Tukārām (1608-49); famous poet-saint of western India. A doyen of the *bhakti* movement.

Vallabhācārya (1479-?); a saint and religious leader of western India. He taught his disciples to develop a very intensely personal relationship with God. Founded the doctrine of *Śuddha Advaita*. See Glossary: *Vedānta*.

Vasiṣṭha; sage, the preceptor of Rāma. His teachings to Rāma are contained in the *Yoga Vāsiṣṭha.*

Vivekānanda (Svāmī Vivekānanda) (1863-1902); famous philosopher and sage from Bengal in north-east India, disciple of the well-known sage Rāmākr̥ṣṇa Paramahaṁsa (1836-86).

Watts, Alan (1915-73); English born author, teacher, Orientalist, exponent of mysticism. Earlier an Anglican cleric. Introduced Zen to the Western world.

Wilber, Ken; regarded as the foremost theoretical psychologist in the field of transpersonal and spiritual studies and consciousness research, author of several books.

Wittgenstein, Ludwig (1889-1951); Austrian mathematician and philosopher, author of *Tractatus Logico-Philosophicus.*

Glossary

abhaṅgas: devotional poems in the Marāṭhī language (of western India).

Advaita: adualism (non-dualism) also called monism (see Appendix). The doctrine that nothing exists apart from the one Absolute, and that the separate individual 'soul' does not really exist — it is just an illusion. Or, to put it another way, the 'soul' or 'self' and God are not different – they are one and the same. This is the best known and most generally accepted school of Vedānta in India today (see Vedānta). The most important exponent of this doctrine has been Ādi Śaṅkarācārya. The two famous examples used in *Advaita* are (1) the example of the clay pot (*ghaṭam*) (p. 42), and (2) the rope-snake (*rajju-sarpa*) illusion (p. 68).

ahaṁkāra: egoism, (that which produces) the sense of separate individuality and of personal 'doership'.

arhat, *arhanta*: (Buddhism) a Liberated person, the Buddha.

ātma-darśana: Self-knowledge, that is, Enlightenment.

ātman: 'soul' or individualised consciousness (as ordinarily understood). But in actuality (as shown in this book, and according to *Advaita* as well), the *ātman* is itself the *param-ātman* (Supreme Consciousness or God). Hence sages often use the term *ātman* to mean the Universal Consciousness (e.g., Ramaṇa Maharṣi)[1]. This latter use

---

1. Osborne, Arthur, *Ramana Maharshi and the Path of Self-Knowledge*, p. 204.

is denoted in some books separately as *Ātman* (with a capital A). But in this book no such distinction is made.

avatāra: incarnation or descent of God in human form (specifically of the god Viṣṇu, the Preserver, of the Hindu trinity). Hindu mythological tradition speaks of ten *avatāras* (of which the tenth, *kalki*, is yet to take birth). The references in Kabīr's poem on p. 230 are to these *avatāras*. (See also Kṛṣṇa, Rāma and *Varāha*).

Bhagavad Gītā: the best known of the Hindu spiritual texts. It forms a part of the epic, the *Mahābhārata*, and contains the philosophical advice given by Kṛṣṇa to his disciple, Prince Arjuna on the battlefield.

Bhāgavat (*Srimad Bhāgavatam*): sacred text depicting the life of Kṛṣṇa along with philosophical discussions, emphasising mainly the path of *bhakti* (devotion).

bhakti: devotion, love of God. Hence *bhakta*, devotee; *bhakti mārga*; path of devotion.

bīdī: crude hand-made variety of local Indian cigarette rolled out of a type of leaf.

Bodhi tree: the tree under which the Buddha was sitting when Enlightenment occurred. (Lit. the tree of wisdom; *bodhi*, wisdom, Enlightenment).

Brahma sūtras: (*sūtra*; maxim) famous basic treatise on Vedānta composed by the sage Vyāsa. Also called *Vedānta sutras*.

Brahman: the Reality, the Absolute, or All-that-is. Synonymous with the Tao, Buddha-nature, etc. (see p. 228). It is beyond comprehension because it is *nirguṇa*, without attributes. It is unknowable, because it is That which is doing the knowing.

Brahma-niṣṭhā: abidance in *Brahman*.

Ch'an: see Zen.

dhyāna: deep, rapt contemplation with unbroken concentration. One usually proceeds from *japa* (incantation) to *dhyāna* to *savikalpa samādhi* and finally *nirvikalpa samādhi*.

Diamond sūtra: famous Buddhist text containing discourses of the Buddha.

fakīr: (Urdu) religious mendicant or ascetic, usually Muslim.

*guṇa*s: fundamental attributes, qualities or natural traits (innate tendencies) described both in humans as well as in inanimate matter. There are three: *sattva*, *rajas*, and *tamas*. *Sattva* is the highest and stands for purity, goodness, nobility, light. *Rajas* stands for activity, energy, and *tamas* for darkness, inertia and evil. Thus *guṇātīta*; beyond the (three) *guṇa*s.

guru: preceptor, teacher or guide, especially spiritual.

gyāna: see *jñāna*.

Hari: (Lit. 'one who attracts'). Another name for the god Viṣṇu.

jīva: so-called embodied or individual 'soul' (individualised consciousness). See *ātman*.

jñāna (*gyāna*) or *ātma-jñāna*: Self-knowledge (the knowledge that comes with Enlightenment) that is, true knowledge or the intuitive understanding. But in Vedāntic literature, sometimes the term *jñāna* is used specifically to indicate intellectual understanding only, and not the intuitive understanding of Enlightenment, for which the term *vijñāna* is used.

Kābā, (Kābāh, Kā'bāh): most holy place of worship in Islam, situated in Mecca.

Kailās: Himalayan peak holy to the Hindus, who consider it to be the abode of Śiva.

karma: action. But see p. 192.

karma mārga: the path of (worldly) action or the householder's path (as against the path of renunciation, *saṁnyāsa mārga*). See pp. 193-8.

karma phala tyāga: surrender of the fruits (results) of action (to God).

karma yoga: the art of integrating everyday activity with the spiritual quest. See p. 204.

koans: (Zen), short riddles or stories usually presented as conversations between a Master and his disciples, and which are at first sight seemingly absurd, meaningless or contradictory. They may be pithy one-liners ('What is the sound of one hand clapping?' or, 'To understand clearly one has to have just one eye') or may be lengthier versions. Used as themes for meditation or reflection, they aim to defeat the intellect (see p. 68) and to eventually lead to *i-ching* (Great Enquiry), which is similar to Self-enquiry (Who wants to know the answer? Where or to whom does this thought arise?).

Kr̥ṣṇa (? *circa* 1500 BC): king of Dvārkā in western India, and legendary sage of the *Bhagavad Gītā*. He was the son of Devaki, but was later adopted by Yaśodā. He romanced with the *gopīs* (milkmaids) in the forests of Br̥ndāvan, and is said to have lifted the Govardhan Mountain to protect his people during a storm. He is named as the eighth *avatāra*. (See p. 230).

līlā: sport, play, entertainment.

mahābhogi, *mahābhoktā*: supreme enjoyer.

mahāvākya: most sublime pronouncement. Four famous Upaniṣadic statements are thus known: *ahaṁ brahmāsmi* (I am *Brahman*), *tat tvam asi* (That thou art), *ayam ātmā brahma* (This self is *Brahman*), and *prajñānam brahma* (Consciousness is *Brahman*). These state the core of the Vedāntic (*Advaita*) philosophy.

mahāyogi: supreme *yogi*.

manana: reflection. Constant turning over of the teaching in the mind, and examining it in the light of one's own logic and reason.

manas: roughly translated as mind, but actually the faculty which is responsible for doubting and the sense of volition or doership. See p. 95, 98-9.

mantra: sacred verbal formula.

mārga: path. In the spiritual context, mode of approach in the quest for 'union' with God (that is, Enlightenment). The three traditionally described *mārga*s are those of *karma* (action), *bhakti* (devotion) and *jñāna* (knowledge).

mauna: silence. The deeper meaning is silence of the mind, that is, absence of me-based (unnecessary) thinking.

māyā: the cosmic delusion by means of which the One appears as the many. See p. 41-4.

mullā, *mullāh*: a Muslim learned in Islamic doctrine and law.

mumukṣu: a person desirous of Liberation.

Natarāja: Śiva depicted in a dancing pose, symbolising the Cosmic Dance (of creation and destruction).

Nāth pantha (*Nāth* sect): a lineage of sages to which belonged the illustrious Jñāneśvar, as also Nisargadatta Mahārāj of this century.

navavidhā bhakti: traditionally described nine modes or methods of practising *bhakti*, beginning with the simplest — listening (*śravaṇam*), and ending with the ultimate — self-surrender (*ātma-nivedanam*).

Neti-neti: (not this, not this), the Upaniṣadic negative way of describing the Absolute by considering descriptions one by one and rejecting them till none are left, thus indicating that It is beyond concepts.

nididhyāsana: cogitation, deep and intense mental deliberation.

nirguṇa: without qualities or attributes. Thus *nirguṇa Brahman* is a term used to describe the attributeless, inconceivable Absolute as it is in reality, as against *saguṇa Brahman*, the Absolute with attributes conceived of by the human mind.

nirvikalpa: devoid of thought or conceptualisation, devoid of distinction (*vikalpa*, distinction) — here referring to the conceptual distinction between 'me' and the 'other' or 'me' and *Brahman*.

nirvikalpa samādhi (*kevala nirvikalpa samādhi*): highest state of trance (in sitting meditation) completely devoid of all (*kevala*, total, complete) thought or conceptualisation, in which therefore distinction of 'me' and the 'other' is lost, but only temporarily (for the duration of the *samādhi*). (See pp. 75-9 and Appendix). Unfortunately, *sahaja samādhi* (see later) is also called *sahaja nirvikalpa samādhi*, and in some works this is shortened to *nirvikalpa samādhi*, causing confusion.

niṣkāma: without (selfish) desire. (See p. 61-4).

niṣṭhā: faith, also (see p. 40) mental fixedness or steadiness achieved by dint of practice (by spiritual effort).

nistraiguṇya: not affected by or concerned with the three *guṇas*.

nivṛtti: withdrawing from worldly concerns.

Paramātman: 'Oversoul', Supreme Self, Universal Consciousness (*param*, supreme). In other words, God. But actually the *ātman* is itself the *paramātman* (see *ātman*).

parāvṛtti: complete transformation (*parā*, inverted, inside-out; *vṛtti*, state, condition, existence).

parvardigār: (Urdu) God, the Almighty.

pītāmbar: an Indian silken lower garment, in which Kṛṣṇa is traditionally depicted.

prajñā: (*pra*, source, origin, beginning; *jña*, to know, to be aware of) Pure Awareness, Primordial Consciousness, that is, Consciousness upstream of thought or conceptualisation and (therefore) devoid of the sense of individuality (see pp.122-3, 178-9). Also, the second or direct mode of knowing (see p. 47).

Prakṛti: Primordial Nature.

prārabdha: current effect of past actions. Could be understood to mean present (me-based) conditioning caused by past (me-based) actions (see p. 64).

pravṛtti: active participation in worldly affairs.

Rāma: legendary king of Ayodhyā in north India perhaps a few centuries before Kṛṣṇa. He was the son of Daśaratha, and is considered the seventh *avatāra* of Viṣṇu. He vanquished the Lankan king Rāvaṇa (who had abducted his wife Sītā).

Rukmiṇi: consort of Viṭhobā.

sādhaka: one who practises *sādhanā*, that is, a spiritual aspirant.

sādhanā: means of Enlightenment, spiritual practice or discipline (spiritual effort).

sādhu: ascetic, holy man (but one who has not formally accepted the *saṁnyāsa mārga*). Also, a good or virtuous man.

sahaja: natural, spontaneous, effortless.

sahaja niṣṭhā: spontaneous (effortless) abidance in *Brahman* (in other words, *sahaja stithi*).

sahaja samādhi (*sahaja nirvikalpa samādhi*): spontaneous or effortless thought-free state of the Liberated One. (As contrasted with the thought-free state of *nirvikalpa samādhi* which is a result of effort). *Sahaja samādhi* is said to be thought-free only with respect to unnecessary (me-based) thinking, as explained in this book (chapter 5). Unlike *nirvikalpa samādhi*, it is not a state of trance, and is compatible with necessary thought and all everyday activity.

sahaja stithi: natural state. Term used to describe the state of the Liberated One, syn. with *sahaja samādhi*.

samādhi: *sam* (together) + *ā* (to) + *dhi* (put together), thus, (re)unification of the apparently separate individual consciousness with the Universal Consciousness. Could therefore mean (1) trance, superconscious state (in which this unification occurs, albeit temporarily), and also (2) the state of the Liberated One (in which the unification is permanent).

saṁnyāsa mārga: the path of renunciation or monasticism (see pp. 192-8). Thus, *saṁnyāsi*; a renunciate. One who has formally (and irrevocably) joined a monastic order (unlike a *sādhu*).

saṁsāra: worldly life.

sat-cit-ānanda: the minimum description required if asked to describe the qualityless, attributeless Absolute (*Brahman*): *sat* (existence or Is-ness) to show that it exists, *cit* (consciousness), to show that it is of the nature of consciousness, sentience or awareness, and *ānanda* (bliss, contentment) in the sense of being complete, self-sufficient, without want, therefore content and blissful by itself. These are not its qualities or characteristics, but rather its essential nature.

satori: the Zen term for Enlightenment.

savikalpa: in which thought (conceptualisation) is present.

savikalpa samādhi: absorption in the object of thought because of intense mental concentration upon that object. A state of trance in sitting meditation prior (and inferior) to *nirvikalpa samādhi*.

Self-enquiry: a method advocated by Śrī Ramaṇa Maharṣi ('Who am I? — '*Nān Yār*?' in Tamil). It is mentioned in the Śrī *Vāsiṣṭa Saṅgraha* (II, 44-6), and is also known in Buddhist literature (Ch'an: *i-ching* or Great Enquiry) — "inquiring after the inquirer himself" (Ku-yin). It is not a method of sitting meditation. It is rather a method of introspective investigation or 'looking inward' to see if at all there is any real 'me' or 'self' within. After hearing (from the *guru* or scriptures) that there is in fact no separate 'me' or 'self', the method of Self-enquiry attempts to confirm this truth practically for oneself. Whereas all other methods assume a 'doer' of those respective methods, Self-enquiry strikes at the very root of doership by questioning 'who' is the 'doer' of any method (or the 'thinker' of any thoughts)! The object of Self-enquiry is thus not to get an answer (say like 'I am *Brahman*') but rather to *feel* the absence of any entity whatsoever. Self-enquiry is thus the method to end all methods. For a detailed discussion, see Osborne, Arthur, *The Teachings of Bhagavan Sri Ramana Maharshi in His Own Words*, pp.130-67.

siddha: the Liberated One (lit. the accomplished one).

siddhīs; miraculous (paranormal) powers said to result from *yogic* practices.

śiṣya: disciple.

sitting meditation: wilful practice of a meditative technique, usually in the sitting posture, as a means to Enlightenment (as commonly understood by the term 'meditation'). This term is used to specify such meditation because the word 'meditation' is often used differently by sages (p.181-2).[2] In Zen, sitting meditation is called *Zazen*.

Śiva: one of the gods of the Hindu trinity. Śiva is the Destroyer.

Śivaliṅga: originally a phallic symbol (*liṅga*, phallus), but now worshipped as the symbol (*liṅga*, symbol) of the god Śiva.

Smṛtis: works by the sages Manu, Parāśara, and Yājñavalkya and a host of other texts, which build further on the basic teachings of the Vedas. Considered subordinate in authority to the Vedas.

śravaṇa: hearing, attentive listening (also by implication, reading). *Śravaṇa, manana, nididhyāsana* are the three traditionally advocated means to reach the (intellectual) understanding of the Reality.

Śrutis: the Vedas (lit. that which is heard, that is, 'revealed' knowledge; deeper meaning: that which was intuited in the mystical state, and not composed when in the human frame of mind. The term could also indicate that the Vedas were handed down by word of mouth).

Sūfism: mystic tradition in Islam.

Śūnyavāda: (the doctrine of Void), the doctrine of the Buddhist Mādhyamika school of Nāgārjuna. It disproves all theories about the Absolute without proposing any of its own, thus indicating that the Absolute is *śūnyatā* (Void), beyond all concepts.

tantra: a religious treatise teaching worship of deities by means of magical formularies for the attainment of paranormal powers. Also the system based on this.

Taoism: Chinese philosophy somewhat similar to *Advaita*

2. Lutyens, Mary, *Krishnamurti: The Open Door*, pp. 62-4.

founded by Lao Tzu and Chuang Tzu about 2,500 years ago. Tao (meaning 'way') is both the path as well as the Goal that is, the Self or the Absolute. The Tao is present everywhere and in all things, but cannot be described in words. Taoist teaching stresses spontaneity (*wu wei*, non-action).

tathāgata: (Buddhism) a Liberated person, the Buddha (lit. one who has 'been there').

tathatā: (Buddhism) 'suchness', the essential, true nature of things, as they really are.

tattva: essence, true or essential nature; thus the true nature of the human 'soul' (and material world) as being identical with the Supreme Spirit.

turīya: (lit. the fourth) the fourth state of consciousness of the Liberated One. In a deeper sense, a name of the transcendental *Brahman* (or the Awareness or *prajñā*) which both transcends and pervades the three states of waking, dream and deep sleep.

upadeśa: teaching, instruction or guidance given by a *guru* to his disciple.

Upaniṣads: the concluding sections of the Vedas containing the Vedānta philosophy.

varāha: a boar. The reference (p. 230) is to the third *avatāra* of Viṣṇu, which is said to have taken the form of a boar, and lifted the earth on its tusks.

Vedānta: (*anta*, end, essence) concluding portion of the Vedas (including the Upaniṣads) containing their essence (see p. 193). A system of philosophy ascribed to the sage Vyāsa and discussed mainly in the Upaniṣads, *Brahma-sūtras* and the *Bhagavad Gītā*. These basic Vedāntic texts have been interpreted in slightly different manners by different commentators giving rise to the various schools of Vedānta philosophy. Of these, the most comprehensive and generally accepted is *Advaita*. The others are: *Dvaita* (dualism) of Mādhvācārya, the doctrine that the 'soul' (or 'self') and God are eternally separate; *Viśiṣṭa Advaita* (qualified monism) of Rāmānuja, which states that the individual 'souls' are very close to God and a part of him, but not one and the same ('like seeds in a pomegranate'); and *Śuddha Advaita* ('pure' monism) of Vallabhācārya which, though called 'pure', still makes a fine distinction between the individual 'souls' and God, saying that they are related 'as sparks to a fire'.

Vedas: most ancient sacred literature of the Hindus (see Śrutis).

vijñāna: In Buddhism, it means the first or symbolic mode of knowing (see pp. 46-8) and it is in this sense that the word is used in this book. However, in Hinduism, it means the true (intuitive) knowledge of the Self (see *jñāna*) and thus corresponds to the Buddhist term *prajña*.

Viṭhobā (*Viṭṭhal*, *Viṭhū*): the god Viṣṇu especially as manifested at Paṇḍharpūr, a famous place of pilgrimage in Maharashtra in western India. Here he is seen with his consort Rukmiṇi standing on a brick (Marāthī: *vīṭha*, brick; *ubhā*, standing) with his hands on his hips. Viṭhobā was the favourite god of the *bhakti* movement of mediaeval Maharashtra.

yajña: an offering to God, a religious sacrifice.

Yoga Vāśiṣṭha: a voluminous work containing the teachings of the sage Vaśiṣṭha to his disciple, the young Rāma. The *Śri Vāśiṣṭha Saṅgraha* is a condensation of the original.

yoga: 'integrating' or 'joining together' (from *yuj*, yoke, joining together). It refers to the (re)unification or (re)integration of the apparently separate individual consciousness with the Universal Consciousness. Also, any system or discipline ('method') which leads to such unification is termed a *yoga*. Thus at some places in the *Bhagavad Gītā* for example, it is used to mean *karma yoga*. (For other meanings see p. 192).

The systematised methods of *yoga* fall generally into two categories: (1) *rāja yoga*, the easier system of *yoga* which 'even kings can practise' (*rāja*, king), expounded mainly by Patañjali. It comprises some eight types of practices, including non-violence, mind-control, etc., hence also called *aṣṭāṅga* (eight-limbed) *yoga*. The *āsana*s (*yogāsana*s) or physical postures (what is colloquially understood by '*yoga*') form just one of these eight subdivisions; (2) the more strenuous *haṭha yoga*, rigorous, forced meditation often in extremely difficult postures taught in some other texts like the *Śiva Saṁhita*.

sahaja yoga: lit. spontaneous, effortless or easy *yoga*. This term should ideally be used to describe the method of direct awakening by means of understanding and introspection as taught by Hui Neng, Ramaṇa Maharṣi, Nisargadatta Mahārāj, etc. and as explained in this book. It is called effortless because it de-emphasises all other spiritual exercises or disciplines. Interestingly, Jesus' statement "My yoke is easy" (Mathew 11:30) could have a similar deeper meaning. However, the term *sahaja yoga* is used by some sects to indicate certain particular methods or spiritual disciplines, which they advocate.

yogi, an adept at *yoga*: The exact meaning will depend on the type of *yoga* being referred to.

Zazen: (Zen) sitting meditation.

Zen (Ch'an): important school of Buddhism from China and Japan. The word Zen is Japanese for the Chinese Ch'an, which in turn is derived from the Indian *dhyāna*. Zen teaches non-duality, oneness of everything and sudden, direct awakening. It emphasises spontaneity and intuitive understanding.

Bibliography

Goddard, Dwight, *A Buddhist Bible*, quoted in *Buddhism and Christianity in the Light of Hinduism* by Arthur Osborne, p. 114 and also in *The Teachings of Bhagavan Sri Ramana Maharshi in His Own Words* by Arthur Osborne, (5th edn.), p. 228.

Harshananda, Swami, *A Dictionary of Advaita Vedānta*, Ramakrishna Math, Bangalore, 1995.

Balsekar, Sri Ramesh, *A Duet of One* (*Ashtavakra Gita* — translation and commentary), Advaita Press.

Brunton, Paul, *A Search in Secret India*, B.I. Pub., 1970, reprint 1994.

(Eng. Tr.) Tapasyananda, Swami, *Adhyatma Ramayana*, 1st edn., 1985, Sri Ramakrishna Math, Madras.

(Ed.) Bhat, V.R., *Ānandabodhāmṛt*, Sri Anandashram, Khar Math, 1999.

Nityaswarupananda, Swami, *Aṣṭāvakra Saṁhitā*, Advaita Ashrama, Calcutta, 9th impression, 1996.

Nikhilānanda, Swāmi, *Ātmabodha*: *Self-Knowledge of Śrī Śaṅkarācārya*, Sri Ramakrishna Math, Madras, 10th impression, 1997.

Mello, S.J., Anthony de, *Call to Love — Meditations*, Gujarat Sahitya Prakash, 1991.

(Eng. Tr. with elucidation) Trasi, Dr. N.M., *Changdev Pasashti*, (unpublished).

Balsekar, Ramesh, *Consciousness Speaks*, Advaita Press, 1992.

Consciousness Writes, conversations by air-mail with Ramesh Balsekar, Zen Publications.

Diwakar, R.R., (1980), *Bhagawan Buddha*, 78-86, Bharatiya Vidya Bhavan, Bombay quoted in *In J. of Psych.* article '*J. Krishnamurti's Teachings — Relevance to Mental Health*'.

Suzuki, D.T., *Essays in Zen Buddhism*, Third Series, Rider & Co., London, 1970.

Balsekar, Ramesh S., *Experiencing the Teaching*, Advaita Press, Los Angeles, 1988.

(ed. and pub.) Hattiangadi, Dr. G.S., *Fifty Years of Bliss*, for Shri Chitrapur Math, Shirali, North Kanara, 1965.

Jayakar, Pupul, *Fire in the Mind*, Penguin, 1995.

Asimov, Isaac, *Ghosts*, from Introduction.

Subedar, Manu, *Gita the Mother*, Kalyani Pub., N. Delhi, 1972, rpt. 1991.

Gray's Anatomy, 33rd edn.,1962, (pp. 152, 1025-30).

Coomaraswamy, Ananda K., *Hinduism and Buddhism*, (New York: Philosophical Library), pp. 18, 69 quoted in *Spectrum of Consciousness*.

Müller, Prof. F. Max, *Ramakrishna — His Life and Sayings*, Pub. Advaita Ashrama, Calcutta, 1992 edn.

I am That, conversations with Sri Nisargadatta Maharaj, Chetana, Pvt. Ltd., 2nd edn., 1976.

Krishnamurti, J., quoted in article 'J. Krishnamurti's teachings — Relevance to Mental Health' by A. Venkoba Rao, in *Indian Journal of Psychiatry*, Oct. 1995, 37(4), p. 155-60.

Rucker, Rudy, *Infinity and the Mind*, Bantam Books, 1983.

Weisz and Schopler, Morgan, King, *Introduction to Psychology*, Tata McGraw-Hill, 7th edn.

J. Krishnamurti as I Knew Him, Susunaga Weeraperuma, Chetana Pub., p. 89. (The words quoted were spoken by Adikaram, Weeraperuma's mentor.)

Singh, Dr. Jaidev and Singh, Dr.Vasudev, *Kabir Vani Piyush* (Hindi), Vishvavidyalay Prakashan, Varanasi, 1988.

Lutyens, Mary, *Krishnamurti: The Open Door*, Avon Books, New York, 1991.

Krishnamurti's talks in America, 1954 (Verbatim Report), Pub. Krishnamurti Writings Inc., Ojai, California.

(Eng. Tr.) Tapasyananda, Swami, *Laghuvasudeva Mananam*, 1st edn., Sri Ramakrishna Math.

Kretschmer, W., "Meditative Techniques in Psychotherapy", in *Altered States of Consciousness*, ed. by C.T. Tart, London & New York, 1969.

Man and the Universe, Commins and Linscott.

(ed.) Commins, Saxe and N. Linscott, Robert, *Man and the Universe*, *the Philosophers of Science*, Washington Square Press, New York, 1969

Mathnawi, Jalalu'din Rumi.

(Tr.) Blakney, R.B., *Meister Eckhart*, Harper Torchbooks, 1941, New York.

Mountain Path, 1993, article by Godman, David.

Mountain Path, Dec'95, p. 77. *Article: Ramana Maharshi and Buddhist non-dualism* by Len Hixon.

Schroedinger, Erwin, *My View of the World*, London, Cambridge Univ. Press, 1964.

(Tr.) Tagore, Rabindranath, *One Hundred Poems of Kabir*, Macmillan, 1972.

Mello, S.J., Anthony de, *One Minute Wisdom*, S.J., Gujarat Sahitya Prakash, Anand.

Tilak, Bāl Gaṅgādhar, *Orion*.

Osborne, Arthur, *Collected Works of Sri Ramana Maharshi.*

Balsekar, Ramesh S., *Pointers from Nisargadatta Maharaj*, Chetana Pub., Bombay, 1st edn., 1982.

Krishnamurti, J., *Questions and Answers*, K.F.I., 1982, reprint 1993.

Osborne, Arthur, *Ramana Maharshi and the Path of Self-Knowledge*, B.I. Pub., 1973 edn.

Radhakrishnan, S., *Religion and Culture*, Hind Pocket Books, 1968.

Reported in the feature 'An Infinite Voyage' broadcast on 'Discovery' TV Channel on November 6, 1995, 10.30 p.m. IST.

Sarth Amrithanubhav ani Changdev Pasashti, (Marathi) ed. by H.B.P.D. Deshpande, Sarathi Prakashan, Pune, 1988.

Bhide, B.A., *Sarth Sri Jnaneshwari* (Marathi), 7th edn., 1989, Pub. K.B. Dhavale.

Savill's System of Clinical Medicine, pp.1367-69, 14th edn.

Śrī Jnanadeva, *Bhāvārtha-Dīpikā: Jñāneśvarī*, English translation by R.K. Bhagwat, Samata Books, Madras, 1979.

Jog-maharaj, Vishnubuva, *Sri Amrithanubhav*, Yashwant Prakashan, Pune, 4th edn., 1988.

Swarupananda, Swami, *Śrimad Bhagavad Gītā*, Advaita Ashrama, Calcutta, 16th impression, 1996.

(Eng. Tr.) Sukthankar, Bhalchandra Sitaram, *Srimad Bhagavad Gita-Rahasya* by Bal Gangadhar Tilak, 6th edn., 1986, Geeta

Printers, Pune.

(Tr.) Goswami C.L., *Śrīmad Bhāgavata Mahāpurāṇa*, Gita Press, Gorakhpur, 3rd edn., 1995.

Sri Ramana Maharshi quoted in *Sunbeam*, April 1981, p. 22. Shri Chitrapur Math, Sri Anandashram, Bombay.

Sunbeam, Feb. 1979, pp.1-3, and April 1978, pp.1-3. Shri Chitrapur Math, Sri Anandashram, Bombay.

Krishnamurti, J., quoted by Asit Chandmal in *Sunday Times* article.

Talks with Ramana Maharshi, p. 385, 1994 edn. quoted in *Mtn. Path*, June 1995, p. 41.

Talks with Ramana Maharshi, p. 436, quoted in *Mtn. Path*, Dec' 95, p. 76.

Guyton, Arthur C., *Textbook of Medical Physiology*, 7th edn., 1986.

Wilber, Ken, *The Atman Project*, The Theosophical Publishing House, Wheaton, U.S.A., 1989.

The Bhagavad Gita with the commentary of Sri Sankaracharya, English tr. by Sastry, Alladi Mahadeva, Samata Books, Madras, 1977 edn. (1992 rpt.).

The Bṛhadāraṇyaka Upaniṣad, Sri Ramakrishna Math, Madras, 1951.

Bronowski, J., *The Common Sense of Science*, Cambridge, Harvard Univ. Press, 1955, p. 137.

The Complete Works of Swami Vivekananda, Vol. II, Mayavati Memorial Volume, Advaita Ashram, Calcutta.

The Concise Oxford Dictionary, 17th edn.

Huxley, Aldous, *The Doors of Perception*, London, 1954.

(Eng. Tr.) Samvid, Compiled by Sri Jnanananda Bharati, *The Essence of Yogavaasishtha* [*Śrī Vāsiṣṭha Saṅgraha*], Samata Books, Madras, 1st edn. 1982, 2nd rpt. 1998.

Krishnamurti, J., *The Flight of the Eagle,* K.F.I., 1982.

Goenka, S.N., *The Gracious Flow of Dharma*, 1994, Vipassana Research Institute.

Osborne, Arthur, *The Incredible Sai Baba*, Orient Longmans.

Krishnamurti, J., *The Last Talks*, K.F.I., 1989, rpt. 1992.

Craveri, Marcello, *The Life of Jesus — An Assessment through Modern Historical Evidence*, Panther History.

Steiner, R., *The Philosophy of Freedom*, London, Rudolf Steiner Press.

Heisenberg, Werner, *The Physicist's Conception of Nature*, Harcourt,

Brace, 1958.

Chang, G.C.C., *The Practice of Zen*, New York: Harper and Row (Perennial Library), 1970

DeMello, Anthony, *The Prayer of the Frog*, Gujarat Sahitya Prakash, 1989.

Goswami, Amit, *The Self-Aware Universe*, 1993, G.P. Putnam's sons, New York.

Mello, Anthony de, *The Song of the Bird*, Gujarat Sahitya Prakash, Anand, 1989.

Wilber, Ken, *The Spectrum of Consciousness*, The Theosophical Publishing House, Wheaton, Illinois, USA; 1977, reprint 1985.

The Spiritual Teaching of Ramana Maharshi, Berkeley, Shambala, 1972.

The Student's Sanskrit-English Dictionary, Vaman Shivram Apte, Motilal Banarsidass, Delhi, 2nd edn., 1970.

Report in the *The Sunday Review of The Times of India* of March 10, 1996, about psychologist V.S. Ramachandran of the University of California, speaking at the Society of Neuroscience meeting in San Diego in November 1995.

Osborne, Arthur, *The Teachings of Bhagavan Sri Ramana Maharshi In His Own Words,* 5th edn., Ramanasramam.

De Cusa, Nicolas, *The Vision of God.*

Watts, Alan W., *The Way of Zen*, Penguin Books.

Krishnamurti, J., *The Wholeness of Life*, K.F.I., 1978.

Blofeld, J., *The Zen Teaching of Huang Po*, Grove Press, N.Y., 1966.

Report in *Times of India*, 6.4.1996.

Truth and Actuality, Krishnamurti Foundation India, 1977 (1995 reprint).

Carlos G. Valles S.J., *Unencumbered by Baggage*, Gujarat Sahitya Prakash, 3rd edn., 1988.

(Eng. Tr.) Madhavananda, Swami, *Vivekacūḍāmaṇi of Śrī Śaṅkarācārya*, Sri Ramakrishna Math, Madras, 10th impression, 1997.

(Ed.) John White, *What is Enlightenment*, Jeremy P. Tarcher Inc., Los Angeles, 1st edn.

Schroedinger, Erwin, *What is Life? and Mind and Matter,* London: Cambridge Univ. Press, 1969.

(Eng. Tr.) Mahadevan, Dr. T.M.P., *Who Am I? (Nān Yār)* of Sri Ramana Maharshi, Ramanasramam, 12th edn., 1969.

Index